REMEMBER

RADIO'S GOLDEN YEARS ©

CREATED BY FRANK BRESEE AND BOBB LYNES,
THIS SPECIAL NOSTALGIC FEATURE TAKES YOU
BACK TO THE YEARS WHEN THE THEATRE OF
THE MIND ENTERTAINED THE WORLD WITH
COMEDY, DRAMA, MUSIC AND VARIETY

IT INFORMS YOU ABOUT THE CREATORS
AND STARS OF THIS GREAT ERA

For information, please contact Frank Bresee Productions, PO Box 1222, Hollywood, CA 90078

Cover designed by Ray Ferry

Library of Congress Cataloging in Publication Data

    1. Radio Shows of the 20th Century 2. Biography

Printed in China

Second Printing: May, 1999

FOREWORD

by

Norman Corwin

History is told in many ways: cave paintings, hieroglyphs, documents, journals, books, murals, memoirs, political atlases, encyclopedias and variants of them all. A relatively recent addition to these forms is the informational cartoon, of which a richly entertaining gallery is now in your hands.

Frank Bresee and Bobb Lynes know the golden age of radio as few others, having observed it, contributed to it, and been long immersed in its many phases. Bresee's GOLDEN DAYS OF RADIO series alone has flourished for very close to half a century, 29 of those years via the Armed Forces Radio Service. And Bobb Lynes' art is just the right vehicle for Bresee's wide ranging research.

Among several striking aspects of this compendium are a wealth of information encapsulated in each panel, fortified by the strength of Lynes' line. He achieves remarkable likeness in simple strokes (note especially Bogart, Bette Davis, Jean Hersholt, Hedda Hopper, Ray   Collins, Mortimer Snerd, Everett Sloane, Orson Welles, Al Jolson, Janet Waldo, Edward R. Murrow). To me the marvel of the panels is that although most teem with information (some populated by as many as 14 or 15 portraits and related texts) they never seem overcrowded. In addition to identifying the casts, writers, directors and production staffs of the program cited, as well as the stations or networks that carried them, the sponsors, agencies, logos, catchwords, idioms; even, sometimes, as the panel on Stan Freberg, a picture of a ticket to the program.

I was enchanted by a number of compelling singularities in this work, such as the following:

Eddie Cantor created the slogan "March of Dimes" for Franklin D. Roosevelt.

"Duffy" never appeared on Duffy's Tavern.

Don McNeill's Breakfast Club was the longest running daytime radio program of all time—coast to coast every morning for 35 years.

"Sorry Wrong Number" was repeated on the Suspense program eight times.

Among premiums offered by the comedy team of Stoopnagle and Budd were round dice for listeners who would rather play marbles.

Jack Benny was the only performer to have the top rated show on both NBC and CBS.

Over the years of Bride and Groom, more than 1000 couples were married on the air.

In his early days Arthur Godfrey appeared on WJSV as "Red Godfrey," the WarblingBanjoist.

It Pays To Be Ignorant, a comedy quiz show, asked such recondite questions as "What color is a white horse?" and "What material is a silk dress made of?"

In a panel on cigarette commercials, a dozen packages from the old days (Chesterfield, Old Gold, Lucky Strike, Kool, etc.) are illustrated and a pocket history of tobacco-sponsored programs given, but Bresee and Lynes are careful to note in a box at the bottom of the page, "This is not an advertisement or endorsement."

Jimmy Fidler, a Hollywood columnist, always signed off his program with, "Good night to you, and I do mean you."

Reader, you'll have a good time browsing through this book, and I do mean you!

ACKNOWLEDGEMENTS

A big thank you to all the radio performers, producers, directors, writers, and <u>sponsors</u> from radio's golden days.

Also a personal thanks to the following persons who have added to the value of this publication with their knowledge and experience: Barbara Watkins, John Dunning, Jim Harmon, David Collins, Charles Stumph, David Berger, Ron & Linda Downey, Harrison Summers, Tom DeLong, Bill Owen & Frank Bruxton, Eric Rhodes, Stuart Lubin, Jack Mathis, Dave Holland, John & Larry Gassman, Anthony Tollin, Milt Larsen, Tom Tumbusch, Jack French, Eddie Leroy, Marty Halperin, Jay Hickerson, Dick Bank, Randy Eidemiller and Chris Lembesis.

We also want to thank the following magazines and publications: *Radio Life, TV-Radio Mirror, Radio Guide, Radio Stars, Tune-In, Tele-Views, Sperdvac Newsletter, Hello Again, Life, Look, Colliers, Saturday Evening Post, Variety, Big Reel, Hollywood Reporter, Billboard, Classic Images* and *Past Times*.

In addition a monumental thank you to the Pacific Pioneer Broadcasters—Hollywood.

—Frank Bresee & Bobb Lynes

RADIO'S GOLDEN YEARS ©

by FRANK BRESEE & BOBB LYNES

BUD ABBOTT & LOU COSTELLO

COMEDIANS BUD ABBOTT & LOU COSTELLO BEGAN THEIR RADIO CAREER AS GUESTS IN A "ONE TIME ONLY" SPOT ON THE CBS KATE SMITH SHOW IN 1938; THEY WERE SO POPULAR THEY RETURNED WEEK AFTER WEEK FOR 50 WEEKS!

IN 1939 THEY WERE SIGNED BY UNIVERSAL PICTURES FOR A LONG SERIES OF FILMS THAT MADE THE STUDIO THE SUCCESS IT IS TODAY: "BUCK PRIVATES", "IN THE NAVY", "HOLD THAT GHOST" AND "ABBOTT AND COSTELLO MEET FRANKENSTEIN"

LOU COSTELLO'S CATCH LINE: "I'M A BAAAD BOY!"

SPONSOR: CAMEL CIGARETTES

THEIR OWN RADIO SHOW BEGAN ON NBC'S THURSDAY NIGHT LINE-UP IN OCTOBER, 1942, LATER MOVED TO ABC SATURDAY MORNINGS THEIR AUDIENCE NUMBERED 20 MILLION LISTENERS WEEKLY

THEIR MOST FAMOUS ROUTINE WAS THE BASEBALL COMEDY SKETCH "WHO'S ON FIRST?"

VOCALISTS INCLUDED CONNIE HAINES & MARILYN MAXWELL

ANNOUNCER: KEN NILES

RADIO'S GOLDEN YEARS.©

by FRANK BRESEE & BOBB LYNES

THIS POPULAR SHOW WAS FIRST HEARD ON NBC ON JANUARY 24, 1942 (JUST AFTER THE START OF WORLD WAR II) WHICH PROBABLY ACCOUNTS FOR MUCH OF ITS POPULARITY. IT WAS FAMILY-ORIENTED AND BROUGHT US MANY HAPPY MEMORIES OF THE DAYS WHEN FAMILIES WERE TOGETHER....

ABIE'S IRISH ROSE

ABIE'S IRISH ROSE HAD ORIGINALLY BEEN ONE OF BROADWAY'S GREAT STAGE HITS RUNNING OVER 2,000 PERFORMANCES BY 1927. IT WAS THE HUMAN STORY OF TWO CULTURES, CATHOLIC AND JEWISH, WHO RESOLVED THEIR DIFFERENCES THROUGH LOVE AND UNDERSTANDING...

SPONSOR: DRENE SHAMPOO

ANNOUNCER: HOWARD PETRIE

NEW YORK CAST: SYDNEY SMITH, CLAYTON COLLYER, BETTY WINKLER, WALTER KINSELLA, MENASHA SKULNIK, ANNA APPEL, BILL ADAMS, ALAN REED, RICHARD COOGAN, PAUL DOUGLAS & MERCEDES McCAMBRIDGE.....

THE WEEKLY HALF-HOUR RAN ON NBC UNTIL 1944....

THEME: "MY WILD IRISH ROSE"

RADIO'S GOLDEN YEARS ©
by FRANK BRESEE & BOBB LYNES

ACADEMY AWARD

ACADEMY AWARD PRESENTED RADIO VERSIONS OF MANY MOTION PICTURES THAT HAD WON THE COVETED AWARD, USING THE ORIGINAL FILM CASTS WHENEVER POSSIBLE. THE STAR-STUDDED WEEKLY SERIES DEBUTED ON CBS ON MARCH 30, 1946 AND LASTED UNTIL DECEMBER 18, 1946... LESS THAN A YEAR

SOME PRODUCTIONS: "JEZEBEL," "KITTY FOYLE," "STAGECOACH," "MALTESE FALCON," "KEYS OF THE KINGDOM," "PORTRAIT OF JENNY," "THE INFORMER," "LOST HORIZON," "A STAR IS BORN" & "SUSPICION"

SQUIBB

ACADEMY AWARD FEATURED: GINGER ROGERS, BETTE DAVIS, HUMPHREY BOGART, RANDOLPH SCOTT, CLAIRE TREVOR, HENRY FONDA, GREGORY PECK AND MORE...

ANNOUNCER: HUGH BRUNDIGE

RADIO'S GOLDEN YEARS ©

by FRANK BRESEE & BOBB LYNES

the ALDRICH FAMILY

HENRY! HENRY ALDRICH!... COMING, MOTHER!

THE ALDRICH FAMILY BEGAN ON RADIO AS A SKIT ON RUDY VALLEE'S RADIO SHOW IN 1938, THEN ON TO KATE SMITH'S SHOW FOR 40 WEEKS....

A SUMMER REPLACEMENT FOR JACK BENNY IN 1939 LEAD TO A REGULAR SPOT ON NBC-BLUE IN 1940....

CREATOR-WRITER WAS CLIFFORD GOLDSMITH

Post's GRAPE-NUTS

CEREAL BEVERAGE

"There's a Reason"

SPONSOR: GENERAL FOODS

JELL-O VANILLA PUDDING

HOUSE JAMESON (FATHER), KATHARINE RAHT (MOTHER), EZRA STONE (HENRY), ANN LINCOLN (MARY) WERE IN THE ORIGINAL CAST......

LATER, CHARITA BAUER WAS "MARY", EDDIE BRACKEN WAS "DIZZY"; JACKIE KELK WAS "HOMER"

NORMAN TOKAR

RAYMOND IVES

DICK JONES

KELK   STONE

MANY ACTORS PLAYED HENRY OVER THE YEARS: EZRA STONE, NORMAN TOKAR, DICK JONES, RAYMOND IVES AND AGAIN EZRA STONE; THEN BOBBY ELLIS UNTIL THE END OF THE SERIES IN 1953...

ANNOUNCERS: HARRY VON ZELL DAN SEYMOUR

BOBBY ELLIS

RADIO'S GOLDEN YEARS ©

by FRANK BRESEE & BOBB LYNES

the FRED ALLEN Show

FRED ALLEN WAS ONE OF THE MOST POPULAR COMEDIANS OF THE 20ᵀᴴ CENTURY, NOT ONLY AS AN AUTHOR, BUT AS A PERFORMER WITH ONE OF THE MOST LISTENED-TO RADIO SHOWS DURING THE 30s & 40s...

HIS SHOW BEGAN ON OCTOBER 23, 1932 & LASTED UNTIL JUNE 26, 1949

SPONSORS: SAL HEPATICA, LINIT, IPANA TOOTHPASTE, TEXACO, TENDERLEAF TEA & FORD MOTORS

HIS WIFE PORTLAND HOFFA SHE APPEARED ON HIS SHOW EVERY WEEK...

HE IS FAMOUS FOR HIS ALLEN'S ALLEY SEGMENT OF HIS WEEKLY SHOW

FEATURED PLAYERS ON HIS PROGRAM WERE: PARKER FENNELLY ("TITUS MOODY"), MINERVA PIOUS ("MRS. NUSSBAUM"), PETER DONALD ("AJAX CASSIDY"), ALAN REED ("FALSTAFF OPENSHAW") AND KENNY DELMAR ("SENATOR CLAGHORN")

ANNOUNCERS:
KENNY DELMAR   HARRY VON ZELL

AFTER RETIRING FROM RADIO, HE CONTINUED TO WRITE AND LATER BECAME A VERY POPULAR PANELIST ON CBS-TV'S "WHAT'S MY LINE?"

5

RADIO'S GOLDEN YEARS©
by FRANK BRESEE & BOBB LYNES

the STEVE ALLEN Show

THIS MULTIMEDIA PERFORMER, WRITER & MUSICIAN BEGAN HIS CAREER IN RADIO IN ARIZONA & BECAME PROMINENT ON MUTUAL'S "SMILE TIME" IN 1946 (SHOW ALSO FEATURED WENDELL NOBLE AND JUNE FORAY)

IN 1949 STEVE BEGAN A LATE NIGHT DISC JOCKEY SHOW, "BREAKING ALL RECORDS" ON LOS ANGELES' CBS STATION, KNX; SHOW BECAME SO POPULAR THAT IT WAS MOVED TO AN AUDIENCE STUDIO AT COLUMBIA SQUARE FROM 12 MIDNIGHT TO 1 A.M. WHERE STEVE PLAYED PIANO & AD-LIBBED WITH PEOPLE IN THE AUDIENCE

STEVE HAS WRITTEN OVER 40 BOOKS

IN THE EARLY FIFTIES STEVE MOVED TO N.Y.C. AND BEGAN "THE "TONIGHT" SHOW ON NBC-TV

STEVE HAS WRITTEN OVER 4000 SONGS & RECORDED DOZENS OF RECORD ALBUMS

RADIO'S GOLDEN YEARS©

by FRANK BRESEE & BOBB LYNES

DON AMECHE

DON AMECHE HAD A LONG AND DISTINGUISHED CAREER. YEARS BEFORE HE BECAME THE #1 BOX OFFICE MOVIE STAR IN THE COUNTRY WITH FILMS LIKE "ALEXANDER GRAHAM BELL" & "SWANEE RIVER", HE WAS A VERY POPULAR RADIO STAR....

SOME OF THE PROGRAMS ON WHICH HE WAS FEATURED:
FIRST NIGHTER (CBS, 1929-36)
BETTY & BOB (BLUE-NBC, 1933)
GRAND HOTEL (BLUE-NBC, 1933)
JACK ARMSTRONG (CBS, 1934)
CHASE & SANBORN HOUR, WITH BERGEN & McCARTHY, W.C. FIELDS (NBC, 1936-40)
DON AMECHE SHOW (NBC, 1946)
OLD GOLD SHOW (CBS, 1947)
THE DRENE SHOW WITH THE BICKERSONS, WITH FRANCES LANGFORD (NBC, 1946)

(REAL NAME: DOM AMICI)

DON AMECHE AS "JOHN BICKERSON"

FRANCES LANGFORD AS "BLANCHE BICKERSON"

THE BICKERSONS

THE BICKERSONS, CREATED AND WRITTEN BY PHIL RAPP FEATURED SOME OF RADIO'S FUNNIEST DOMESTIC COMEDY ROUTINES, MANY OF WHICH WERE LATER RELEASED ON RECORDS

RADIO'S GOLDEN YEARS©

by FRANK BRESEE & BOBB LYNES

AMOS N' ANDY

LISTENERS TOOK NOTICE OF RADIO WHEN AMOS N' ANDY WENT ON THE COAST-TO-COAST NBC NETWORK ON AUGUST 19, 1929....

EARLY ANNOUNCER WAS BILL HAY; LATER HARLOW WILCOX, KEN CARPENTER AND ART GILMORE

FREEMAN GOSDEN   CHARLES CORRELL
CREATORS AND STARS OF AMOS N' ANDY

ERNESTINE WADE WAS "SAPPHIRE" STEVENS"

IN THE SHOW'S EARLY YEARS GOSDEN (AMOS & THE KINGFISH) AND CORRELL (ANDY) PLAYED ALL THE PARTS. LATER CAST INCLUDED HATTIE McDANIEL, AMANDA RANDOLPH, LOU LUBIN, ROY GLENN, JOHNNY LEE, JAMES BASKETT & MORE.....

Campbell's Quality

Rinso

Rexall

Pepsodent
TOOTH PASTE · CONTAINS I₂

SPONSORS: CAMPBELL'S SOUPS, PEPSODENT TOOTHPASTE, RINSO SOAP AND REXALL DRUG STORES

RADIO'S GOLDEN YEARS. ©

by FRANK BRESEE & BOBB LYNES

John J. Anthony GOODWILL HOUR

JOHN J. ANTHONY'S GOODWILL HOUR BEGAN AUGUST 1, 1937 ON MBS & WAS HEARD EVERY SUNDAY NIGHT. MR. ANTHONY WOULD ANSWER DIFFICULT PROBLEMS OF HIS GUESTS WITH A BRIEF AND SIMPLE RESOLUTION..HIS CONCEPT WAS BASED ON THE GOLDEN RULE; SOMETIMES HE WOULD SCOLD A GUEST ON THE AIR WHEN THEY WOULD CONFESS AN INFIDELITY

BETWEEN 1940-43 THE SERIES WAS HEARD ON NBC-BLUE; LATER BACK ON MUTUAL

ANNOUNCER: ROLAND WINTERS

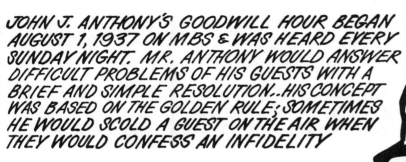

Ironized Yeast

SPONSORS: IRONIZED YEAST, CARTERS LIVER PILLS, CLARK CHEWING GUM & STERLING DRUGS

JOHN J. ANTHONY
(REAL NAME: LESTER KROLL)

CATCH PHRASES:
"PLEASE DON'T TOUCH THE MICROPHONE"
"WHAT IS YOUR PROBLEM, MADAME?"
"NO NAMES, PLEASE"

IN THE 1960'S MR. ANTHONY MOVED TO LOS ANGELES AND CONDUCTED ONE OF THE FIRST PHONE-IN TALK SHOWS ON KLAC

RADIO'S GOLDEN YEARS©

by FRANK BRESEE & BOBB LYNES

ARMSTRONG Theatre of Today

IN OCTOBER, 1941 THE ARMSTRONG THEATRE OF TODAY DEBUTED ON THE SATURDAY MORNING CBS LINE-UP.

BREAKING FROM TRADITION, THE SHOW BEGAN WITH A FEW MINUTES OF WORLD NEWS BY "ARMSTRONG'S NEWS REPORTER," AND THEN INTO THE DRAMA....

THE STORIES WERE USUALLY LIGHT-HEARTED COMEDIES, PERFECT FOR SATURDAY MORNING LISTENERS. THE FINAL YEAR WAS 1954

ARMSTRONG COMMERCIALS: ELIZABETH RELLER AND JULIE CONWAY

THE SERIES FEATURED THE BEST NEW YORK RADIO ACTORS: STAATS COTSWORTH, RICHARD KOLLMAR, ELSPETH ERIC, PAUL McGRATH, MARILYN ERSKINE, ALFRED DRAKE, SANDRA GOULD AND NANETTE FABRAY

ANNOUNCER: TOM SHIRLEY

NEWS REPORTER: GEORGE BRYAN

ARMSTRONG'S LINOLEUM and LINOFLOR

Custom Laid or Standard Designs

SPONSORS: ARMSTRONG CORK CO., THEN CREAM OF WHEAT

RADIO'S GOLDEN YEARS.©
by FRANK BRESEE & BOBB LYNES

ARCHIE ANDREWS

CREATED AND DRAWN BY BOB MONTANA, ARCHIE ANDREWS WAS RIGHT OUT OF THE COMIC PAGES. THE POPULAR NEWSPAPER STRIP CAME TO RADIO IN 1943 ON THE BLUE NETWORK AS A 15-MINUTE FIVE-A-WEEK AFTERNOON TEENAGE SHOW. IT IS BEST REMEMBERED, HOWEVER, AS A 30 MINUTE SATURDAY MORNING FEATURE ON NBC....

AS IN THE STRIP, THE RADIO SERIES FEATURED THE FUNNY EXPERIENCES OF A GROUP OF HIGH SCHOOL STUDENTS IN THE TOWN OF RIVERDALE

OVER THE YEARS ARCHIE WAS PLAYED BY CHARLES MULLEN, JACK GRIMES, BURT BOYER & BOB HASTINGS

JACK GRIMES

CAMERON ANDREWS

ALICE YOURMAN

VIVIAN SMOLEN

BOB HASTINGS

GLORIA MANN

ROSEMARY RICE

"JUGHEAD"-HARLAN STONE, CAMERON ANDREWS
"VERONICA"-GLORIA MANN, VIVIAN SMOLEN
"BETTY"-- DORIS GRUNDY, ROSEMARY RICE

ANNOUNCERS: KENNETH BANGHART DICK DUDLEY ROBERT WARREN

OTHER CAST MEMBERS: VINTON HAYWORTH, JOEY GEFFEN, ALICE YOURMAN & ARTHUR KOHL

SPONSORS: SWIFT & COMPANY AND KRAFT FOODS

RADIO'S GOLDEN YEARS©

by FRANK BRESEE & BOBB LYNES

Gene AUTRY's MELODY RANCH

ORVON GENE AUTRY "THE SINGING COWBOY" BEGAN HIS CAREER ON KVOO-TULSA IN 1929, BECAME STAR OF WLS-CHICAGO'S BARN DANCE, MOVED ON TO REPUBLIC WESTERN MUSICALS IN 1935. CBS BEGAN GENE'S "MELODY RANCH" ON JANUARY 7, 1940, INTERRUPTED BY W.W. II, AND RUNNING UNTIL 1956.... REGULAR CAST INCLUDED PAT BUTTRAM, JOHNNY BOND, CASS COUNTY BOYS, CARL COTNER'S BAND & THE PINAFORES

PAT BUTTRAM

CARL COTNER

JOHNNY BOND

CHARLES LYON

LOU CROSBY
ANNOUNCERS

GENE'S HIT RECORDS INCLUDED "SILVER-HAIRED DADDY OF MINE," "RUDOLPH, THE RED-NOSED REINDEER," & HIS THEME SONG "BACK IN THE SADDLE AGAIN"

GENE'S ONLY SPONSOR: WRIGLEY'S DOUBLEMINT GUM.....

WRIGLEY'S DOUBLEMINT CHEWING GUM

WRIGLEY'S DOUBLEMINT CHEWING GUM

GENE SERVED IN THE ARMY AIR CORPS IN BURMA FROM 1942 TO 1945

GENE LATER OWNED GOLDEN WEST BROADCASTING (TV & RADIO) & CALIFORNIA ANGELS BASEBALL TEAM

RADIO'S GOLDEN YEARS©

by FRANK BRESEE & BOBB LYNES

BABY SNOOKS

FAMOUS BROADWAY STAR, FUNNY GIRL FANNY BRICE DEVELOPED THE CHARACTER OF 7-YEAR-OLD "BABY SNOOKS" WHILE IN THE ZIEGFELD FOLLIES....

ANNOUNCERS: JOHN CONTE, HARLOW WILCOX, HARRY VON ZELL, DON WILSON

SPONSORS: MAXWELL HOUSE, POST TOASTIES, SANKA, JELLO AND TUMS

WHEN "THE ZIEGFELD FOLLIES" OF THE AIR" BEGAN ON CBS IN 1936, BABY SNOOKS WAS AN IMPORTANT PART OF THE SHOW; FOR THE NEXT 15 YEARS SHE WAS A REGULAR FEATURE ON CBS AND NBC NETWORKS....

BABY SNOOKS' FRUSTRATED "DADDY" WAS HANLEY STAFFORD

SANKA COFFEE

Post's TOASTIES Corn Flakes

REGULAR GRIND MAXWELL HOUSE Coffee

JELL-O PUDDINGS THREE MARVELOUS FLAVORS

TUMS FOR ACID INDIGESTION

RADIO'S GOLDEN YEARS ©

by FRANK BRESEE & BOBB LYNES

ART BAKER

ART BAKER AND HIS NOTEBOOK DEBUTED ON LOS ANGELES RADIO POWERHOUSE KFI ON SEPTEMBER 8, 1938. HIS RADIO CAREER BEGAN IN 1936 ON A LOCAL SHOW "TAPESTRIES OF LIFE."

HIS HOME-SPUN PHILOSOPHY WAS SO MUCH ENJOYED BY WEST COAST LISTENERS, IT WAS'NT LONG BEFORE HIS SHOW WAS SYNDICATED COAST-TO-COAST, LASTING FOR OVER A DECADE.

ART BAKER HOSTED QUIZ AND AUDIENCE PARTICIPATION SHOWS: "PULL OVER NEIGHBOR," "PEOPLE ARE FUNNY," & "HOLLYWOOD IN PERSON."

ART WAS ALSO ANNOUNCER FOR: HEDDA HOPPER'S HOLLYWOOD, POT O' GOLD AND BOB HOPE SHOW

HE ALSO ACTED IN MANY FILMS INCLUDING: "STATE OF THE UNION," "SPELLBOUND," "DAISY KENYON" & "TASK FORCE"

HE WAS ON EARLY LOS ANGELES TELEVISION AND WAS THE ORIGINAL HOST FOR "YOU ASKED FOR IT"

RADIO'S GOLDEN YEARS ©

by FRANK BRESEE & BOBB LYNES

ANDRÉ BARUCH

ANNOUNCER ANDRÉ BARUCH WAS ONE OF THE MOST IMPORTANT PERSONALITIES IN BROADCASTING FOR OVER A QUARTER OF A CENTURY.

HE WAS BORN IN PARIS, FRANCE AND WAS EDUCATED AT COLUMBIA UNIVERSITY IN THE U.S.

ANDRÉ BARUCH WAS THE ANNOUNCER FOR MANY FAMOUS PROGRAMS: YOUR HIT PARADE (22 YEARS RADIO & TV), THE SHADOW, JUST PLAIN BILL, JOHN'S OTHER WIFE, BOBBY BENSON'S B-BAR-B RIDERS, THE FRED WARING SHOW, KATE SMITH HOUR (RADIO & TV), MYRT & MARGE, AMERICAN ALBUM OF FAMILIAR MUSIC AND MANY OTHERS....

HE WAS ALSO THE VOICE OF PATHÉ NEWSREELS (22 YEARS) AND BROOKLYN DODGERS' PLAY-BY-PLAY ANNOUNCER...

HIS COMMERCIALS READ LIKE A WHO'S WHO OF ADVERTISING: LUCKY STRIKE, BAYER ASPIRIN, OLDSMOBILE, GENERAL FOODS, GENERAL MILLS, SPEIDEL WATCH BANDS, RAMADA INN, FORMULA 405, HOLIDAY INN, DUPONT, MORE!

ANDRÉ WAS MARRIED TO BIG BAND SINGER BEA WAIN AND AT ONE TIME THEY HAD THEIR OWN DAILY BEA & ANDRÉ SHOW ON FLORIDA'S WMJR/WPBR

DURING THE 1980S BEA AND ANDRÉ REVIVED YOUR HIT PARADE (SYNDICATED) PLAYING ORIGINAL HIT SONGS WITH THEIR COMMENTS ON THE TIMES.....

RADIO'S GOLDEN YEARS ©

by FRANK BRESEE & BOBB LYNES

JOHN BARRYMORE

JOHN BARRYMORE WAS ONE OF THE GREAT ACTORS OF THE STAGE AND HIS GENIUS WAS ALSO ENJOYED IN EARLY MOTION PICTURES, AND LATER, ON RADIO....

HE SUBSTITUTED FOR HIS BROTHER LIONEL ON DICKENS' CHRISTMAS CAROL IN 1938 AND IN 1937 DID THE NBC SERIES "JOHN BARRYMORE READS SHAKESPEARE"

RADIO APPEARANCES INCLUDED GUESTING ON KATE SMITH HOUR, BERGEN & McCARTHY AND THE TEXACO STAR THEATRE....

SOME FAMOUS ROLES: (STAGE) MACBETH, HAMLET, OTHELLO, ROMEO, RICHARD III (FILMS) "DON JUAN," "BEAU BRUMMEL," "TWENTIETH CENTURY"

HIS GREATEST FAME ON RADIO WAS WITH RUDY VALLEE AS A REGULAR ON RUDY'S SEALTEST SHOW IN 1940

AFTER REHEARSING RUDY'S MAY 14, 1942 SHOW, BARRYMORE BECAME ILL, WAS HOSPITALIZED AND DIED A FEW WEEKS LATER....

RADIO'S GOLDEN YEARS.©

by FRANK BRESEE & BOBB LYNES

JACK BENNY

JACK BENNY WAS THE ONLY PERFORMER TO HAVE THE NUMBER 1 RATED SHOW ON BOTH NBC AND CBS

SPONSORS: CANADA DRY, CHEVROLET, JELL-O, GRAPE-NUTS FLAKES, LUCKY STRIKE

LUCKY STRIKE "IT'S TOASTED"

Post's GRAPE-NUTS

JELL-O SIX DELICIOUS FLAVORS

CANADA DRY

CHEVROLET

CAST REGULARS: EDDIE (ROCHESTER) ANDERSON, DENNIS DAY, PHIL HARRIS, MARY LIVINGSTONE, MEL BLANC AND ANNOUNCER DON WILSON

CBS TELEVISION

JACK BENNY MOVED INTO TV (IN THE 1950s) WITH HIS SAME CAST AND SAME HIGH RATINGS...

BENNY HAD A RUNNING ON-AIR FEUD (FOR LAUGHS) WITH COMIC FRED ALLEN

HIS SHOW DEBUTED ON NBC-BLUE MAY 2, 1932, AND LATER MOVED TO CBS, ENDING ON MAY 22, 1955; RE-RUNS 'TIL 1958

RADIO'S GOLDEN YEARS ©

by FRANK BRESEE & BOBB LYNES

BEULAH

BEULAH WAS FIRST HEARD AS FIBBER McGEE'S MAID ON NBC ON JANUARY 25, 1944, WAS SO POPULAR THAT "SHE" SPUN-OFF INTO "THE MARLIN HURT & BEULAH SHOW" ON CBS ON JULY 2, 1945, LASTING UNTIL MARCH 21, 1946 WHEN MARLIN HURT (THE STAR) SUDDENLY DIED AT AGE 40.

"MARLIN HURT & BEULAH SHOW" CAST INCLUDED JOHN BROWN, CAROL STEWART, KEN NILES; PHIL LESLIE WAS THE WRITER, PRODUCER-DIRECTOR WAS HELEN MACK

"BEULAH" WAS REVIVED ON APRIL 2, 1947 ON ABC (AGAIN PLAYED BY A WHITE MAN, BOB CORLEY); BECAME A 15-MINUTE NIGHTLY SERIAL ON CBS THAT FALL, STARRING HATTIE McDANIEL

MARLIN HURT PLAYED HIMSELF, BILL JACKSON (BEULAH'S FRIEND) AND BEULAH!

RUBY DANDRIDGE LILLIAN RANDOLPH

SPONSORS: TUMS, PROCTER & GAMBLE

BEULAH'S SERIAL CAST INCLUDED HUGH STUDEBAKER, JESS KIRKPATRICK, MARY JANE CROFT & LOIS CORBETT; RUBY DANDRIDGE & ERNEST WHITMAN

LOUISE BEAVERS, LILLIAN AND AMANDA RANDOLPH ALSO PLAYED BEULAH BEFORE THE SHOW ENDED IN 1954

RADIO'S GOLDEN YEARS ©
by FRANK BRESEE & BOBB LYNES

EDGAR BERGEN & CHARLIE McCARTHY

EDGAR BERGEN AND HIS FAMOUS DUMMY WERE FIRST HEARD ON RUDY VALLEE'S RADIO HOUR ON NBC DEC. 17, 1936... RETURNING MANY TIMES UNTIL THEY BEGAN THEIR OWN WEEKLY SHOW SIX MONTHS LATER

BERGEN & McCARTHY WERE ON THE RADIO FROM MAY 9, 1937 TO JULY 1, 1956

BERGEN & McCARTHY'S PAL WAS THE POPULAR WOODEN-HEAD MORTIMER SNERD

CAST REGULARS INCLUDED W.C. FIELDS, DON AMECHE AND DOROTHY LAMOUR

SPONSORS: CHASE AND SANBORN COFFEE, COCA-COLA, KRAFT, R. HUDNUT AND & CBS RADIO

LONGTIME ANNOUNCER: BILL BALDWIN

ORCHESTRA LEADER: RAY NOBLE

HIS DAUGHTER, CANDICE BERGEN IS POPULAR TV STAR OF "MURPHY BROWN"

RADIO'S GOLDEN YEARS ©

by FRANK BRESEE & BOBB LYNES

MILTON BERLE

ONE OF THE GREAT STARS OF SHOW BUSINESS JOINED THE RANKS OF RADIO PERSONALITIES ON SEPT. 6, 1936 ON CBS. BY 1939 HE WAS HOSTING A SHOW FOR QUAKER OATS: "STOP ME IF YOU'VE HEARD THIS ONE"

OVER THE YEARS BERLE STARRED ON VARIOUS SHOWS AND BY 1944 HE BEGAN "LET YOURSELF GO" WHICH LASTED THREE YEARS

IN 1947 MILTON BEGAN THE MILTON BERLE SHOW, A SITUATION COMEDY WHICH FEATURED BERT GORDON, PERT KELTON, JACK ALBERTSON, ARNOLD STANG. AND ARTHUR Q. BRYAN. ORCHESTRA LEADER: RAY BLOCH

SPONSORS: QUAKER OATS CAMPBELL SOUPS, EVERSHARP, PHILIP MORRIS & TEXACO....

ANNOUNCERS: FRANK GALLUP, KEN ROBERTS

IN 1948 HE DEBUTED ON NBC-TV'S "TEXACO STAR THEATRE" AND BECAME "MISTER TELEVISION"

RADIO'S GOLDEN YEARS ©

by FRANK BRESEE & BOBB LYNES

BEN BERNIE

BEN BERNIE, "THE OLD MAESTRO" HAD ONE OF THE MOST ADMIRED SENTIMENTAL ORCHESTRAS OF THE 1930's AND 1940's

"AU REVOIR, PLEASANT DRE-AMS.... THINK OF US WHEN REQUESTING YOUR THEMES. UNTIL THE NEXT TIME WHEN, YOU MAY ALL TUNE IN AGAIN...KEEP THE OLD MAESTRO ALWAYS IN YOUR SCHEMES.....YOWSAH, YOWSAH, YOWSAH!"

A TRUE RADIO PIONEER HE WAS FIRST HEARD OVER LOCAL NEW YORK STATION WJZ IN 1923, OVER THE YEARS HIS SHOW WAS ON CBS, NBC BLUE NETWORKS

A VAUDEVILLE VETERAN, BERNIE HOSTED ONE OF RADIO'S MOST POPULAR VARIETY PROGRAMS FEATURING OUTSTANDING ARTISTS OF THE DAY AS GUESTS

THEMES: "IT'S A LONESOME OLD TOWN" & "AU REVOIR"

IN THE EARLY '30s HE AND WALTER WINCHELL CREATED A FRIENDLY "FEUD" WITH BOTH TRADING AMUSING INSULTS ON THE RESPECTIVE PROGRAMS

SPONSORS: MENNEN SHAVE CREME, PABST BEER, U.S. RUBBER CO., AMERICAN CAN CO., LADY ESTHER, HALF AND HALF TOBACCO, WRIGLEY GUM AND BROMO-SELTZER

RADIO'S GOLDEN YEARS©

by FRANK BRESEE & BOBB LYNES

Big Jon & Sparkie
NO SCHOOL TODAY

NO SCHOOL TODAY WITH BIG JON AND SPARKIE WAS A POPULAR CHILDRENS PROGRAM OF THE 1950s AND FEATURED JON ARTHUR

THE SERIES REVOLVED AROUND BIG JON AND HIS CAST OF DELIGHTFUL CHARACTERS AND "THE LITTLE ELF FROM THE LAND OF MAKE-BELIEVE: "SPARKIE"

THE SHOW FEATURED SONGS AND STORIES FOR THE KIDS; BUT MANY PARENTS ALSO ENJOYED THEM

JON ARTHUR'S RECORDED SPEEDED-UP VOICE WAS SPARKIE'S VOICE,...

"SPARKIE"

HOST-CREATOR: JON ARTHUR GOERSS

THEME: "TEDDY BEARS PICNIC"

FROM 1950 TO 1958 THE SHOW WAS HEARD ON ABC

22

RADIO'S GOLDEN YEARS©

by FRANK BRESEE & BOBB LYNES

the BIG SHOW

THE BIG SHOW TRULY WAS. IT BEGAN AS A SUNDAY EVENING RADIO EXTRAVAGANZA ON NBC NOVEMBER 11, 1950 AND LASTED UNTIL APRIL 20, 1952....

OPENING.... TALULLAH:
"FOR THE NEXT HOUR AND THIRTY MINUTES, THIS PROGRAM WILL PRESENT—IN PERSON—THE BRIGHTEST STARS IN SHOW BUSINESS. MY NAME, DAHLINGS IS TALLULAH BANKHEAD"

EACH WEEK THE BRIGHTEST STARS OF SHOW BUSINESS WERE FEATURED. FRED ALLEN (OUT OF RETIREMENT) WAS A REGULAR SUPPORTING STAR. GUESTS INCLUDED: BOB HOPE, ETHEL MERMAN, JIMMY DURANTE, FANNY BRICE, FRANKIE LAINE, GROUCHO MARX, MARTIN & LEWIS AND MORE

THE 90-MINUTE LIVE SPECTACULAR FEATURED LEGENDARY BROADWAY ACTRESS TALLULAH BANKHEAD AS "MISTRESS OF CEREMONIES"

ANNOUNCERS: JIMMY WALLINGTON, ED HERLIHY

ANACIN

Chesterfield

SPONSORS: RCA, ANACIN AND CHESTERFIELD CIGARETTES

RCA

CLOSING THEME: "MAY THE GOOD LORD BLESS AND KEEP YOU"

WRITERS INCLUDED GOODMAN ACE, SELMA DIAMOND, GEORGE FOSTER

MEREDITH WILLSON'S ORCHESTRA SUPPLIED THE MUSIC

RADIO'S GOLDEN YEARS ©

by FRANK BRESEE & BOBB LYNES

BIG TOWN

BIG TOWN, STARRING MOTION PICTURE ACTOR EDWARD G. ROBINSON, BEGAN ITS LONG RUN IN 1937 ON CBS

ROBINSON ORIGINATED ROLE OF STEVE WILSON, MANAGING EDITOR OF THE ILLUSTRATED PRESS, A CRUSADING NEWSPAPER THAT FOUGHT CRIME AND CRIMINALS ON ITS PAGES CLAIRE TREVOR WAS LORELEI KILBOURNE, SOCIETY EDITOR

OTHER CAST MEMBERS: GALE GORDON, LOU MERRILL, CY KENDALL, JACK SMART, PAULA WINSLOWE, MASON ADAMS & LARRY HAINES

ED PAWLEY BECAME STEVE WILSON IN 1942 AND PLAYED THE PART UNTIL THE END OF THE SERIES IN 1952.
ONA MUNSON ALSO PLAYED LORELEI; LATER, FRAN CARLON HAD THE PART

SPONSORS: RINSO SOAP, LIFEBOUY SOAP & BAYER ASPIRIN

LIFEBUOY HEALTH SOAP

Bayer-Tablets of Aspirin 5grs each Genuine

RINSO

DWIGHT WEIST (NEW YORK)

ANNOUNCERS: CARLTON KADELL KEN NILES (HOLLYWOOD)

24

RADIO'S GOLDEN YEARS ©

by FRANK BRESEE & BOBB LYNES

BOB & RAY

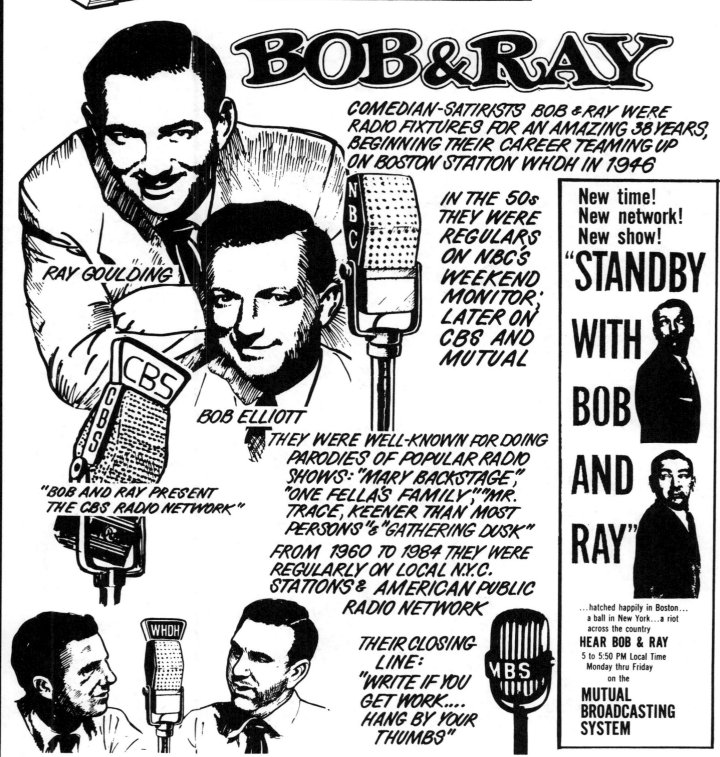

COMEDIAN-SATIRISTS BOB & RAY WERE RADIO FIXTURES FOR AN AMAZING 38 YEARS, BEGINNING THEIR CAREER TEAMING UP ON BOSTON STATION WHDH IN 1946

IN THE 50s THEY WERE REGULARS ON NBC'S WEEKEND MONITOR; LATER ON CBS AND MUTUAL

RAY GOULDING

BOB ELLIOTT

"BOB AND RAY PRESENT THE CBS RADIO NETWORK"

THEY WERE WELL-KNOWN FOR DOING PARODIES OF POPULAR RADIO SHOWS: "MARY BACKSTAGE," "ONE FELLA'S FAMILY," "MR. TRACE, KEENER THAN MOST PERSONS" & "GATHERING DUSK"

FROM 1960 TO 1984 THEY WERE REGULARLY ON LOCAL N.Y.C. STATIONS & AMERICAN PUBLIC RADIO NETWORK

THEIR CLOSING LINE: "WRITE IF YOU GET WORK.... HANG BY YOUR THUMBS"

New time!
New network!
New show!

"STANDBY WITH BOB AND RAY"

...hatched happily in Boston... a ball in New York...a riot across the country
HEAR BOB & RAY
5 to 5:50 PM Local Time
Monday thru Friday
on the
MUTUAL BROADCASTING SYSTEM

RADIO'S GOLDEN YEARS.©

by FRANK BRESEE & BOBB LYNES

BOBBY BENSON AND THE B·BAR·B RIDERS

FAMOUS OPENING:
"HERE THEY COME! THEY'RE RIDING FAST AND THEY'RE RIDING HARD! IT'S TIME FOR ACTION AND ADVENTURE IN THE MODERN WEST WITH BOBBY BENSON AND THE B-BAR-B RIDERS! AND OUT IN FRONT, ASTRIDE HIS GOLDEN PALOMINO AMIGO, IT'S THE COWBOY KID HIMSELF, BOBBY BENSON! BEEE-BAR-BEEEE!"

WANAMAKER

BILLY HALOP

IVAN CURY

BOBBY McKNIGHT

CLIVE RICE

BOBBY WAS A TEN-YEAR OLD KID WHO OWNED A BIG RANCH IN TEXAS

BOBBY BENSON BEGAN AS A LOCAL KIDS ADVENTURE SERIAL IN BUFFALO, NEW YORK IN 1931, MOVED TO CBS (1932-36) AS BOBBY BENSON AND THE H-BAR-O RANGERS. THE SERIES WAS REVIVED ON MUTUAL IN 1949 AS BOBBY BENSON AND THE B-BAR-B RIDERS AND RAN UNTIL 1955....

ANNOUNCER: CARL WARREN

THE FIRST BOBBY WAS RICHARD WANAMAKER THEN, BILLY HALOP, LATER: CLIVE RICE, (CLYDE CAMPBELL) BOBBY McKNIGHT AND IVAN CURY

A YOUNG DON KNOTTS PLAYED "WINDY WALES" (MBS SERIES)

TEX RITTER PLAYED ON THE CBS SERIES
PRODUCER: HERB RICE
WRITER: JIM SHEAN
DIRECTOR: BOB NOVAK

SPONSORS: HECKER'S H-O CEREALS AND KRAFT FOODS

"HARKA", THE INDIAN AND "IRISH" WERE PLAYED BY CRAIG McDONNELL

BOB HAAG WAS FOREMAN "TEX MASON"

NOTE: IN THE 1980s DON KNOTTS CO-STARRED WITH TEX RITTER'S SON JOHN IN THE TV HIT "THREE'S COMPANY"

RADIO'S GOLDEN YEARS ©

by FRANK BRESEE & BOBB LYNES

BOSTON BLACKIE

BOSTON BLACKIE WENT ON THE AIR ON NBC IN 1944 AS A SUMMER REPLACEMENT FOR AMOS N' ANDY

THE RADIO SERIES FEATURED CHESTER MORRIS IN THE TITLE ROLE, A PART HE CREATED IN THE COLUMBIA PICTURES BOSTON BLACKIE FILMS

"BOSTON BLACKIE! ENEMY TO THOSE WHO MAKE HIM AN ENEMY.... FRIEND TO THOSE WHO HAVE NO FRIEND!"

RICHARD LANE WAS (MOVIES & RADIO) "INSPECTOR FARADAY"

CHESTER MORRIS

THE ZIV SERIES STARRED NEW YORK RADIO ACTOR RICHARD KOLLMAR

BLACKIE WAS A PRIVATE DETECTIVE WHO WORKED IN NEW YORK CITY, SOLVING CRIMES FOR ANYONE WHO PAID HIM HIS DAILY FEE...

IN 1945 THE ZIV RADIO SYNDICATION COMPANY BEGAN A NEW SERIES OF BOSTON BLACKIE PROGRAMS, WHICH WAS ON THE AIR FOR OVER 10 YEARS

REGULAR CAST INCLUDED: RICHARD LANE, LESLEY WOODS, MAURICE TARPLIN, FRANK ORETH, TONY BARRETT & MORE

RICHARD KOLLMAR WAS MARRIED TO FAMOUS NEWSPAPER COLUMNIST DOROTHY KILGALLEN. FOR A TIME, THEY HAD AN EARLY MORNING SHOW (DOROTHY & DICK) ON WOR-MUTUAL

ANNOUNCERS: HARLOW WILCOX (NBC) LARRY ELLIOT (ZIV)

SPONSOR: RINSO SOAP (NBC)

Rinso

ZIV ALSO PRODUCED A ½ HOUR TV VERSION OF BOSTON BLACKIE WITH KENT TAYLOR IN THE 1950s

RADIO'S GOLDEN YEARS.

by FRANK BRESEE & BOBB LYNES

BOX 13

BOX 13 WAS A POPULAR SYNDICATED DETECTIVE/ADVENTURE RADIO SERIES STARRING PARAMOUNT FILM STAR ALAN LADD AS "DAN HOLIDAY."...

A NEWSMAN WHO WAS ALSO AN AUTHOR OF MYSTERY NOVELS, HE WAS ALWAYS ON THE LOOK-OUT FOR UNIQUE MATERIAL FOR HIS BOOKS AND PLACED THIS WANT AD IN THE "STAR TIMES"..."ADVENTURE WANTED, WILL GO ANYWHERE, DO ANYTHING..... WRITE BOX 13." THE AD BROUGHT HIM ALL KINDS OF WEIRD CHARACTERS AND UNEXPECTED DANGERS & ADVENTURES

ALAN LADD
AS DAN HOLIDAY

ASSISTANT, "SUZY" WAS SYLVIA PICKER

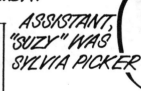

THE SERIES WAS HEARD IN SYNDICATION AND ON THE MUTUAL BROADCASTING SYSTEM STARTING AUGUST 22, 1948

SUPPORT CAST: LURENE TUTTLE, ALAN REED, LUIS VAN ROOTEN

TRANSCRIBED AT RADIO RECORDERS IN HOLLYWOOD FOR MAYFAIR PRODUCTIONS

RADIO'S GOLDEN YEARS ©

by FRANK BRESEE & BOBB LYNES

the EDDIE BRACKEN Show

PARAMOUNT PICTURE PERSONALITY, EDDIE BRACKEN STARRED IN HIS OWN RADIO SITUATION COMEDY BEGINNING ON CBS IN 1945. WHILE TRYING TO HELP HIS FRIENDS OUT OF SCRAPES, HE SEEMED TO CREATE MORE PROBLEMS!

ALSO FEATURED ON THE SHOW WERE: WILLIAM DEMAREST, ANN RUTHERFORD, JANET WALDO, CATHY LEWIS, WALLY MAHER & IRENE RYAN

ANNOUNCER: JOHN WALD

TEXACO DEALERS PRESENT EDDIE BRACKEN SHOW

CATHY LEWIS

TEXACO T REG.T.M.

SPONSOR: TEXACO GASOLINE

29

RADIO'S GOLDEN YEARS ©

by FRANK BRESEE & BOBB LYNES

DON McNEILL'S

BREAKFAST CLUB

THE BREAKFAST CLUB WAS THE LONGEST RUNNING DAYTIME RADIO PROGRAM OF ALL TIME. IT WAS ON THE AIR COAST-TO-COAST EVERY MORNING FOR 35 YEARS! (JUNE 23,1933 TO DEC. 27,1968)

SHOW ORIGINATED FROM THE SHERMAN HOUSE IN CHICAGO

SPONSORS: GENERAL MILLS, SWIFT & COMPANY AND PHILCO

PHILCO

Swift's Premium HAM

Betty Crocker Bisquick

FREE! Betty Crocker's Bisquick Cook Book with the package

WHEATIES

"Breakfast of Champions"

REGULARS OVER THE YEARS: JIM & MARIAN JORDAN (1930s) JOHNNY DESMOND, JACK OWENS, SAM COWLING & FRAN ALLISON.....

HOST OF THE PROGRAM WAS DON McNEILL

THEME SONG —
"GOOD MORNING BREAKFAST CLUB-ERS ITS TIME TO SING YA — ANOTHER CHEERY GREETING; SO MAY WE BRING YA; FOUR CALLS FOR BREAKFAST! OUR HAPPY CALL FOR BREAKFAST!"

BREAKFAST CLUB WAS ONE OF THE EARLY RADIO PROGRAMS TO ALSO BE SIMULCAST ON TV (1954)

RADIO'S GOLDEN YEARS©

by FRANK BRESEE & BOBB LYNES

BREAKFAST IN HOLLYWOOD

BREAKFAST IN HOLLYWOOD WAS AN EARLY MORNING DAILY, HALF-HOUR PROGRAM THAT DELIGHTED WOMEN LISTENERS FROM COAST-TO-COAST

IT BEGAN AS BREAKFAST AT SARDI'S AND DEBUTED ON NBC-BLUE IN 1941, LATER MOVING TO ABC... TOM BRENEMAN WOULD MOVE THROUGH HIS AUDIENCE AND INTERVIEW LADIES IN THE RESTAURANT, ASK CRAZY QUESTIONS AND LOOK FOR THE LADY WITH THE SILLIEST HAT.... AND WEAR IT!

ORCHIDS FROM CEDRIC'S FLORIST WERE GIVEN TO THE ELDEST GUEST EACH MORNING. THE JOKE OF THE DAY FROM "UNCLE CORNEY" AND A WISHING RING CEREMONY HELPED MAKE THE SHOW ONE THE MOST OF POPULAR DAYTIME RADIO PROGRAMS

SPONSOR: KELLOGG'S

Kellogg's

HOST
TOM BRENEMAN

JOHN NELSON

ANNOUNCERS:
CARL WEBSTER
PIERCE

A LATER HOST WAS GARRY MOORE....

THE PROGRAM WAS SO POPULAR THAT, IN 1947, A FEATURE FILM WAS MADE OF "BREAKFAST IN HOLLYWOOD" STARRING TOM BRENEMAN

RADIO'S GOLDEN YEARS

by FRANK BRESEE & BOBB LYNES

THE BLACK MUSEUM

THE BLACK MUSEUM WAS HOSTED BY ONE OF RADIO'S GREAT PERFORMERS.... ORSON WELLES

HOST: ORSON WELLES

THE WEEKLY MURDER MYSTERY SERIES FEATURED DRAMATIZED STORIES FROM LONDON'S SCOTLAND YARD, WHERE IS HOUSED AN UNBELIEVEABLE ARRAY OF CRIMINAL ARTIFACTS....

THE PROGRAM AIRED IN THE UNITED STATES, TUESDAYS AT 8 PM ON THE MUTUAL BROADCASTING SYSTEM FROM JANUARY TO DECEMBER, 1952

THE TRANSCRIBED SERIES WAS PRODUCED AT THE BRITISH BROADCASTING COMPANY IN LONDON....

THE SERIES WAS SO POPULAR IT CONTINUES TO BE HEARD IN RE-RUNS TO THIS DAY

RADIO'S GOLDEN YEARS ©
by FRANK BRESEE & BOBB LYNES

BLIND DATE

ARLENE FRANCIS WAS THE LOVELY "FEMCEE" OF THE POPULAR SHOW "BLIND DATE" WHICH BEGAN ON NBC JULY 8, 1943. THE PROGRAM FEATURED 6 SERVICEMEN AND A BEAUTIFUL MODEL. THE MODEL WOULD ASK THE MEN (WHO WERE HIDDEN BEHIND A WALL) QUESTIONS AND CHOOSE ONE FOR A DATE BASED ON THE ANSWERS EACH G.I. WOULD GIVE. (25 YEARS LATER, THE SHOW WAS SEEN ON TV AS "THE DATING GAME")

MISS FRANCIS WAS ALSO A REGULAR ON "AFFAIRS OF ANN SCOTLAND," "THE HOUR OF CHARM," "WHAT'S MY NAME?," "BETTY & BOB." SHE ALSO HOSTED NBC-TV'S "HOME" SHOW & WAS A PANELIST ON "WHAT'S MY LINE?"

SPONSORS:
MAXWELL HOUSE COFFEE & HINDS HAND CREAM

ARLENE FRANCIS GUIDED THE SHOW FOR ITS 3 SUCCESSFUL YEARS ON RADIO

HER HUSBAND WAS THE FAMOUS NEW YORK RADIO ACTOR MARTIN GABEL

RADIO'S GOLDEN YEARS.©

by FRANK BRESEE & BOBB LYNES

AH, AH, AH... DON'T TOUCH THAT DIAL... IT'S TIME FOR
BLONDIE!

BLONDIE AND DAGWOOD BEGAN AS A COMIC STRIP CREATED BY CHIC YOUNG IN 1930, BECAME POPULAR IN MOTION PICTURES IN 1938 AND BEGAN THEIR WEEKLY RADIO SHOW ON CBS ON JULY 3, 1939 AND RAN LATER ON THE BLUE NETWORK, ENDING ON APRIL 20, 1950.....
THE RADIO CAST INCLUDED HANLEY STAFFORD, FRANK NELSON, TOMMY COOK, & ELVIA ALLMAN

HANLEY STAFFORD AS "MR. DITHERS"

SPONSORS: CAMEL CIGARETTES, SUPER SUDS, COLGATE & FORD....

THE SHOW STARRED THE SAME ACTORS AS THE MOVIE SERIES: PENNY SINGLETON AS "BLONDIE" AND ARTHUR LAKE AS "DAGWOOD"

TOMMY COOK AS "ALEXANDER"

RADIO'S GOLDEN YEARS ©

by FRANK BRESEE & BOBB LYNES

BOLD VENTURE

HUMPHREY BOGART AND REAL-LIFE WIFE LAUREN BACALL STARRED IN THIS SYNDICATED RADIO SHOW (BY ZIV) DURING THE 1950-51 SEASON. THE 30-MINUTE WEEKLY ADVENTURE WAS HEARD ON OVER 400 STATIONS IN THE U.S.A.

ANNOUNCER: JOHN HIESTAND

THEY SPENT MANY ADVENTURES ON THEIR BOAT "THE BOLD VENTURE" AND A STRANGE ASSORTMENT OF CON MEN & DRIFTERS HELPED MAKE THE SHOW ONE OF THE MOST POPULAR ADVENTURES OF THE SEASON....

BOGART PLAYED "SLATE SHANNON" OWNER OF A CUBAN HOTEL. BACALL PLAYED "SAILOR DUVAL" (SLATE'S WARD AFTER HER FATHER DIED)

KING MOSES, A CALYPSO SINGER, SANG MUSICAL BRIDGES WHICH MOVED THE STORIES ALONG...

THEME MUSIC PROVIDED BY DAVID ROSE

A TOTAL OF 78 EPISODES WERE BROADCAST

Bride & Groom

BRIDE AND GROOM BEGAN ON ABC IN 1945, WHERE IT REMAINED FOR HALF A DOZEN YEARS......
COUPLES WERE INTERVIEWED ON THE AIR AND THEY TOLD THE STORY OF HOW THEY MET AND FELL IN LOVE. THE HOST WOULD BRING OUT UNIQUE AND FUNNY THINGS IN THEIR RELATIONSHIP, THEN SEND THEM TO A WEDDING CHAPEL NEXT DOOR TO THE STUDIO, TO BE MARRIED.
AS THE COUPLE SAID THEIR WEDDING VOWS, ANNOUNCER JACK McELROY WOULD CROON A LOVE SONG. SEVERAL COMMERCIALS LATER AND A LIST OF FABULOUS PRIZES, THE NOW HAPPILY-MARRIED COUPLE WOULD RETURN TO THE STUDIO FOR A GOODBYE TO LISTENERS AND A KISS FROM THE EMCEE

SDAY, JAN. 12, 1950

GOOD ON ABOVE DATE ONLY

Please present this card
to attend
The Wedding Reception of
Bride and Groom
Chapman Park Hotel
615 South Alexandria Avenue
Doors Open at 10:45 A. M.
Doors Close at 11:00 A. M.
One

ANNOUNCER:
JACK McELROY

HOST-EMCEE:
JOHN NELSON

MUSIC:
GAYLORD CARTER

OVER THE YEARS MORE THAN 1,000 COUPLES WERE MARRIED ON THE SHOW

MASTERSON   NELSON   REDDY

SPONSOR:
STERLING
DRUGS

THE SHOW WAS CREATED AND PRODUCED BY "THE THREE JOHN COMPANY"...JOHN NELSON, JOHN MASTERSON AND JOHN REDDY

RADIO'S GOLDEN YEARS ©
by FRANK BRESEE & BOBB LYNES

BUCK ROGERS IN THE 25th CENTURY

BUCK ROGERS IN THE 25TH CENTURY BEGAN IN AMAZING STORIES MAGAZINE, MOVED TO THE COMIC STRIPS, THEN WAS ADAPTED TO AND DEBUTED ON CBS RADIO NOVEMBER 7, 1932 AS A DAILY 15-MINUTE SERIAL.

IN THE STORY, ANTHONY "BUCK" ROGERS, DURING WORLD WAR I, IS TRAPPED IN SUSPENDED ANIMATION AND WAKES UP IN THE FANTASTIC WORLD OF THE 25TH CENTURY WITH SPACE SHIPS, RAY GUNS AND GRAVITY BELTS!

BUCK WAS PLAYED BY CURTIS ARNELL, LATER JOHN LARKIN, MATT CROWLEY GIRLFRIEND WILMA DEERING WAS ADELE RONSON, LATER VIRGINIA VASS

BUCK'S ENEMIES: KILLER KANE AND ARDELA VALMER

ANNOUNCERS: FRED UTTAL, PAUL DOUGLAS DR. HUER WAS PLAYED BY EDGAR STEHLI

SPONSORS: KELLOGG'S, COCOMALT, CREAM OF WHEAT AND POPSICLE

WRITER-DIRECTOR WAS JACK JOHNSTONE (WHO LATER DID SUPERMAN, MAN CALLED X, JOHNNY DOLLAR, OTHERS)

IN 1946-47 THE SERIES WAS HEARD ON MUTUAL

RADIO'S GOLDEN YEARS©

by FRANK BRESEE & BOBB LYNES

BULLDOG DRUMMOND

BULLDOG DRUMMOND WAS ONE OF THE MANY RADIO SERIES DEVELOPED FROM A POPULAR MOTION PICTURE. IT BEGAN IN SEPTEMBER 1941 ON WOR-NEW YORK AND WAS HEARD COAST-TO-COAST ON THE MUTUAL BROADCASTING SYSTEM

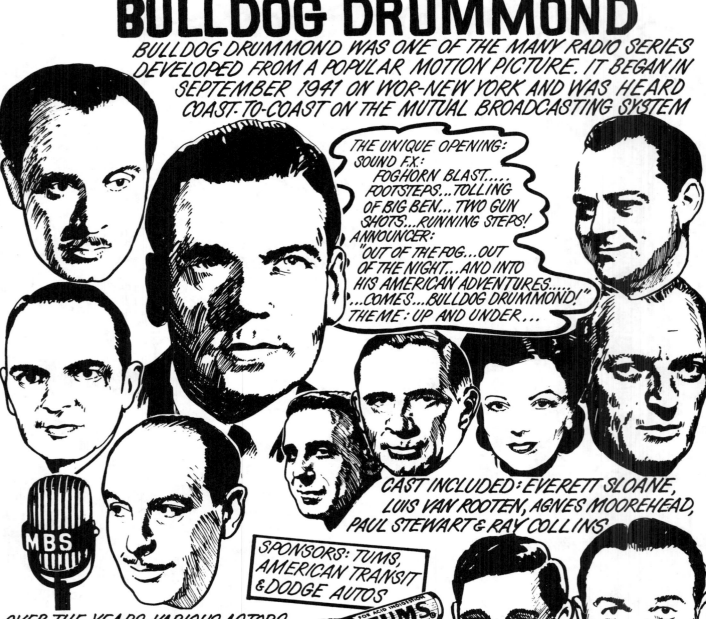

THE UNIQUE OPENING:
SOUND F.X.:
FOGHORN BLAST.....
FOOTSTEPS...TOLLING
OF BIG BEN...TWO GUN
SHOTS...RUNNING STEPS!
ANNOUNCER:
"OUT OF THE FOG...OUT
OF THE NIGHT...AND INTO
HIS AMERICAN ADVENTURES.....
...COMES....BULLDOG DRUMMOND!"
THEME: UP AND UNDER...

CAST INCLUDED: EVERETT SLOANE, LUIS VAN ROOTEN, AGNES MOOREHEAD, PAUL STEWART & RAY COLLINS

SPONSORS: TUMS, AMERICAN TRANSIT & DODGE AUTOS

OVER THE YEARS, VARIOUS ACTORS PLAYED HUGH DRUMMOND: GEORGE COULOURIS, SANTOS ORTEGA, AND BEST REMEMBERED...NED WEVER DURING A SECOND RUN IN THE 1950s, THE LEAD WAS SIR CEDRIC HARDWICKE

ANNOUNCERS:
KEN ROBERTS   TED MEYERS

RADIO'S GOLDEN YEARS ©

by FRANK BRESEE & BOBB LYNES

BOB BURNS

COMEDIAN BOB BURNS, BETTER KNOWN AS "THE ARKANSAS TRAVELER" BEGAN HIS RADIO CAREER ON RUDY VALLEE'S SHOW IN 1935. HE WAS SUCH A HIT, THAT BING CROSBY HIRED HIM AS A FOIL ON HIS SHOW. THE 26-WEEK CONTRACT TURNED INTO SIX YEARS!

BOB BURNS' OWN SHOW BEGAN ON CBS IN 1941, TWO YEARS LATER MOVED TO NBC FOR SIX MORE YEARS...

CAST REGULARS: GINNY SIMMS, SHIRLEY ROSS, EDNA MAY OLIVER, & MANTAN MORELAND

BURNS SPUN YARNS, TOLD JOKES, AND PLAYED HIS STRANGE, HOME-MADE MUSICAL INSTRUMENT CALLED A "BAZOOKA"

SPONSORS: CAMPBELL SOUPS, LEVER BROS., LIFEBOUY SOAP, AMERICAN FOODS, KOLYNOS TOOTH PASTE & DREFT SOAP

LIFEBUOY HEALTH SOAP

Campbell's Quality

DURING WORLD WAR II, THE U.S. ARMY DEVELOPED A SPECIAL WEAPON TO LAUNCH HIGH VELOCITY MORTARS... IT WAS NAMED "THE BAZOOKA" AFTER BURNS' MUSICAL INSTRUMENT.

MUSIC: RAY SINATRA ORCHESTRA

RADIO'S GOLDEN YEARS©

by FRANK BRESEE & BOBB LYNES

GEORGE & GRACIE BURNS & ALLEN

GEORGE BURNS AND GRACIE ALLEN WAS ONE OF THE LONGEST RUNNING AND MOST POPULAR HUSBAND AND WIFE RADIO TEAMS.....

THEY WERE ON THE AIR FROM FEBRUARY 15, 1932 UNTIL MAY 17, 1950, WHEN THEY MOVED TO TELEVISION

GEORGE & GRACIE TEAMED TOGETHER IN VAUDEVILLE IN THE TWENTIES

CHARACTER ACTORS WHO WERE REGULARS ON THE SHOW: MEL BLANC, ELVIA ALLMAN, GALE GORDON AND HANS CONRIED

SPONSORS: SWAN SOAP, MAXWELL HOUSE COFFEE & GRAPE-NUTS

Post's GRAPE-NUTS

SWAN

FOR GLASS COFFEE-MAKERS
MAXWELL HOUSE Coffee

ANNOUNCERS: JOHN CONTE, HARRY VON ZELL, BILL GOODWIN, TOBE REED

IN 1940 GRACIE ALLEN RAN FOR U.S. PRESIDENT (FOR LAUGHS) ON THE SURPRISE PARTY TICKET

GEORGE BURNS CELEBRATED HIS 100TH BIRTHDAY ON JANUARY 20, 1996 AND DIED 7 WEEKS LATER...

RADIO'S GOLDEN YEARS©

by FRANK BRESEE & BOBB LYNES

Billie Burke

THE BILLIE BURKE SHOW BEGAN ON CBS IN 1944; CONTINUED UNTIL 1946, WAS HEARD EVERY SATURDAY MORNING COAST-TO-COAST FOLLOWING "LET'S PRETEND"

THE SHOW FEATURED MISS BURKE IN HER FAMILIAR ROLE AS A SCATTER-BRAINED LADY WITH A HEART OF GOLD

ANNOUNCERS: MARVIN MILLER, TOM DIXON

THE SUPPORTING CAST INCLUDED EARLE ROSS, LILLIAN RANDOLPH, MARVIN MILLER, ARTHUR Q. BRYAN, HATTIE McDANIEL & FRANKLIN BRESEE

BILLIE BURKE CAME TO RADIO FROM BROADWAY ("ZIEGFELD FOLLIES") AND MOVIES (THE GOOD WITCH GLINDA IN "THE WIZARD OF OZ")

CBS

CBS

LISTERINE TOOTH PASTE

SPONSOR: LISTERINE TOOTHPASTE

RADIO'S GOLDEN YEARS ©

by FRANK BRESEE & BOBB LYNES

CALLING ALL CARS!

CALLING ALL CARS WAS ONE OF THE BEST REMEMBERED POLICE-DETECTIVE SHOWS DURING THE EARLY DAYS OF RADIO....

IT DEBUTED IN NOVEMBER 1933, AS A WEDNESDAY NIGHT FEATURE ON CBS RADIO; LATE IN 1934 IT MOVED TO FRIDAY NIGHTS WHERE IT RAN FOR THE NEXT FIVE YEARS

OPENING: "CALLING ALL CARS: ATTENTION ALL CARS; ROBBERY IN PROGRESS AT 5TH AND MAIN; PROCEED AT ONCE, THAT IS ALL.....ROSENQUIST"

NARRATOR: FREDERICK W. LINDSEY

THE BEST-REMEMBERED VOICE WAS THAT OF REAL-LIFE POLICE DISPATCHER, SGT. JESSE ROSENQUIST

THE SERIES FEATURED ACTUAL STORIES OF THE LOS ANGELES POLICE DEPARTMENT, MUCH AS DRAGNET DID YEARS LATER

DIRECTOR: WILLIAN N. ROBSON

CAST: BILL ZUCKERT, ROBERT DRYDEN, JACKSON BECK, ETC.

RIO GRANDE

SPONSOR: RIO GRANDE GASOLINE

RADIO'S GOLDEN YEARS ©

by FRANK BRESEE & BOBB LYNES

CAVALCADE OF AMERICA

THE CAVALCADE OF AMERICA WAS ONE OF THE MOST PRESTIGEOUS SHOWS ON THE AIR. IT DEBUTED ON CBS ON OCT. 9, 1935, MOVING TO NBC IN 1939. THE WEEKLY SERIES COMBINED AUTHENTIC HISTORICAL EVENTS IN EXCITING DRAMATIZATIONS. SPECIAL WRITERS FOR THE PROGRAM INCLUDED MAXWELL ANDERSON, STEPHEN VINCENT BENET, CARL SANDBURG AND ROBERT SHERWOOD

GUEST STARS: CLARK GABLE, ORSON WELLES, RAYMOND MASSEY, CHARLES LAUGHTON, LIONEL BARRYMORE, TYRONE POWER, ALFRED LUNT & LYNN FONTANNE, MORE

RADIO SUPPORT CAST: AGNES MOOREHEAD, JOHN McINTIRE, JEANETTE NOLAN, RAYMOND EDWARD JOHNSON, RAY COLLINS, OTHERS

DUPONT

SPONSOR: DUPONT

ANNOUNCER: CLAYTON COLLYER

MUSIC: DONALD VOORHEES, ROBERT ARMBRUSTER

PRODUCER: ROGER PRYOR

CAMEL CARAVAN
WITH
VAUGHN MONROE
AND HIS ORCHESTRA

THE CAMEL CARAVAN STARRING VAUGHN MONROE WAS A MUSICAL VARIETY SHOW ON CBS WHICH BEGAN IN 1942 AND LASTED FOR TEN YEARS. IT WAS BROADCAST FROM NEW YORK CITY AND TRAVELLED TO MANY REMOTE LOCATIONS AROUND AMERICA...

VAUGHN MONROE RECORDED FOR RCA VICTOR AND DURING HIS LONG CAREER PRODUCED MANY HITS, INCLUDING: "RUM AND COCA-COLA," "THERE I'VE SAID IT AGAIN," "SEEMS LIKE OLD TIMES," "TALLAHASSEE," "GHOST RIDERS IN THE SKY," "RACING WITH THE MOON" AND "MULE TRAIN"

RCA **RCA Victor**
RADIO'S GREATEST VALUE · A SERVICE OF THE RADIO CORP. OF AMERICA

THEME SONG:
"RACING WITH THE MOON"

ANNOUNCER:
HUGH CONOVER

SPONSOR:
CAMEL CIGARETTES

CAMEL
TURKISH & DOMESTIC BLEND CIGARETTES
CHOICE QUALITY

DURING THE LATE FORTIES VAUGHN MONROE STARRED IN WESTERN FILMS FOR REPUBLIC STUDIOS

RADIO'S GOLDEN YEARS ©

by FRANK BRESEE & BOBB LYNES

the JUDY CANOVA Show

COMEDIENNE JUDY CANOVA WAS FIRST HEARD (WITH HER BROTHERS) IN A MUSICAL-COMEDY ACT ON THE RUDY VALLEE SHOW IN THE LATE THIRTIES. IN JULY 1943 SHE BEGAN HER SHOW ON CBS (LATER NBC)

WITH A CAST OF RADIO PERSONALITIES WHICH INCLUDED HANS CONRIED, VERNA FELTON, SHELDON LEONARD, MEL BLANC, RUBY DANDRIDGE & JOE KEARNS

SPONSORS: COLGATE TOOTHPASTE, SEALTEST PRODUCTS

Sealtest CREAM

COLGATE RIBBON DENTAL CREAM

ANNOUNCER: HOWARD PETRIE

MEL BLANC PLAYED JUDY'S PA AND PEDRO WHOSE POPULAR INTRO WAS: "PARDON ME FOR TALKING IN YOUR FACE, SENOREETA!"

45

RADIO'S GOLDEN YEARS ©

by FRANK BRESEE & BOBB LYNES

EDDIE CANTOR

EDDIE CANTOR WAS THE FIRST OF THE BIG TIME COMEDIANS TO TAKE RADIO BY STORM; HIS SHOW WAS HEARD FROM SEPT. 13, 1931 TO OCT. 8, 1953, ON BOTH NBC or CBS

HE BROUGHT MANY ENTERTAINERS TO RADIO FOR THE FIRST TIME: GEORGE BURNS & GRACIE ALLEN, BOBBY BREEN, DEANNA DURBIN, DINAH SHORE & EDDIE FISHER

♪ "I LOVE TO SPEND EACH WEDNESDAY WITH YOU...." ♪

ANNOUNCERS: JIMMY WALLINGTON (NEW YORK) HARRY VON ZELL (HOLLYWOOD)

REGULARS ON HIS SHOW: BERT GORDON (THE MAD RUSSIAN) & HARRY EINSTEIN (PARKYAKARKAS)

Pabst Blue Ribbon

SPONSORS: CHASE & SANBORN COFFEE, PEBECO TOOTHPASTE, TEXACO, CAMEL CIGARETTES, SAL HEPATICA AND PABST BEER.....

REGULAR GRIND STAR BRAND PRESSURE PACKED Chase & Sanborn COFFEE GROUND & DOMESTIC

CAMEL

Sal Hepatica ORIGINAL! Effervescent Saline Combination CAREFULLY BLENDED WELL BALANCED LAXATIVE & CATHARTIC

ACO

WALLINGTON

VON ZELL

EDDIE CANTOR CREATED THE SLOGAN "MARCH OF DIMES" FOR PRESIDENT FRANKLIN D. ROOSEVELT.....

RADIO'S GOLDEN YEARS©

by FRANK BRESEE & BOBB LYNES

CAPTAIN MIDNIGHT!

SKELLY S

ANNOUNCER DON GORDON

Captain Midnight's **SECRET SQUADRON** 1942 BOOK OF OFFICIAL CHARTS, CODES AND SEC...

CAPTAIN MIDNIGHT BEGAN ON RADIO AT CHICAGO'S WGN FOR ONLY THE MIDWEST SPONSORED BY SKELLY OIL COMPANY IN 1939. THE 15 MINUTE DAILY SERIAL WENT TO MUTUAL ON SEPT. 30, 1940....

HE WAS JOINED IN HIS FLYING ADVENTURES BY SECRET SQUADRON MEMBERS "CHUCK RAMSEY," "PATSY DONOVAN" (LATER "JOYCE RYAN") & "ICHABOD MUDD"

CAST OVER THE YEARS: BILL ROSE, JOHNNY COONS, MARILOU NEUMAYER, ART HERN, FINNEY BRIGGS RENÉE RODIER & HUGH STUDEBAKER....

EACH EPISODE FEATURED A SECRET MESSAGE TO THE LISTENERS WHO USED VARIOUS CODE-O-GRAPHS TO DE-CODE THE WORDS....

WILLIS (BILL) BOUCHEY WAS THE CAPTAIN FOR SKELLY

ED PRENTISS STARRED ON MBS UNTIL DEC. 15, 1949

OVALTINE

SPONSORS: SKELLY OIL & OVALTINE

ANNOUNCERS: TOM MOORE & PIERRE ANDRE

THE EVIL VILLAIN "IVAN SHARK" WAS BORIS APLON

RADIO'S GOLDEN YEARS ©

by FRANK BRESEE & BOBB LYNES

Can You Top This!

HARRY HERSHFIELD

PETER DONALD

MBS

SENATOR FORD

JOE LAURIE, JR.

"SENATOR" ED FORD WAS A VAUDEVILLE VETERAN
HARRY HERSHFIELD, CARTOONIST (CREATOR OF
"ABE KABIBBLE") & AFTER-DINNER SPEAKER
JOE LAURIE, JR. VAUDEVILLE VET & COMEDY
WRITER (EDDIE CANTOR & AL JOLSON)

CAN YOU TOP THIS BEGAN AS A LOCAL PANEL SHOW
ON WOR DECEMBER 9, 1940. THE LISTENERS WERE
ASKED TO SEND IN JOKES TO BE TOLD BY PETER
DONALD AND THE PANEL OF COMEDY EXPERTS
WOULD TRY TO GET BIGGER LAUGHS WITH JOKES
ON THE SAME SUBJECT. THE PANEL NEVER KNEW
IN ADVANCE WHAT THE JOKES WOULD BE AND
RELIED ON THEIR KNOWLEDGE OF HUMOR TO
COME UP WITH THE AD-LIBBED TOPPERS....

THE SERIES MOVED TO NBC
IN 1942, THEN MBS (1948-50)
LATER ABC, ENDING ON
NBC IN 1954

ABC

Ford

COLGATE DENTAL CREAM with GARDOL

Mars

SNICKERS

milky way

milky way BAR

SPONSORS:
COLGATE, FORD
& MARS CANDY

RADIO'S GOLDEN YEARS ©

by FRANK BRESEE & BOBB LYNES

CARNATION CONTENTED HOUR

THE CARNATION CONTENTED HOUR WAS A VARIETY PROGRAM OF POPULAR MUSIC WHICH DEBUTED ON NBC IN 1932 AND WAS HEARD FOR AN AMAZING 15 YEARS; IN THE LATE 40s & EARLY 50s ON CBS

ORCHESTRAS LED BY:
FRANK BLACK,
PERCY FAITH,
TED DALE

THE CARNATION HOUR FEATURED AN IMPRESSIVE LIST OF POPULAR SINGERS AND MUSICIANS: BUDDY CLARK, DINAH SHORE, TONY MARTIN, JANE POWELL AND DICK HAYMES

BUDDY CLARK

PERCY FAITH

ANNOUNCER:
JIMMY WALLINGTON

SPONSOR:
CARNATION
MILK PRODUCTS

VELVETIZED
Carnation
EVAPORATED
MILK

RADIO'S GOLDEN YEARS.©

by FRANK BRESEE & BOBB LYNES

JACK CARSON Show

WARNER BROTHERS MOTION PICTURE STAR JACK CARSON BEGAN HIS OWN RADIO PROGRAM ON CBS IN JUNE, 1943. THIS WEDNESDAY NIGHT ROMP WAS A SITUATION COMEDY OF SORTS, WITH CARSON IN THE MIDDLE.....

HIS MAIN FOIL WAS BRITISH ACTOR ARTHUR TREACHER. ALSO EDDIE MARR AS A HUSTLING SALESMAN WHO SOLD ANYTHING FROM A FROZEN ESKIMO TO A WOODEN INDIAN....

SCATTERBRAINED IRENE RYAN (LATER, BEVERLY HILLBILLIES' GRANNY ON TV) WAS ALONG FOR LAUGHS, AS WAS 8-YEAR OLD NORMA JEAN NILSSON MEL BLANC AND DAVE WILLOCK

MUSIC: FREDDY MARTIN, LATER FRANK DeVOL

SPONSORS: CAMPBELL SOUP AND SEALTEST

Campbell's Quality

Sealtest ICE CREAM

VOCALIST: DALE EVANS

ANNOUNCERS: DEL SHARBUTT, HOWARD PETRIE

LATER, THE PROGRAM MOVED TO NBC AS "THE SEALTEST VILLAGE STORE" CO-STARRING EVE ARDEN WITH FRANK DeVOL'S ORCHESTRA....

NATIONAL BROADCASTING COMPANY. INC
HOLLYWOOD STUDIOS
SUNSET AND VINE

| Mon.-Oct. 20 See Reverse Side | PREVIEW SEALTEST VILLAGE STORE STARRING JACK CARSON with EVE ARDEN FRANK DeVOL'S ORCHES ★ CHILDREN ... | STU |

50

RADIO'S GOLDEN YEARS ©

by FRANK BRESEE & BOBB LYNES

CBS RADIO WORKSHOP

SOME STORIES FEATURED:
"MARS IS HEAVEN"
"REPORT ON THE WEANS"
"KING OF THE CATS"
"NIGHTMARE"
"JIMMY BLUE EYES"
"ANALYSIS OF SATIRE"
"1,489 WORDS"

THE CBS RADIO WORKSHOP WAS THE PRESTIGE DRAMATIC ANTHOLOGY SHOW OF RADIO. IT BEGAN AS A SUSTAINED SERIES, THE COLUMBIA WORKSHOP, ON CBS IN 1936, WHICH RAN OFF AND ON UNTIL 1947. REVIVED BY CBS IN 1956, THE WORKSHOP PRESENTED AS THE OPENING PROGRAM ALDOUS HUXLEY NARRATING HIS FAMOUS "BRAVE NEW WORLD"

HOLLYWOOD'S FINEST ACTORS WERE HEARD WEEKLY: JOHN DEHNER, WM. CONRAD, VIC PERRIN, JOE KEARNS, SAM EDWARDS, LURENE TUTTLE, STAN FREBERG, DAWS BUTLER, JUNE FORAY, PARLEY BAER, RAYMOND BURR, JACK KRUSCHEN, BYRON KANE, HOWARD McNEAR, LOU KRUGMAN EDWARD R. MURROW AND THEN-SENATOR JOHN F. KENNEDY!

OTHER WRITERS' WORKS FEATURED WERE RAY BRADBURY, ARCHIBALD MacLEISH, ROBERT NATHAN, NORMAN CORWIN, MORE

PRODUCER-DIRECTORS: WM. N. ROBSON, WM. FROUG, JACK JOHNSTONE, ELLIOTT LEWIS, PAUL ROBERTS & DEE ENGLEBACH

ANNOUNCERS: HUGH DOUGLAS, BOB HITE, GEORGE WALSH & TED PEARSON

MUSIC: BERNARD HERRMANN, AMERIGO MORENO, LEITH STEVENS

RADIO'S GOLDEN YEARS ©

by FRANK BRESEE & BOBB LYNES

CHANDU THE MAGICIAN

FRANK CHANDLER, AN AMERICAN-BORN MYSTIC, LEARNED THE SECRETS OF THE EAST FROM A YOGI IN INDIA. USING HIS OWN POWERS, HE COMBATED EVIL ALL OVER THE WORLD AS HE BECAME KNOWN AS "CHANDU, THE MAGICIAN."....

THE 15 MINUTE NIGHTLY SERIES BEGAN ON KHJ IN 1932, MOVED TO THE MUTUAL-DON LEE NETWORK AND RAN UNTIL 1936. THE SHOW WAS REVIVED ON JUNE 28, 1948 FOR THE WEST COAST ON MBS-DONLEE; LATER AS A 30-MINUTE WEEKLY, ENDING ON ABC IN 1950....

IRENE TEDROW

TOM COLLINS

THE FIRST CHANDU: GAYNE WHITMAN, LATER HOWARD HOFFMAN AND TOM COLLINS (1940s MBS SERIES)

WHITE KING

LEE MILLAR

SPONSORS: WHITE KING SOAP (WEST), BEECH-NUT GUM (EAST)

VEOLA VONN

ANNOUNCER: HOWARD CULVER

DIRECTOR: CYRIL ARMBRISTER

MUSIC: FELIX MILLS, RAYMOND PAIGE, LATER KORLA PANDIT AT THE ORGAN.....

SUPPORT CAST: OLAN SOULÉ, LEON JANNEY, IAN MARTIN, BRYNA RAEBURN, LUIS VAN ROOTEN, IRENE TEDROW VEOLA VONN, LEE MILLAR AND JOY TERRY

RADIO'S GOLDEN YEARS ©
by FRANK BRESEE & BOBB LYNES

CHESTERFIELD SUPPER CLUB

FEATURING THE TOP MUSIC OF THE TIME, THE CHESTERFIELD SUPPER CLUB BEGAN IN DECEMBER 1944 ON NBC AND RAN UNTIL 1954...

THE 15-MINUTE SHOW AIRED FIVE NIGHTS A WEEK STARRING PERRY COMO (MON.-WED.-FRI.) AND JO STAFFORD (TUES.-THURS.)

NATIONAL BROADCASTING COMPANY. INC
HOLLYWOOD STUDIOS
SUNSET AND VINE

The CHESTERFIELD SUPPER CLUB
STARRING
JO STAFFORD
★ CHILDREN UNDER 14 WILL NOT BE ADMITTED ★

23
Tue.-Sept.
See Reverse Side

LATER STARS WERE: PEGGY LEE, JOHNNY JOHNSTON, BILL LAWRENCE

SINGING GUESTS INCLUDED BUDDY CLARK, DICK HAYMES, FRANKIE LAINE, OTHERS

ANNOUNCERS: MARTIN BLOCK (NEW YORK)

TOM REDDY (HOLLYWOOD)

THEMES: "SMOKE DREAMS" AND "A CIGARETTE, SWEET MUSIC & YOU"

SPONSOR: CHESTERFIELD CIGARETTES

RADIO'S GOLDEN YEARS ©

by FRANK BRESEE & BOBB LYNES

CIGARETTE COMMERCIALS

DURING RADIO'S FORMATIVE YEARS, FROM THE THIRTIES THROUGH THE FIFTIES, MOST OF THE CIGARETTE COMPANIES SPONSORED RADIO SHOWS. THEY BROUGHT US THE BIGGEST STARS AND THE FINEST ENTERTAINMENT, AT HOME...AND FOR FREE!

LUCKY STRIKE BROUGHT US "YOUR HIT PARADE"& "THE JACK BENNY SHOW," CHESTERFIELD PRESENTED "THE BING CROSBY SHOW," "THE BOB HOPE SHOW," PERRY COMO AND ARTHUR GODFREY; ALSO "GLENN MILLER TIME," THE SUPPER CLUB" WITH PEGGY LEE & JO STAFFORD. CAMEL SPONSORED "ABBOTT & COSTELLO" "BLONDIE," BOB CROSBY & BOB HAWK.

PHILIP MORRIS BROUGHT US "CANDID MICROPHONE," "CRIME DOCTOR" & RALPH EDWARDS'"THIS IS YOUR LIFE". RALEIGH SPONSORED "PEOPLE ARE FUNNY," RED SKELTON, HILDEGARDE & "BREAK THE BANK."

OLD GOLD PRESENTED "POT O' GOLD," "THE BICKERSONS," "STOP THE MUSIC"& FRANK SINATRA. PALL MALL PRESENTED "THE BIG STORY," AND "RIPLEY'S BELIEVE IT OR NOT." L&M SPONSORED "GUNSMOKE" AND "DRAGNET"

THIS IS NOT AN ADVERTISEMENT OR ENDORSEMENT

54

RADIO'S GOLDEN YEARS©

by FRANK BRESEE & BOBB LYNES

The CISCO KID

O. HENRY'S "FAMOUS ROBIN HOOD OF THE OLD WEST" THE CISCO KID WAS FIRST HEARD ON WOR-MUTUAL ON OCTOBER 2, 1942 STARRING JACKSON BECK AS "CISCO" WITH LOUIS SORIN AS "PANCHO" AND RAN FOR ABOUT ONE SEASON

OPENING....
PANCHO: "CISCO! THEE SHERIFF HE IS GEETING CLOSER!"
CISCO: "THIS WAY, PANCHO! VAMANOS!"

IT CAME BACK TO MUTUAL-DON LEE FROM HOLLYWOOD IN 1946 WITH JACK MATHER (CISCO) & HARRY LANG (SOMETIMES MEL BLANC) AS PANCHO, ALTERNATING WITH RED RYDER MONDAY, WEDNESDAY & FRIDAY

JACKSON BECK

HARRY LANG

SPONSORS: BUTTER-NUT/WEBER'S/ KILLPATRICK'S BREAD

Butter-nut BREAD

JACK MATHER

MBS

RADIO'S GOLDEN YEARS.©

by FRANK BRESEE & BOBB LYNES

COMMAND PERFORMANCE U.S.A
ARMED ★ FORCES ★ RADIO ★ SERVICE

COMMAND PERFORMANCE WAS A RADIO SPECTACULAR.....FROM EARLY 1942 UNTIL AFTER WORLD WAR TWO, IT WAS BROADCAST BY SHORTWAVE TO AMERICAN G.I.s FIGHTING OVERSEAS ON ARMED FORCES RADIO SERVICE (AFRS)...

VIRTUALLY ALL MOVIE, STAGE, RADIO & RECORDING STARS APPEARED ON COMMAND PERFORMANCE

EACH SHOW FEATURED MORE STARS ON ONE HALF HOUR PROGRAM THAN MIGHT BE APPEARING ON ALL WEEKLY NETWORK SHOWS COMBINED!

GUESTS WITH THE MOST APPEARANCES WERE: DINAH SHORE (35 TIMES); BING CROSBY (29) BOB HOPE (26) JIMMY DURANTE (19) FRANCES LANGFORD (18) JUDY GARLAND (15) VIRGINIA O'BRIEN (13)

THE LAST COMMAND PERFORMANCE WAS A SPECIAL COMMEMORATING THE 35TH ANNIVERSARY OF THE SHOW IN 1977 HOSTED BY BOB HOPE

ANNOUNCERS: KEN CARPENTER (145 TIMES), HARRY VON ZELL, JIMMY WALLINGTON & DON WILSON

LINA ROMAY

RADIO'S GOLDEN YEARS ©

by FRANK BRESEE & BOBB LYNES

JOHN CONTE

JOHN CONTE WAS ONE OF RADIO'S EARLIEST MASTER OF CEREMONIES. OVER THE YEARS HE WAS ASSOCIATED WITH MOST OF THE POPULAR ENTERTAINERS IN SHOW BUSINESS, INCLUDING FANNY BRICE (BABY SNOOKS) AND FRANK MORGAN (THE WIZARD OF OZ)

HE WAS FEATURED ON:
MAXWELL HOUSE COFFE TIME
IT HAPPENED IN HOLLYWOOD
SCREEN GUILD PLAYERS
COMMAND PERFORMANCE
MAIL CALL
TEENTIMER CANTEEN
MY GOOD WIFE WITH ARLENE FRANCIS
JOHN CONTE SHOW
TREASURY OF MUSIC

CONTE WORKED ON CBS, NBC, ABC AND AFRS NETWORKS

JOHN CONTE WAS HOST OF THE FIRST ALL-COLOR DAILY ONE HOUR SHOW "MATINEE THEATRE" ON NBC-TV

JOHN CONTE CONTINUED HIS CAREER IN BROADCASTING, LATER WAS OWNER-OPERATOR OF THE WELL-KNOWN PALM SPRINGS NBC-TV STATION, KMIR

RADIO'S GOLDEN YEARS ©

by FRANK BRESEE & BOBB LYNES

MEET CORLISS ARCHER

F. HUGH HERBERT'S PLAY "KISS AND TELL" WAS THE BASIS FOR THE TEENAGE SITUATION COMEDY SERIES MEET CORLISS ARCHER, WHICH BEGAN ON CBS IN 1943 (LATER ON ABC) ENDING ON CBS IN 1955...

PRISCILLA LYON WAS THE FIRST CORLISS, THEN JANET WALDO PLAYED THE PART MOST OF THE TIME. CORLISS ARCHER AND A DATE WITH JUDY WERE SIMILAR TO EACH OTHER... JANET & LOUISE ERICKSON, (JUDY) EACH PLAYED PARTS ON THE OTHER'S SHOWS!

BOYFRIEND DEXTER FRANKLIN WAS PLAYED BY IRVING LEE, BILL CHRISTY... AND BEST REMEMBERED.... SAM EDWARDS

DAVID HUGHES

JANET WALDO

FATHER, HARRY ARCHER WAS FRANK MARTIN, THEN FRED SHIELDS

ANNOUNCERS: JOHN HIESTAND, DEL SHARBUTT KEN CARPENTER & JACK NARZ

MRS. ARCHER WAS ALWAYS IRENE TEDROW

DURING THE FINAL YEAR (1954-55) LUGENE SANDERS WAS CORLISS, DAVID HUGHES PLAYED DEXTER

DEXTER'S GREETING: "OH, CORR-LAISS!" WAS A RUNNING JOKE ON THE SHOW....

SPONSORS: ANCHOR HOCKING GLASS, TONI PERMANENTS, CARTER'S LITTLE LIVER PILLS, CAMPBELL'S SOUPS, PEPSODENT TOOTH- PASTE AND ELECTRIC COMPANIES of AMERICA

RADIO'S GOLDEN YEARS ©

by FRANK BRESEE & BOBB LYNES

NORMAN CORWIN

RADIO'S NORMAN CORWIN WROTE, PRODUCED AND DIRECTED SOME OF THE MOST ACCLAIMED AND HONORED WORKS EVER HEARD ON RADIO. HE BROUGHT HIS GENIUS FOR PERFECT WORDS TO CBS'S "COLUMBIA WORKSHOP" IN 1938 AND BY 1944 WAS CREATING CLASSICS ON "COLUMBIA PRESENTS CORWIN," A DRAMATIC ANTHOLOGY SERIES WHICH FEATURED MANY OF HOLLYWOOD'S BEST ACTORS: CHARLES LAUGHTON, ELSA LANCHESTER, FREDRIC MARCH, BURL IVES, MORE....

DURING WORLD WAR II CORWIN CREATED MANY SPECIAL PROGRAMS FOR CBS: "WE HOLD THESE TRUTHS" (DEC. 15, 1941) "ON A NOTE OF TRIUMPH" (V-E DAY, MAY 8, 1945), "14 AUGUST 1945" (V-J DAY) & "THE UNDECIDED MOLECULE" (JULY 17, 1945), PLUS THE 26-WEEK SERIES "THIS IS WAR."

DURING THE McCARTHY ERA CORWIN FOUGHT "WITCH HUNTS" & BLACK-LISTS.

ON AUGUST 14, 1995 A STIRRING, REVISED VERSION OF "14 AUG. '45" WRITTEN BY MR. CORWIN, WAS PRESENTED ON PUBLIC RADIO

OVER THE YEARS HE HAS BEEN HONORED WITH MANY AWARDS, INCLUDING: THE ONE WORLD AWARD, TWO PEABODY AWARDS, AN EMMY, A GOLDEN GLOBE, AN OSCAR NOMINATION, A GOLDEN MIKE (PACIFIC PIONEER BROADCASTERS) AND INDUCTION IN THE RADIO HALL OF FAME IN CHICAGO

NORMAN CORWIN HAS AUTHORED MANY BOOKS & IS A LEADING AUTHORITY ON THE GOLDEN AGE OF RADIO

RADIO'S GOLDEN YEARS©

by FRANK BRESEE & BOBB LYNES

DAVID HARDING, COUNTERSPY

OPENING:
"WASHINGTON CALLING DAVID HARDING, COUNTERSPY"
"WASHINGTON CALLING DAVID HARDING, COUNTERSPY"
"HARDING, COUNTERSPY, CALLING WASHINGTON"

DAVID HARDING, COUNTERSPY WAS A VERY POPULAR SERIES DURING WORLD WAR II AND MANY YEARS THEREAFTER, RUNNING FROM MAY 18, 1942 TO NOVEMBER 29, 1957

THE PLOTS USUALLY CONCERNED COUNTER-SPIES IN THE UNITED STATES WHO WERE "ESPECIALLY APPOINTED TO INVESTIGATE AND COMBAT THE ENEMIES OF OUR COUNTRY, BOTH AT HOME AND ABROAD"; DURING THE WAR, IT WAS THE NAZI FIFTH COLUMNISTS & THE JAPANESE BLACK DRAGON SOCIETY

ANNOUNCERS:
BOB SHEPARD
ROGER KRUPP

DAVID HARDING WAS PLAYED BY DON McLAUGHLIN, HIS ASSISTANT PETERS WAS MANDEL KRAMER

CREATED BY PHILLIPS H. LORD (WHO CREATED "GANGBUSTERS")

SPONSORS: MAIL POUCH TOBACCO, SCHUTTER CANDY, PEPSI-COLA, GULF OIL AND ANAHIST COLD MEDICINE

Pepsi-Cola®

SUPER ANAHIST
APC COMPOUND
WITH VITAMIN C
COLDS IN ALL STAGES
SIMPLE HEADACHES
HAY FEVER

GULF

RADIO'S GOLDEN YEARS ©
by FRANK BRESEE & BOBB LYNES

CRIME DOCTOR

CRIME DOCTOR WAS THE STORY OF DOCTOR BENJAMIN ORDWAY, WHO AS A SPECIALIST IN CRIMINAL PSYCHIATRY, SOLVED MYSTERIES AND CRIMES AND BROUGHT TO JUSTICE HUNDREDS OF CRIMINALS DURING HIS SEVEN YEARS ON THE AIR.....

THE WEEKLY SERIES WAS BROADCAST FROM CBS' NEW YORK STUDIOS FROM AUGUST, 1940 UNTIL OCTOBER, 1947. IT WAS A SUNDAY NIGHT FEATURE ON CBS WITH ONE OF THE HIGHEST HOOPER RATINGS OF ANY DETECTIVE/MYSTERY SHOW ON THE AIR

OVER THE YEARS THE TITLE ROLE WAS PLAYED BY:
JOHN McINTIRE
HUGH MARLOWE
EVERETT SLOANE
RAY COLLINS
HOUSE JAMESON
(FROM 1943 TO 1947)

CAST: JEANETTE NOLAN, ELSPETH ERIC, EDGAR STEHLI, WALTER VAUGHN & EDITH ARNOLD

ANNOUNCER: CHARLES O'CONNOR

SPONSOR: PHILIP MORRIS

RADIO'S GOLDEN YEARS.©

by FRANK BRESEE & BOBB LYNES

CASEY, CRIME PHOTOGRAPHER

CRIME PHOTOGRAPHER CAME TO CBS JULY 7, 1943 UNDER THE TITLE "FLASHGUN CASEY, CHANGED TO CASEY, PRESS PHOTOGRAPHER, THEN CASEY, CRIME PHOTOGRAPHER... FINALLY SIMPLY CRIME PHOTO-GRAPHER. HE WAS A DETECTIVE-REPORTER FOR THE MORNING EXPRESS WHO DID HIS REPORTING WITH A CAMERA. HE OPERATED OUT OF THE BLUE NOTE CAFE WHERE HIS FRIEND ETHELBERT WAS BARTENDER

JAN MINER

BECK

GIBSON

STAATS COTSWORTH WAS CASEY

REGULAR CAST: JOHN GIBSON (ETHELBERT), JACKSON BECK (INSPECTOR LOGAN). CASEY'S GIRLFRIEND ANNIE WAS PLAYED BY LESLEY WOODS, JAN MINER AND OTHERS

WRITTEN BY ALONZO DEEN COLE
DIRECTOR: JOHN DIETZ
THE SERIES RAN UNTIL 1950, WAS REVIVED IN 1953, ENDING IN 1955

ANNOUNCERS: TONY MARVIN, BILL CULLEN

SPONSORS: ANCHOR-HOCKING GLASS, TONI HOME PERMANENT AND PHILIP MORRIS CIGARETTES

RADIO'S GOLDEN YEARS©
by FRANK BRESEE & BOBB LYNES

the BING CROSBY Show

HE WAS FAMOUS FOR THE PARAMOUNT "ROAD" PICTURES WITH HIS FRIEND BOB HOPE

BING CROSBY'S RADIO CAREER BEGAN IN AUGUST 1931 AND LASTED UNTIL THE SIXTIES; OVER THE YEARS, HIS SHOW WAS HEARD ON CBS, NBC AND ABC.. GUEST STARS INCLUDED BOB BURNS, LINA ROMAY, LIONEL BARRYMORE, AL JOLSON, FRANK SINATRA, HUMPHREY BOGART, ETC..

SPONSORS INCLUDED CREMO CIGARS, WOODBURY SOAP, KRAFT FOODS, PHILCO, G-E AND CHESTERFIELD CIGARETTES....

PRODUCED B
INSERT YOUR
Philco Radio Time
STARRING
BING CROSBY
NOT TO BE PLAYED BEFORE March 5, 1947 OR AFTER March 7, 1947
PROGRAM 21
START OUTSIDE
...RICAN BROADCASTING COMPANY.

IN OCTOBER 1946, CROSBY BEGAN PRE-RECORDING HIS SHOW FOR ABC; THE FIRST STAR TO RECORD A NETWORK PROGRAM

BING CROSBY'S RECORDING OF "WHITE CHRISTMAS" HAS SOLD MORE THAN ANY OTHER RECORD ISSUED (OVER 7 MILLION AND COUNTING!)

"WHERE THE BLUE OF THE NIGHT MEETS THE GOLD OF THE DAY..."

MUSIC DIRECTOR: JOHN SCOTT TROTTER

HIS ANNOUNCER FOR MANY YEARS: KEN CARPENTER

RADIO'S GOLDEN YEARS ©
by FRANK BRESEE & BOBB LYNES

DANGEROUS ASSIGNMENT

EACK WEEK STEVE WAS SENT TO A DIFFERENT PART OF THE GLOBE TO SOLVE A CRIME OR TAKE CARE OF A PROBLEM..

BAGHDAD!
MARTINIQUE!
SINGAPORE!

ACADEMY AWARD NOMINEE BRIAN DONLEVY STARRED AS STEVE MITCHELL, INTERNATIONAL TROUBLESHOOTER ON THIS WEEKLY NBC SERIES WHICH DEBUTED IN JULY 1949 AND RAN UNTIL 1953 BEFORE MOVING TO TV.....

YEAH, DANGER IS MY ASSIGNMENT. I GET SENT TO A LOT OF PLACES I CAN'T EVEN PRONOUNCE. THEY ALL SPELL THE SAME THING, THOUGH....TROUBLE!

WHEATIES
"breakfast of Champions"

BREAKFAST OF CHAMPIONS"

SPONSORS: WHEATIES & FORD

Ford

HOLLYWOOD'S BEST RADIO ACTORS APPEARED: PAUL FREES, BILL CONRAD, PARLEY BAER, VIRGINIA GREGG, PEGGY WEBBER

STEVE'S "CHIEF" WAS HERB BUTTERFIELD

ANNOUNCER: JOHN STORM

RADIO'S GOLDEN YEARS.©

by FRANK BRESEE & BOBB LYNES

A DATE with JUDY

A DATE WITH JUDY WAS A POPULAR RADIO SITUATION COMEDY WHICH DEBUTED ON NBC JUNE 24, 1941 AS A SUMMER REPLACEMENT FOR BOB HOPE, GOT A REGULAR SPOT IN 1943, UNTIL 1949; ENDING ON ABC IN 1950

JUDY FOSTER WAS A 15 YEAR OLD WHO FACED THE USUAL ADOLESCENT PROBLEMS. THE FIRST JUDY WAS ANN GILLIS, LATER DELLIE ELLIS; FINALLY LOUISE ERICKSON

HER FAVORITE BOYFRIEND WAS OOGIE PRINGLE; HER BIGGEST PROBLEM WAS HER BROTHER RANDOLPH

JUDY'S PARENTS WERE PLAYED BY PAUL McGRATH, JOE KEARNS & JOHN BROWN; MARGARET BRAYTON, BEA BENADERET & LOIS CORBETT

GIRLFRIEND MITZI OR GLORIA WAS PLAYED BY LURENE TUTTLE, LOUISE ERICKSON; FINALLY SANDRA GOULD

LOUISE ERICKSON

OOGIE WAS RICHARD CRENNA

DIX DAVIS

RANDOLPH WAS TOMMY BOND, LATER DIX DAVIS

WRITER: ALEEN LESLIE

DIRECTOR: HELEN MACK

ANNOUNCER: MARVIN MILLER

SPONSORS: PEPSODENT, TUMS, FORD, SAL HEPATICA & REVERE CAMERAS

RADIO'S GOLDEN YEARS.©

by FRANK BRESEE & BOBB LYNES

JOAN DAVIS

COMEDIENNE JOAN DAVIS FIRST APPEARED AS A GUEST ON THE NBC RUDY VALLEE SHOW IN 1941; WAS SUCH A SENSATION THAT SHE BECAME A REGULAR IN 1942. JOAN PLAYED A MAN-CRAZY, SLIGHTLY OFF-BEAT GAL WHO CHASED EVERY MALE ON THE SHOW INCLUDING VALLEE

IN 1945 JOAN DAVIS MOVED TO CBS WITH HER OWN SHOW "JOANIE'S TEA ROOM". HER ANNOUNCER/SIDE-KICK WAS HARRY VON ZELL......

WHEN RUDY JOINED THE COAST GUARD IN 1943, JOAN DAVIS TOOK OVER THE SHOW ("SEALTEST VILLAGE STORE")

Sealtest

SWAN

SPONSORS: SEALTEST, LEVER BROS. & ROI-TAN CIGARS

IN 1946 HER SHOW WAS RE-TITLED "LEAVE IT TO JOAN" WITH WALLY BROWN, VERNA FELTON & SHARON DOUGLAS

RADIO'S GOLDEN YEARS©

by FRANK BRESEE & BOBB LYNES

DAYTIME SERIALS

OVER THE YEARS, THROUGH THE 1930's, 1940's AND INTO THE 1950's RADIO NETWORKS FEATURED SOAP OPERAS FROM MORNING 'TIL NIGHT; WITH CONTINUING STORYLINES, MOST OF THE PROGRAMS WERE 15 MINUTES LONG, HEARD FIVE TIMES A WEEK, MONDAY THROUGH FRIDAY. THE STORIES WERE CALLED "SOAP OPERAS" BECAUSE THEY WERE AIMED PRIMARILY AT THE WOMEN'S AUDIENCE AND WERE MOSTLY SPONSORED BY SOAP PRODUCTS.....

THE DAILY DRAMAS INVOLVED THE HEROINES (AND HEROES) IN FAMILY TROUBLES, MARITAL DIFFICULTIES, ILLNESSES, AMNESIA, LOST RELATIVES, MURDERS & JUST EVERYDAY DOMESTIC PROBLEMS....

SOME SPONSORS: GENERAL FOODS, CARNATION MILK, PRUDENTIAL INSURANCE, WHITEHALL PHARMICALS, AMERICAN HOME PRODUCTS, ANACIN, & KOLYNOS, PHILLIPS MILK OF MAGNESIA, BAYER ASPIRIN, PROCTOR & GAMBLE, GENERAL MILLS, DUZ SOAP AND RINSO, COLGATE-PALMOLIVE-PEET, LEVER BROS. & MORE...

JUST PLAIN BILL
ARTHUR HUGHES
"BILL DAVIDSON"

THE BEST ANNOUNCERS IN RADIO WORKED THESE SERIALS: GEORGE ANSBRO, DAN SEYMOUR, JOHN REED KING, CHARLES STARK, BERT PARKS, JIM AMECHE, FORD BOND, RALPH EDWARDS, BUD COLLYER, DON PARDO AND MORE.....

RADIO'S GOLDEN YEARS ©

by FRANK BRESEE & BOBB LYNES

DEATH VALLEY DAYS

DEATH VALLEY DAYS WAS AN ANTHOLOGY SERIES OF TRUE DRAMAS OF THE OLD WEST, (MOSTLY CALIFORNIA'S HISTORY) AND DEBUTED ON NBC ON SEPTEMBER 30, 1930 AND WAS BROADCAST FOR MANY YEARS FROM SAN FRANCISCO....

OPENING:
"AS THE EARLY MORNING BUGLE CALL OF COVERED WAGONS FADES AWAY AMONG THE ECHOES ANOTHER TRUE DEATH VALLEY DAYS STORY IS PRESENTED FOR YOUR ENTERTAINMENT BY THE PACIFIC COAST BORAX COMPANY, PRODUCERS OF 20 MULE TEAM BORAX PRODUCTS"

THE SHOW WAS NARRATED BY "THE OLD RANGER" PLAYED BY ACTOR JACK MacBRYDE

Name of Program

"DEATH VALLEY DAYS"

Produced For

4/7/38

Part No. 1

tart.

PLAYING T

Mint.   Sec.

oadcast hold this disc for instructions

PRODUCED BY
MacGREGOR & SOLLIE
RECORDING LABORATORIES, INC.
865 Mission Street
SAN FRANCISCO, CALIF.
MS A 14
FORM NO. MS 81

LATER HOSTS: STANLEY ANDREWS AND (ON TV) RONALD REAGAN AND ROBERT TAYLOR

ANNOUNCER:
DRESSER DAHLSTEAD

OVER THE YEARS (1930-1945) THE SERIES WAS HEARD ON NBC, THE BLUE NETWORK & CBS

SPONSOR:
20 MULE TEAM
BORAX & BORAXO

BORAX

RADIO'S GOLDEN YEARS ©

by FRANK BRESEE & BOBB LYNES

Vaughn DeLeath

VAUGHN DeLEATH WAS RADIO'S FIRST SINGER AND WAS KNOWN AS "THE ORIGINAL RADIO GIRL"

SHE WAS ONLY 19 YEARS OLD (IN 1920) WHEN SHE FIRST SANG INTO A MICROPHONE

VAUGHN DeLEATH WAS CALLED RADIO'S FIRST FEMALE "CROONER" BECAUSE OF HER STYLE OF SINGING CLOSE TO A MICROPHONE

WITHIN A FEW YEARS MISS DeLEATH WAS A REGULAR ON RADIO AND IN 1931 WAS HIRED BY CBS FOR A TWICE-A-WEEK 15 MINUTE SHOW

SHE ALSO PIONEERED TELEVISION, APPEARING IN 1930 ON EARLY EXPERIMENTAL BROADCASTS....

HER THEME: "RED SAILS IN THE SUNSET"

RADIO'S GOLDEN YEARS.©

by FRANK BRESEE & BOBB LYNES

DENNIS DAY, THE POPULAR VOCALIST IRISH TENOR ON THE JACK BENNY SHOW, BEGAN HIS OWN HALF-HOUR WEEKLY SITUATION COMEDY ON NBC IN 1946....

A DAY IN THE LIFE OF
DENNIS DAY

DENNIS PLAYED A SODA JERK AT WILLOUGHBY'S DRUG STORE. HE WAS WELL-MEANING, BUT ON EACH SHOW HE HAD HIS PROBLEMS, ESPECIALLY WITH HIS GIRLFRIEND, MILDRED.

DENNIS DAY PLAYED DENNIS DAY

DURING THE SHOW DAY WOULD SING SEVERAL SONGS

MILDRED ANDERSON: BETTY MILES LATER, BARBARA EILER
MR. ANDERSON: DINK TROUT
MRS. ANDERSON: BEA BENADERET
MR. WILLOUGHBY: JOHN BROWN

SPONSOR: COLGATE-PALMOLIVE

FRANK BARTON

VERNE SMITH

JIMMY WALLINGTON

ANNOUNCERS:

THE COMEDY WAS HEARD ON NBC FROM 1946 TO 1951 FROM HOLLYWOOD

RADIO'S GOLDEN YEARS ©
by FRANK BRESEE & BOBB LYNES

Dick TRACY

IT'S TIME FOR DICK TRACY..... PROTECTOR OF LAW & ORDER!

ALL OF THE CHARACTERS IN CHESTER GOULD'S VERY POPULAR COMIC STRIP, DICK TRACY, WERE BROUGHT TO RADIO IN 1935, INCLUDING: PAT PATTON (TRACY'S SIDE-KICK), JUNIOR (TRACY'S ADOPTED SON), TESS TRUE-HEART (TRACY'S GIRL-FRIEND), PLUS FLAT-TOP AND VITAMIN FLINTHEART

THE FAST-MOVING RADIO ADVENTURES WERE VERY SIMILAR TO THE COMICS AND WOULD OFTEN RUN CONCURRENTLY, WITH TRACY SOLVING MYSTERIES & ARRESTING CRIMINALS

CHESTER GOULD

DICK TRACY © TRIBUNE SYND.

DICK TRACY WAS PLAYED ON ABC BY NED WEVER

THE SERIES BEGAN ON MUTUAL IN 1935, MOVED TO NBC-BLUE FROM 1937 TO 1939. BY 1945 IT WAS HEARD ON THE BLUE NETWORK (LATER ABC) AND IN 1946 WAS A SHORT-LIVED SATURDAY EVENING SHOW, ENDING IN 1948....

SUPPORT CAST: RALPH BELL, MERCEDES McCAMBRIDGE AND GILBERT MACK

ANNOUNCERS: DON GARDNER, GEORGE GUNN, ED HERLIHY & DAN SEYMOUR

JUNIOR WAS PLAYED BY JACKIE KELK

SPONSORS: QUAKER CEREALS, TOOTSIE ROLLS

Tootsie Rolls

RADIO'S GOLDEN YEARS.©

by FRANK BRESEE & BOBB LYNES

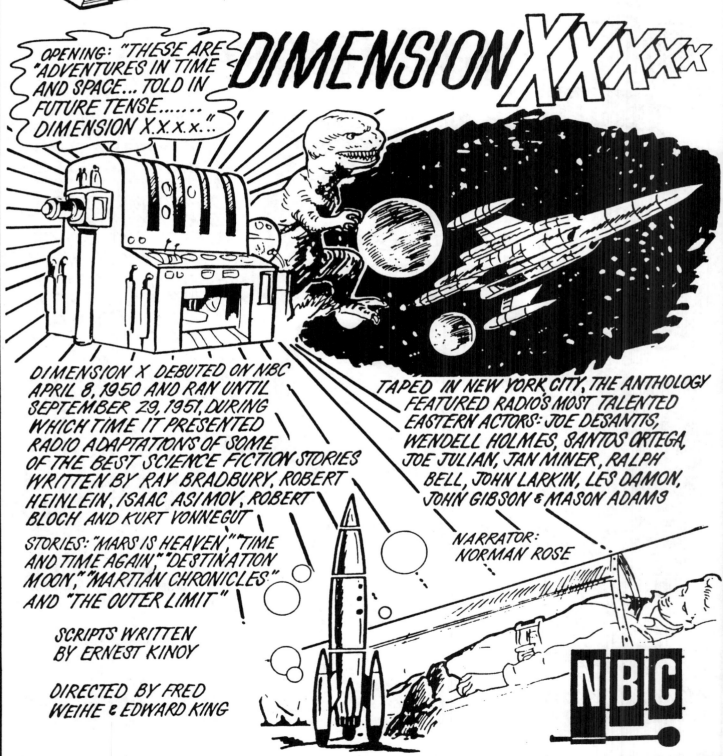

OPENING: "THESE ARE "ADVENTURES IN TIME AND SPACE... TOLD IN FUTURE TENSE........ DIMENSION X.x.x.x..."

DIMENSION XXXxx

DIMENSION X DEBUTED ON NBC APRIL 8, 1950 AND RAN UNTIL SEPTEMBER 29, 1951, DURING WHICH TIME IT PRESENTED RADIO ADAPTATIONS OF SOME OF THE BEST SCIENCE FICTION STORIES WRITTEN BY RAY BRADBURY, ROBERT HEINLEIN, ISAAC ASIMOV, ROBERT BLOCH AND KURT VONNEGUT

STORIES: "MARS IS HEAVEN," "TIME AND TIME AGAIN," "DESTINATION MOON," "MARTIAN CHRONICLES," AND "THE OUTER LIMIT"

SCRIPTS WRITTEN BY ERNEST KINOY

DIRECTED BY FRED WEIHE & EDWARD KING

TAPED IN NEW YORK CITY, THE ANTHOLOGY FEATURED RADIO'S MOST TALENTED EASTERN ACTORS: JOE DESANTIS, WENDELL HOLMES, SANTOS ORTEGA, JOE JULIAN, JAN MINER, RALPH BELL, JOHN LARKIN, LES DAMON, JOHN GIBSON & MASON ADAMS

NARRATOR: NORMAN ROSE

NBC

RADIO'S GOLDEN YEARS ©

by FRANK BRESEE & BOBB LYNES

DORIS DAY

BEFORE BECOMING A MOTION PICTURE STAR, DORIS DAY APPEARED IN A VARIETY OF RADIO PROGRAMS, INCLUDING: YOUR HIT PARADE (WITH FRANK SINATRA), BOB HOPE SHOW (VOCALIST & ACTRESS) AND IN 1952 BEGAN HER OWN HALF HOUR WEEKLY MUSICAL SHOW ON CBS.....

SHE BEGAN HER CAREER AS BAND VOCALIST WITH LES BROWN'S BAND OF RENOWN AND WAS HEARD ON MANY REMOTE BROADCASTS

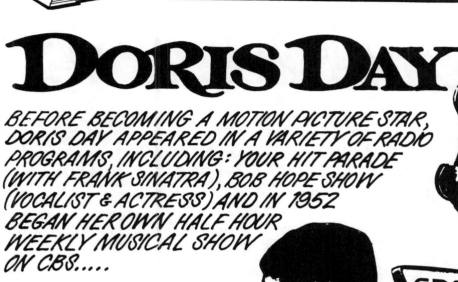

LES BROWN

REAL NAME: DORIS VON KAPPELHOFF

DOES ANYONE KNOW WHY BOB HOPE CALLED HER "JB"?

HIT RECORDS: "SENTIMENTAL JOURNEY," "LOVE SOMEBODY"(WITH BUDDY CLARK), "A GUY IS A GUY," "ITS MAGIC," "SECRET LOVE," "WHAT-EVER WILL BE, WILL BE" AND MORE!

HIT MOVIES: "MY DREAM IS YOURS," "THE MAN WHO KNEW TOO MUCH,""CALAMITY JANE" "TEA FOR TWO," "TEACHER'S PET,""LOVER COME BACK"& MORE

RADIO'S GOLDEN YEARS©

by FRANK BRESEE & BOBB LYNES

DRAGNET

CREATED BY & STARRING JACK WEBB, DRAGNET FEATURED AUTHENTIC STORIES FROM THE FILES OF THE LOS ANGELES POLICE DEPARTMENT WITH THE CO-OPERATION OF W.H. PARKER, L.A. CHIEF OF POLICE. THE PROGRAM DEBUTED ON NBC JUNE 10, 1949 AND RAN UNTIL FEBRUARY 16, 1957

"DRAGNET" THEME COMPOSED BY WALTER SCHUMANN

WRITERS: JIM MOSER, JOHN ROBINSON

THIS IS THE CITY... LOS ANGELES, CALIFORNIA..... IT WAS MONDAY, AUGUST 20TH. IT WAS WARM IN LOS ANGELES. WE WERE WORKING THE DAY WATCH OUT OF HOMICIDE. MY PARTNER'S BEN ROMERO. MY NAME'S FRIDAY. A CALL CAME IN. A MAN HAD JUST JUMPED FROM THE 12TH FLOOR OF THE HOLLYWOOD HOTEL........

WEBB'S PARTNERS WERE PLAYED BY BARTON YARBOROUGH BARNEY PHILLIPS AND BEN ALEXANDER

CATCH PHRASE: "JUST THE FACTS, MA'AM"

SUPPORT CAST: JACK KRUSCHEN, VIC PERRIN, RICHARD BOONE, HERB ELLIS, VIRGINIA GREGG, RAYMOND BURR, PEGGY WEBBER, HARRY BARTELL, HERB BUTTERFIELD, STACY HARRIS AND MORE......

HAL GIBNEY   GEORGE FENNEMAN
ANNOUNCERS
IN ADDITION TO RADIO THE SHOW WAS ALSO A HIT ON TV

SPONSORS: FATIMA CIGARETTES AND CHESTERFIELD CIGARETTES

THE MEMORABLE OPENING: "THE STORY YOU ARE ABOUT TO HEAR IS TRUE. ONLY THE NAMES HAVE BEEN CHANGED TO PROTECT THE INNOCENT."...

RADIO'S GOLDEN YEARS.©

by FRANK BRESEE & BOBB LYNES

Dr. Christian

THE SHOW DEBUTED ON CBS IN NOVEMBER 1937 AND RAN UNTIL JANUARY 1954

THE DR. CHRISTIAN RADIO PROGRAM GREW OUT OF A 1936 FILM "THE COUNTRY DOCTOR" STARRING JEAN HERSHOLT. IT WAS THE STORY OF DR. ALLAN DAFOE, THE CANADIAN DOCTOR FAMOUS FOR DELIVERING THE DIONNE QUINTUPLETS..

BEGINNING IN 1941 THE SHOW DISPENSED WITH PROFESSIONAL WRITERS AND ASKED LISTENERS TO SUBMIT SCRIPTS. IT BECAME "THE ONLY SHOW IN RADIO WHERE THE AUDIENCE WRITES THE SCRIPTS" (WRITERS RECEIVED UP TO $2,000 PER SCRIPT)

STAR OF THE PROGRAM WAS JEAN HERSHOLT, WHO PLAYED "DOCTOR CHRISTIAN" (FROM THE FIRST SHOW TO THE FINAL BROADCAST)

THE PROGRAM TOOK PLACE IN THE MYTHICAL TOWN OF RIVER'S END

CHRISTIAN'S NURSE "JUDY PRICE" WAS PLAYED DURING THE EARLY YEARS BY LURENE TUTTLE & HELEN CLAIRE

COLUMBIA BROADCASTING SYSTEM
COLUMBIA SQUARE PLAYHOUSE
6121 SUNSET BOULEVARD — HOLLYWOOD

STUDIO B CBS

THE 'VASELINE' PROGRAM
Starring
JEAN HERSHOLT
with
ROSEMARY DeCAMP in
"DOCTOR CHRISTIAN"
CHILDREN UNDER TWELVE WILL NOT BE ADMITTED

Wednesday
JULY
31
1946
7:30 p.m.
Doors Close
at 7:25 p.m.

Nº 727

BEST REMEMBERED "JUDY PRICE" WAS ROSEMARY DeCAMP

ANNOUNCER: ART GILMORE

SPONSOR: VASELINE PRODUCTS

JEAN HERSHOLT ALSO PLAYED DR. CHRISTIAN IN SERIES OF FILMS BEGINNING IN 1939; THE MOTION PICTURE ACADEMY'S HERSHOLT HUMANITARIAN AWARD WAS NAMED IN HIS HONOR......

RADIO'S GOLDEN YEARS.©

by FRANK BRESEE & BOBB LYNES

Dr. I.Q.
THE MENTAL BANKER

DR. I.Q., THE MENTAL BANKER, WAS ON THE AIR FROM 1939 THROUGH 1950. THE QUIZ SHOW, HEARD COAST-TO-COAST ON NBC-BLUE, WAS ONE OF THE FIRST PROGRAMS THAT TRAVELLED TO CITIES THROUGHOUT THE U.S. BROADCASTING FROM STAGES OF DIFFERENT THEATRES EACH WEEK... DR. I.Q. WOULD STAND ON STAGE, WHILE SIX ROVING ASSISTANTS, STATIONED IN THE AUDIENCE WOULD INTERVIEW THE CONTESTANTS

LEW VALENTINE

THE FIRST DR. I.Q. WAS LEW VALENTINE, LATER REPLACED BY JIMMY McLAIN WHILE VALENTINE WAS IN THE SERVICE

JIMMY McLAIN

OVER THE YEARS, THOUSANDS OF DOLLARS WERE GIVEN TO CONTESTANTS FOR CORRECT ANSWERS

AN ASSISTANT WOULD SAY "I'VE GOT A LADY IN THE BALCONY, DOCTOR!", TO WHICH DR. I.Q. WOULD REPLY: "SIXTEEN SILVER DOLLARS TO THAT LADY IF SHE CAN ANSWER THIS QUESTION...."

SNICKERS BAR

SPONSOR: MARS CANDY

milky way BAR

Mars

ANNOUNCER: ALAN O. ANTHONY

AN IMPORTANT FEATURE WAS THE TONGUE TWISTER: "JIM IS SLIM, SAID TIM TO KIM; JIM IS SLIM, TIM, TO TIM SAID KIM"

RADIO'S GOLDEN YEARS ©
by FRANK BRESEE & BOBB LYNES

DUFFY'S TAVERN

DUFFY'S TAVERN WAS ONE OF THE MOST POPULAR COMEDY SHOWS OF THE 1940s AND 1950s. IT STARRED ED GARDNER AS "ARCHIE", BARKEEP OF DUFFY'S— A BAR AND RESTAURANT. THE SHOW BEGAN ON CBS MARCH 1, 1941 AND LASTED UNTIL JAN. 18, 1952 ON NBC....

GARDNER'S WIFE AT THE TIME OF ITS DEBUT, SHIRLEY BOOTH, WAS A CAST REGULAR AS "MISS DUFFY." LATER WHEN THE SHOW WAS HEARD FROM NBC HOLLYWOOD, THE PART WAS PLAYED BY SANDRA GOULD AND FLORENCE HALOP......

"DUFFY'S TAVERN...WHERE THE ELITE MEET TO EAT! ARCHIE, THE MANAGER SPEAKIN'.. DUFFY AIN'T HERE... OH HELLO, DUFFY!"

NATIONAL BROADCASTING COMPANY, INC.
HOLLYWOOD STUDIOS
SUNSET AND VINE
VITALIS and MINIT-RUB
PRESENT
DUFFY'S TAVERN
Starring ED GARDNER AS ARCHIE
★ CHILDREN UNDER 14 WILL NOT BE ADMITTED ★
22 See Reverse Side

ANNOUNCERS: JIMMY WALLINGTON, MARVIN MILLER, JACK BAILEY & ROD O'CONNOR

NOTE: "DUFFY" NEVER ACTUALLY APPEARED ON THE SHOW!

OTHER REGULARS ON THE SHOW WERE: CHARLIE CANTOR, EDDIE GREEN, ALAN REED, DICK VAN PATTEN & LURENE TUTTLE

THEME SONG: "WHEN IRISH EYES ARE SMILING"

SPONSORS: IPANA TOOTHPASTE, BLATZ BEER, VITALIS, SCHICK PRODUCTS & MINIT-RUB

RADIO'S GOLDEN YEARS ©

by FRANK BRESEE & BOBB LYNES

DUNNINGER!

THIS PROGRAM FEATURED JOSEPH DUNNINGER, KNOWN AS A MASTER MAGICIAN, HYPNOTIST AND MENTALIST........

HE WAS A FRIEND OF HARRY HOUDINI AND DURING THE 1920s WAS A VAUDEVILLE ENTERTAINER

HE BECAME SO POPULAR AND WELL KNOWN, THAT BY 1943 HE BEGAN HIS OWN RADIO SHOW ON NBC BLUE NETWORK

HIS RADIO SERIES AIRED FROM 1943 TO 1946

DURING THE SHOW, DUNNINGER WOULD PICK PEOPLE AT RANDOM FROM THE AUDIENCE AND TELL THEM THEIR NAMES, ADDRESSES, HOME TOWNS, ETC..

ANNOUNCERS: DON LOWE, ROGER KRUPP

Rinso

LIFEBUOY HEALTH SOAP

SWP

COVER THE EARTH

ORCHESTRA: MITCHELL AYRES

SPONSORS: LEVER BROS. & SHERWIN-WILLIAMS PAINT

HE CLAIMED HE WAS CORRECT AT LEAST 90% OF THE TIME AND HE KEPT RADIO AUDIENCES FASCINATED FOR YEARS

RADIO'S GOLDEN YEARS ©

by FRANK BRESEE & BOBB LYNES

JIMMY DURANTE GARRY MOORE

ANNOUNCER HOWARD PETRIE

ONE OF THE GREATEST COMEDY TEAMS IN RADIO WAS JIMMY DURANTE AND GARRY MOORE.... THEY TEAMED UP ON MARCH 25, 1943, AND SOON THE DURANTE-MOORE SHOW HELD A TOP SPOT ON THE RADIO AIRWAVES

CAST MEMBERS INCLUDED ARTHUR TREACHER, VICTOR MOORE & CANDY CANDIDO

DURANTE ESTABLISHED HIS TRADEMARK SONG "INKA-DINKA-DOO" ON AN EARLY PROGRAM & IT LASTED HIM THROUGH-OUT HIS CAREER

BECAUSE OF THE AGE DIFFERENCE, DURANTE CALLED MOORE "JUNIOR" AND MOORE CALLED DURANTE "SCHNOZZ" BECAUSE OF HIS LARGE NOSE.

SPONSORS: CAMEL CIGARETTES & REXALL DRUGS

CREATOR/PRODUCER WAS PHIL COHAN

MUSIC BY XAVIER CUGAT (LATER, ROY BARGY

DURANTE'S FAMOUS CLOSING: "GOODNIGHT, MRS. CALABASH, WHEREVER YOU ARE"

COLUMBIA BROADCASTING SYSTEM
COLUMBIA SQUARE PLAYHOUSE
6121 SUNSET BOULEVARD — HOLLYWOOD

STUDIO
A
CBS

JIMMY DURANTE AND GARRY MOORE
Presented by
YOUR REXALL DRUGGIST
with
DALE EVANS   HOWARD PETRIE
ROY BARGY ORCHESTRA

FRIDAY
MAY
3
1946
5:30-6 p.m.
Doors Close
at 5:15 p.m.

Nº 1429

CHILDREN UNDER TWELVE WILL NOT BE ADMITTED

RADIO'S GOLDEN YEARS ©

by FRANK BRESEE & BOBB LYNES

EASY ACES

EASY ACES WAS KNOWN AS "RADIO'S LAUGH NOVELTY.". IT WAS ONE OF THE FIRST RADIO SHOWS TO BE SYNDICATED ON LOCAL STATIONS ACROSS THE NATION STARTING MARCH 1, 1932.

THE SHOW WAS ON THE AIR UNTIL JANUARY 17, 1945

JANE ACE WAS THE MASTER OF THE MALAPROP, WITH EXPRESSIONS LIKE: "HE'S A FLY IN THE OATMEAL", "TIME WOUNDS ALL HEELS"& "CONGRESS IS STILL IN SEASON"

THE SHOW STARRED THE REAL HUSBAND &WIFE TEAM OF GOODMAN & JANE ACE

OVER THE YEARS THE COMEDY WAS HEARD ON THE CBS &NBC NETWORKS

GOODMAN ACE LATER WROTE COMEDY FOR TALLULAH BANKHEAD'S "BIG SHOW" AND PERRY COMO'S TV SHOW

RADIO'S GOLDEN YEARS ©

by FRANK BRESEE & BOBB LYNES

EB AND ZEB

EB AND ZEB WAS ONE OF THE EARLY 15 MINUTE DAILY PROGRAMS THAT WAS HEARD DURING RADIO'S FORMATIVE YEARS, PRESENTING HILLBILLY DIALECT HUMOR IN THE LUM AND ABNER TRADITION...

EB AND ZEB WAS A QUARTER HOUR OF LIFE IN RURAL AMERICA AND LISTENERS TO SOME OF THE OLD TRANSCRIPTIONS AGREE, IT WAS A SAMPLE OF 1920s-1930s AMERICAN LIFE.....

AL PEARCE WAS EB

BILL WRIGHT WAS ZEB

THE PROGRAM BEGAN SYNDICATION IN 1932 AND RAN FOR OVER 10 YEARS..... LATER, THE CHARACTERS OF EB AND ZEB WERE BROUGHT BACK ON THE WEEKLY AL PEARCE SHOW ON CBS

SPONSOR: SHELL OIL COMPANY

SHELL

RADIO'S GOLDEN YEARS©

by FRANK BRESEE & BOBB LYNES

ELLERY QUEEN

ELLERY QUEEN WAS BASED ON THE DETECTIVE CHARACTER IN THE POPULAR BEST-SELLING BOOKS AND MAGAZINES CREATED BY FREDRIC DANNAY AND MANFRED LEE

EACH WEEK ELLERY QUEEN WOULD DRAMATIZE A MYSTERY WITH ALL THE IMPORTANT CLUES.....AND NEAR THE END OF EACH PROGRAM, THE DRAMA STOPPED AND AN "ARMCHAIR GUEST DETECTIVE" WAS ASKED TO SOLVE THE CASE _ MANY TIMES THE GUEST WAS WRONG, AND ELLERY NAMED THE "MURDERER"

YOUNG

MARLOWE

DOBKIN

TED DE CORSIA

SANTOS ORTEGA

CULVER

SMITH

INSPECTOR QUEEN WAS: SANTOS ORTEGA, BILL SMITH & HERB BUTTERFIELD
SGT. VELIE WAS: HOWARD SMITH, TED DE CORSIA ED LATIMER & ALAN REED

GIRLFRIEND NIKKI PORTER WAS: MARIAN SHOCKLEY, HELEN LEWIS, BARBARA TERRELL, GERTRUDE WARNER, CHARLOTTE KEANE, KAYE BRINKER & VIRGINIA GREGG

ANNOUNCERS: KEN ROBERTS, BERT PARKS, ERNEST CHAPPELL, DON HANCOCK AND PAUL MASTERSON

THE SERIES BEGAN ON CBS JUNE 18, 1939, MOVED TO NBC (1941-44) BACK TO CBS (1945-47) ENDING ON ABC (1948)

ELLERY QUEEN WAS PLAYED BY HUGH MARLOWE, CARLETON YOUNG, SIDNEY SMITH, LARRY DOBKIN & HOWARD CULVER

SCRIPTS BY FREDRIC DANNAY, MANFRED LEE & ANTHONY BOUCHER

SPONSORS: GULF OIL, BROMO SELTZER AND ANACIN

RADIO'S GOLDEN YEARS©

by FRANK BRESEE & BOBB LYNES

TIRED OF THE EVERYDAY ROUTINE?....
WANT TO GET AWAY FROM IT ALL?....
WE OFFER YOU.....

ESCAPE!

PRODUCER-DIRECTORS:
WILLIAM N. ROBSON
NORMAN MACDONNELL

NARRATORS:
PAUL FREES
WILLIAM CONRAD
LOU KRUGMAN

ANNOUNCER:
ROY ROWAN

THEME:
"NIGHT ON BALD MOUNTAIN"
ORGANIST:
IVAN DITMARS

MUSIC BY CY FEUER; LATER-DEL CASTILLO,
WILBUR HATCH & LEITH STEVENS

ESCAPE WAS ONE OF THE MOST POPULAR HORROR-ADVENTURE ANTHOLOGY SERIES IN THE FORTIES AND FIFTIES....IT WAS "DESIGNED TO FREE YOU FROM FOUR WALLS OF TODAY WITH A HALF HOUR OF HIGH ADVENTURE "PRESENTING STORIES BY THE WORLD'S GREATEST AUTHORS

A FEW OF THE CLASSICS PRESENTED: "THE BIRDS","THE TIME MACHINE,""THREE SKELETON KEY,""LEININGEN VS. THE ANTS," "EARTH ABIDES"&"EVENING PRIMROSE"

HOLLYWOOD'S BEST RADIO ACTORS STARRED: WM. CONRAD, JOHN DEHNER, HARRY BARTELL, BEN WRIGHT, JACK WEBB, VIRGINIA GREGG, PARLEY BAER, LARRY DOBKIN, VIVI JANISS, SAM EDWARDS, JACK KRUSCHEN & MORE

SOUND EFFECTS WERE CREATED BY GENIUSES BILLY GOULD AND CLIFF THORSNESS

SPONSORS:
RICHFIELD OIL
AND CBS RADIO

RICHFIELD

ESCAPE DEBUTED ON CBS JULY 7, 1947 AND RAN UNTIL SEPT. 25, 1954

RADIO'S GOLDEN YEARS.©
by FRANK BRESEE & BOBB LYNES

ETHEL & ALBERT

THE SETTING OF THIS CHARMING SHOW WAS THE MYTHICAL TOWN OF SANDY HARBOR, MINNESOTA. ETHEL & ALBERT WERE A MARRIED COUPLE AND PEG LYNCH PLAYED ETHEL PERFECTLY.....

"ETHEL ARBUCKLE" PEG LYNCH

"ALBERT ARBUCKLE" ALAN BUNCE

CREATED & WRITTEN BY PEG LYNCH

SHE AND ALBERT WERE ALWAYS INVOLVED WITH THE TRIVIAL DAILY EVENTS OF THEIR LIVES & THEIR NEIGHBORS' LIVES

THE 15 MINUTE DAILY COMEDY WAS HEARD ON ABC FOR OVER 6 YEARS, LATER ON NBC & CBS

ANNOUNCERS: GEORGE ANSBRO, FRED COLE, DON LOWE, GLENN RIGGS & HERB SHELTON

PERFORMERS OVER THE YEARS INCLUDED: RICHARD WIDMARK, ED BEGLEY, RAYMOND EDWARD JOHNSON, LEON JANNEY, JULIE STEVENS & DON McLAUGHLIN

THEME MUSIC: "LOVE NEST" & "SIDE BY SIDE"

LATER INCARNATIONS: "THE COUPLE NEXT DOOR" & "THE LITTLE THINGS IN LIFE"

RADIO'S GOLDEN YEARS©

by FRANK BRESEE & BOBB LYNES

FAMOUS NEWSCASTERS

THERE WERE MANY GREAT NEWSCASTERS DURING RADIO'S GOLDEN DAYS

OVER THE YEARS THE RADIO NETWORKS BROUGHT LISTENERS:

GABRIEL HEATTER..."AH, THERE'S GOOD NEWS TONIGHT"

HANS VON KALTENBORN..."THIS IS H.V. KALTENBORN IN WASHINGTON"

FULTON LEWIS, JR....."AND THAT'S THE TOP OF THE NEWS AS IT LOOKS FROM HERE"

DREW PEARSON..."WHOSE PREDICTIONS PROVE TO BE ACCURATE 87% OF THE TIME"

EDWARD R. MURROW...."THIS IS LONDON"

WALTER WINCHELL....."GOOD EVENING MR. & MRS AMERICA & ALL THE SHIPS AT SEA!"

BOAKE CARTER..."CHEERIO!"

PAUL HARVEY...."GOOD.....DAY!"

EDWARD R. MURROW

LOWELL THOMAS

FULTON LEWIS, JR

ROBERT TROUT

ELMER DAVIS

WALTER WINCHELL

DREW PEARSON

PAUL HARVEY

BOAKE CARTER

GABRIEL HEATTER

H.V. KALTENBORN

RADIO'S GOLDEN YEARS.©

by FRANK BRESEE & BOBB LYNES

FAMOUS NEWSCASTERS

THERE WERE MANY GREAT NEWSCASTERS DURING RADIO'S GOLDEN DAYS

OVER THE YEARS THE RADIO NETWORKS BROUGHT LISTENERS:

GABRIEL HEATTER..."AH, THERE'S GOOD NEWS TONIGHT"

HANS VON KALTENBORN..."THIS IS H.V. KALTENBORN IN WASHINGTON"

FULTON LEWIS, JR....."AND THAT'S THE TOP OF THE NEWS AS IT LOOKS FROM HERE"

DREW PEARSON..."WHOSE PREDICTIONS PROVE TO BE ACCURATE 84% OF THE TIME"

EDWARD R. MURROW.... "THIS IS LONDON"

WALTER WINCHELL....."GOOD EVENING MR. & MRS AMERICA & ALL THE SHIPS AT SEA!"

BOAKE CARTER..."CHEERIO!"

PAUL HARVEY...."GOOD.....DAY!"

HE ONCE TOLD A REPORTER_"WHEN I BEGAN BROADCASTING, HERE ARE SOME INTEREST-ING STATISTICS: ERIC SEVERIED WAS 13, HOWARD K. SMITH, 11, WALTER CRONKITE, 9, MIKE WALLACE, 7, DAVID BRINKLEY, 2 AND HARRY REASONER WAS 2 YEARS OLD. JOHN CHANCELLOR, BARBARA WALTERS, ROGER MUDD, TOM BROKAW, DAN RATHER AND NEARLY ALL THE OTHERS WERE NOT EVEN BORN YET!"

UNDOUBTABLY THE MOST FAMOUS OF ALL WAS LOWELL THOMAS, WHO BEGAN BROADCASTING ON PITTSBURGH'S KDKA IN 1925, MOVED ON TO NBC, AND CONTINUED UNTIL HIS LAST CBS SHOW ON MAY 14, 1976!

LOWELL THOMAS' FAMOUS SIGN-OFF: "SO LONG, UNTIL TOMORROW!"

THE FAT MAN

THE FAT MAN (BRAD RUNYON) WAS CREATED ESPECIALLY FOR RADIO BY FAMOUS MYSTERY WRITER DASHIELL HAMMETT ("THE THIN MAN," "MALTESE FALCON") AND WAS HEARD ON ABC FROM JAN. 21, 1946 TO SEPT. 26, 1951

OTHER CAST MEMBERS: ED BEGLEY, BETTY GARDE AND PAUL STEWART

"THERE HE GOES NOW, INTO THAT DRUGSTORE. HE'S STEPPING ON THE SCALE, WEIGHT.....239 POUNDS. FORTUNE..... DANGER! WHOOO IS IT? THE FAT MAN!"

BRAD RUNYON WAS PLAYED BY J. SCOTT SMART

EACH WEEK THE FAT MAN WOULD SOLVE A MYSTERY & BRING CRIMINALS TO JUSTICE; HIS TONGUE-IN-CHEEK DELIVERY MADE THE ONE OF THE MOST POPULAR DETECTIVE SHOWS ON THE AIR....

A SPONSOR.....

RADIO'S GOLDEN YEARS ©

by FRANK BRESEE & BOBB LYNES

FIBBER McGEE & MOLLY

FIBBER McGEE & MOLLY HAD THE NUMBER ONE RADIO SHOW FOR MANY YEARS; NBC WAS THEIR NETWORK FOR ALL 473 PROGRAMS

THEY WERE ON THE AIR FOR OVER 20 YEARS WITH THEIR ANNOUNCER

HARLOW WILCOX

THE COMEDY STARRED THE REAL-LIFE HUSBAND AND WIFE TEAM OF JIM AND MARIAN JORDAN.....

FIBBER & MOLLY LIVED IN THE MYTHICAL TOWN OF WISTFUL VISTA; THEIR ADDRESS WAS 79 WISTFUL VISTA.....

LONGTIME SPONSORS: JOHNSON'S WAX; LATER PET MILK

NATIONAL BROADCASTING COMPANY
RCA BUILDING RADIO CITY STUDIOS NEW YORK

TUES.
13
NOV.
1945

VOID IF SOLD

The Makers of
JOHNSON'S WAX and Self-Polishing
GLO·COAT
FIBBER McGEE and MOLLY

FLOOR
6

SEE REVERSE SIDE

Door Close
9:20 PM

CREATED BY DON QUINN, THE SERIES FEATURED RADIO PERSONALITIES BILL THOMPSON, ARTHUR Q. BRYAN, SHIRLEY MITCHELL & GALE GORDON

DON QUINN

MARLIN HURT WAS THEIR MAID "BEULAH."....

BILLY MILLS WAS THE LONGTIME ORCHESTRA LEADER AND THE KINGSMEN VOCAL GROUP WOULD ENTERTAIN ON EACH SHOW

RADIO'S GOLDEN YEARS ©

by FRANK BRESEE & BOBB LYNES

JIMMY FIDLER
HOLLYWOOD COLUMNIST

UNLIKE HEDDA HOPPER AND LOUELLA PARSONS, WHO TREATED HOLLYWOOD AND THE STARS WITH RESPECT, HOLLYWOOD COLUMNIST JIMMY FIDLER WAS CONSIDERED RADIO'S MOST THREATENING MENACE TO MOVIES & MOVIE PEOPLE....

HE CALLED BAD MOVIES "STINKERS" AND HAD A RATING SYSTEM NEVER BEFORE EQUALLED: FOUR BELLS FOR A TOP FILM, ONE BELL FOR A STINKER!

HE READ OPEN LETTERS TO THE STARS FROM HIS "LITTLE BLACK BOOK", CONDEMNED THEM FOR THEIR "BAD" DEEDS....

HIS FAMOUS SIGN-OFF: "GOOD NIGHT TO YOU, AND I DO MEAN YOU!"

SPONSORS: TANGEE LIPSTICK, DRENE SHAMPOO, TAYTON COSMETICS, ARRID DEODORANT

HE WAS ON THE AIR FOR OVER FOUR DECADES, BEGINNING ON NBC-BLUE IN 1932. BY 1935 HE WAS ON NBC, THEN IN 1936, SWITCHED TO CBS. IN 1942 HE WAS BACK ON THE BLUE NETWORK (ABC) WHERE HE LASTED UNTIL 1950. IN 1951 HE BEGAN A DAILY SYNDICATED SHOW WHICH RAN WELL INTO THE 1970s, (HEARD ON OVER 100 STATIONS.....

RADIO'S GOLDEN YEARS ©

by FRANK BRESEE & BOBB LYNES

FIRST NIGHTER

THE FIRST NIGHTER PROGRAM DEBUTED ON NBC ON DECEMBER 4, 1930 FROM CHICAGO. EARLY STARS OF THE DRAMATIC ANTHOLOGY SERIES WERE DON AMECHE, JUNE MEREDITH & BETTY LOU GERSON.

IN 1936 BARBARA LUDDY & LES TREMAYNE BECAME THE STARS; OLAN SOULÉ WAS MISS LUDDY'S CO-STAR FROM 1943 TO 1949.

THE SHOW WAS ON ALL NETWORKS: NBC, CBS & MUTUAL OVER THE YEARS....

BETTY LOU GERSON

BRET MORRISON

SPONSORS: CAMPANA, MILLER BEER

Campana Italian Balm

Miller Genuine Draft

"MR. FIRST NIGHTER": (HOSTS) WERE CHARLES HUGHES, MACDONALD CAREY, BRET MORRISON, MARVIN MILLER & RYE BILLSBURY

IT WAS REVIVED FOR ONE SEASON IN 1952

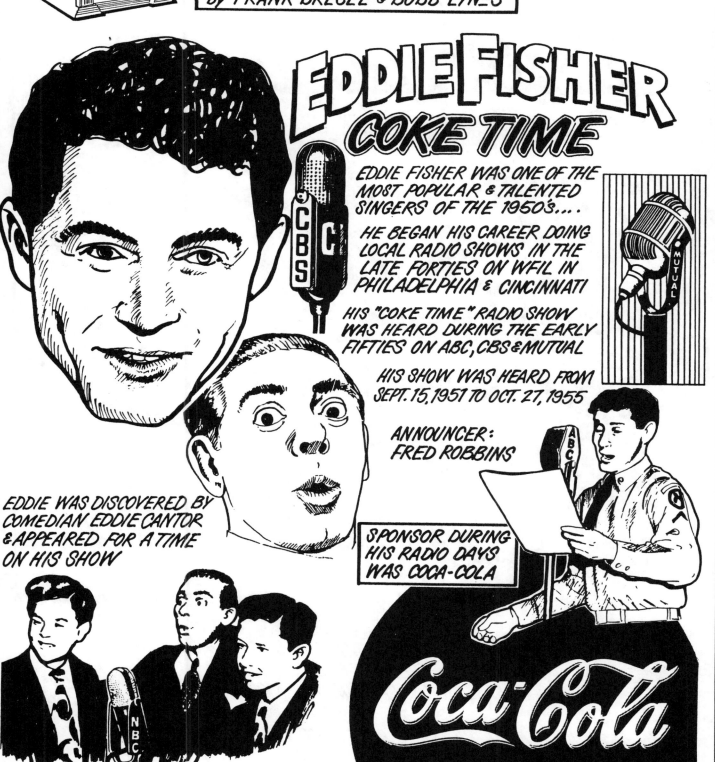

RADIO'S GOLDEN YEARS ©

by FRANK BRESEE & BOBB LYNES

EDDIE FISHER
COKE TIME

EDDIE FISHER WAS ONE OF THE MOST POPULAR & TALENTED SINGERS OF THE 1950's....

HE BEGAN HIS CAREER DOING LOCAL RADIO SHOWS IN THE LATE FORTIES ON WFIL IN PHILADELPHIA & CINCINNATI

HIS "COKE TIME" RADIO SHOW WAS HEARD DURING THE EARLY FIFTIES ON ABC, CBS & MUTUAL

HIS SHOW WAS HEARD FROM SEPT. 15, 1951 TO OCT. 27, 1955

ANNOUNCER: FRED ROBBINS

EDDIE WAS DISCOVERED BY COMEDIAN EDDIE CANTOR & APPEARED FOR A TIME ON HIS SHOW

SPONSOR DURING HIS RADIO DAYS WAS COCA-COLA

Coca-Cola

RADIO'S GOLDEN YEARS.©

by FRANK BRESEE & BOBB LYNES

FLASH GORDON

FLASH GORDON WAS BASED ON THE VERY POPULAR NEWSPAPER COMIC STRIP CREATED AND DRAWN BY ALEX RAYMOND AND BEGAN ON RADIO (MBS) IN 1935 AND CONTINUED FOR MANY YEARS IN SYNDICATION

by ALEX RAYMOND

Flash Gordon artwork © King Features Syndicate

THE EXPLOITS OF FLASH GORDON TOOK PLACE FOR MANY YEARS ON THE PLANET MONGO, WHERE HIS MAJOR ENEMY, THE EVIL MING, THE MERCILESS RULED HIS EMPIRE...

CAST MEMBERS: TEDDY BERGMAN (ALAN REED), EVERETT SLOANE, CHARLIE CANTOR, RAY COLLINS, MORE

GALE GORDON PLAYED FLASH GORDON

FLASH'S FRIENDS WERE DOCTOR ZARKOV, PRINCE BARIN AND GIRLFRIEND DALE ARDEN

PRODUCER: HIMAN BROWN

IN 1936, UNIVERSAL PICTURES RELEASED THE FIRST OF 3 FANTASTIC MOVIE SERIALS ABOUT FLASH STARRING BUSTER CRABBE

RADIO'S GOLDEN YEARS ©

by FRANK BRESEE & BOBB LYNES

FORT LARAMIE

FORT LARAMIE WAS ONE OF THE LAST OF THE WESTERN-TYPE PROGRAMS BROUGHT TO RADIO, DEBUTING ON CBS JANUARY 22, 1956. ACCORDING TO NORMAN MacDONNELL (ALSO PRODUCER-DIRECTOR OF "GUNSMOKE") FORT LARAMIE WAS TO BE "A MONUMENT TO ORDINARY MEN WHO LIVED IN EXTRAORDINARY TIMES IN UNCHARTED COUNTRY IN THE EARLY DAYS OF THE U.S."

THE SERIES CENTERED AROUND THE CAVALRY STATIONED AT WYOMING TERRITORY'S FORT LARAMIE AND CAPT. LEE QUINCE AND THE BRAVE MEN WHO SERVED WITH HIM.......

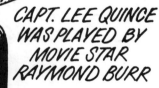

CAPT. LEE QUINCE WAS PLAYED BY MOVIE STAR RAYMOND BURR

SOUND EFFECTS WERE CREATED BY WIZARDS' RAY KEMPER, BILL JAMES, TOM HANLEY

ANNOUNCER: DAN CUBBERLY

REGULAR CAST: VIC PERRIN, HARRY BARTELL AND JACK MOYLES; SUPPORTED BY LARRY DOBKIN, RALPH MOODY, JACK KRUSCHEN, LOU KRUGMAN & MORE.....

THE SERIES WAS BROADCAST SUSTAINED FROM HOLLYWOOD'S CBS COLUMBIA SQUARE STUDIOS

RADIO'S GOLDEN YEARS.©

by FRANK BRESEE & BOBB LYNES

STAN FREBERG WAS THE LAST COMEDIAN TO HAVE HIS OWN REGULAR WEEKLY NETWORK RADIO SHOW...

STAN FREBERG Show

THE STAN FREBERG SHOW, SUSTAINED BY CBS, WENT ON THE AIR FROM HOLLYWOOD IN JULY, 1957 AND RAN FOR 15 SHORT WEEKS.....

DURING THAT TIME SOME OF THE BEST HUMOR AND BITING SATIRE EVER HEARD ON RADIO WAS FEATURED...

CBS RADIO NETWORK
COLUMBIA SQUARE
6121 SUNSET BLVD. - Studio B
THE STAN FREBERG SHOW
with
PEGGY TAYLOR
JUD CONLON'S RHYTHMAIRES
BILLY MAY'S MUSIC
Children between 8 & 12 will be admitted with adults

Wednesday
OCTOBER
16
1957
8-8:30 p.m.
Doors Close
at 7:40 p.m.

Nº 972

REGULARS INCLUDED:
DAWS BUTLER
JUNE FORAY
PETER LEEDS
PEGGY TAYLOR

HIS SHOW FEATURED ROUTINES WHICH BECAME CLASSICS AND MANY WERE RELEASED ON RECORDS BY CAPITOL:

"WUNERFUL, WUNERFUL" A LAWRENCE WELK PARODY (WELK HATED IT!), A SATIRE OF HARRY BELAFONTE'S "BANANA BOAT SONG," A JACK WEBB "DRAGNET" TAKE-OFF & MANY OTHERS

ANNOUNCER:
BUD SEWELL

MUSIC BY:
BILLY MAY ORC.
& JUD CONLON'S
RHYTHMAIRES

RADIO'S GOLDEN YEARS.©

by FRANK BRESEE & BOBB LYNES

FRONTIER GENTLEMAN

FRONTIER GENTLEMAN, STARRED JOHN DEHNER AS J.B. KENDALL, FEATURED AN ENGLISHMAN'S ACCOUNT OF LIFE AND DEATH IN THE 1800s AMERICAN WEST. AS A REPORTER FOR THE LONDON TIMES KENDALL WROTE COLORFUL AND UNUSUAL ACCOUNTS.....

AS A MAN WITH A GUN, HE LIVED AND BECAME PART OF THE VIOLENT YEARS IN THE NEW TERRITORIES

JOHN DEHNER

ORIGINATED AT CBS' HOLLYWOOD STUDIOS, THE SERIES BEGAN ON FEBRUARY 2, 1958

ANNOUNCERS: JOHN WALD, BUD SEWELL, JOHNNY JACOBS & JAMES MATTHEWS

HOLLYWOOD'S BEST ACTORS WERE FEATURED: JOHN McINTIRE, JEANETTE NOLAN, HARRY BARTELL, LARRY DOBKIN, VIRGINIA GREGG, JACK KRUSCHEN, ETC.

RADIO'S GOLDEN YEARS.©
by FRANK BRESEE & BOBB LYNES

GANGBUSTERS

GANGBUSTERS, EACH WEEK DOCUMENTED A CASE FROM LAW ENFORCEMENT FILES, WAS ON RADIO FROM JULY 20, 1935 UNTIL DECEMBER 20, 1957....21 YEARS! THE FIRST PROGRAM TO EFFECTIVELY USE SOUND EFFECTS.... A POLICE SIREN, MACHINE-GUN SPRAYING BULLETS, SCREECHING CAR TIRES, MARCHING FEET... AND GANGBUSTERS WAS ON THE AIR......

DURING GANGBUSTERS' EARLY DAYS STORIES TRACED CRIMINAL CAREERS SUCH AS JOHN DILLINGER, "PRETTY BOY" FLOYD, "BABY-FACE" NELSON AND BONNIE & CLYDE

CREATED & PRODUCED BY PHILLIPS H. LORD, THE SHOW WAS, FOR YEARS, HOST/NARRATED BY COL. H. NORMAN SCHWARZKOPF (BY PROXY)....

GANGBUSTERS.... PRESENTED IN COOPERATION WITH POLICE AND FEDERAL LAW ENFORCEMENT DEPARTMENTS THROUGHOUT THE UNITED STATES!

ANNOUNCERS INCLUDED: CHARLES STARK, FRANK GALLOP AND DON GARDINER

CREATOR PHILLIPS H. LORD

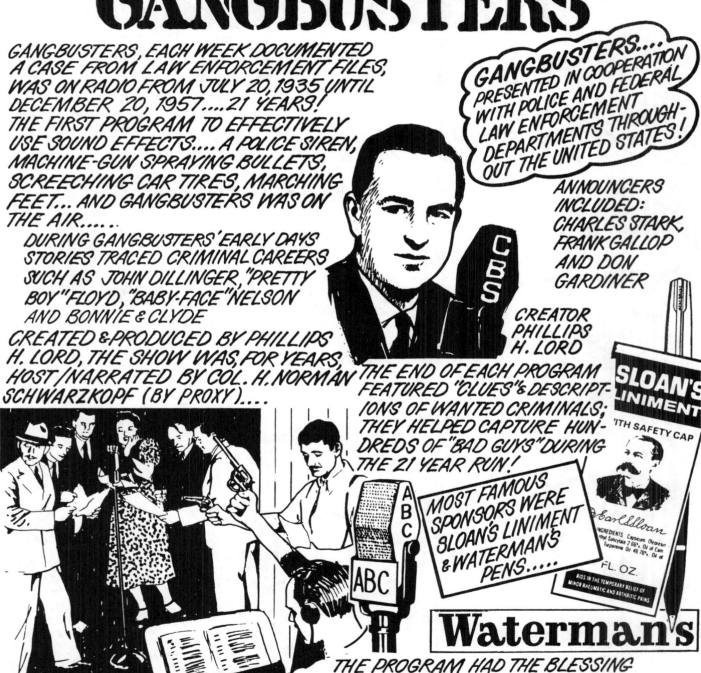

THE END OF EACH PROGRAM FEATURED "CLUES"& DESCRIPTIONS OF WANTED CRIMINALS; THEY HELPED CAPTURE HUNDREDS OF "BAD GUYS" DURING THE 21 YEAR RUN!

MOST FAMOUS SPONSORS WERE SLOAN'S LINIMENT & WATERMAN'S PENS.....

SLOAN'S LINIMENT WITH SAFETY CAP

Waterman's

THE PROGRAM HAD THE BLESSING OF THE NO. ONE "G-MAN" IN THE U.S.- J. EDGAR HOOVER

RADIO'S GOLDEN YEARS©

by FRANK BRESEE & BOBB LYNES

ARTHUR GODFREY

HIS WAS ONE OF THE LONGEST RUNNING AND MOST SUCCESSFUL SHOWS ON DAYTIME NETWORK RADIO....
ARTHUR GODFREY WAS BORN IN 1903 AND BEFORE THE AGE OF 30 WAS APPEARING ON AMATEUR RADIO PROGRAMS

IN JANUARY, 1934 HE BEGAN A SHOW ON WJSV-CBS IN WASHINGTON, D.C. AS "RED" GODFREY, "THE WARBLING BANJOIST"

LONGTIME ANNOUNCER: TONY MARVIN

FOR MANY YEARS GODFREY WAS THE MORNING MAN ON WABC-CBS IN NEW YORK CITY

MUSIC DIRECTOR: ARCHIE BLEYER

AT ONE TIME THE GODFREY SHOW WAS RESPONSIBLE FOR ALMOST 20% OF CBS REVENUES!

PARTIAL LIST OF SPONSORS: LIPTON TEA, CHESTERFIELD, BRISTOL-MYERS, LEVER BROS., PILLSBURY, CHASE & SANBORN, FRIGIDAIRE, MINUTE RICE, LISTERINE, WILDROOT, PEPTO BISMOL, CHRYSLER-PLYMOUTH, STAR KIST TUNA, SCHICK RAZORS, NABISCO AND HERSHEY'S CHOCOLATE

HIS COAST-TO-COAST DAILY 90 MINUTE CBS SHOW BEGAN IN 1945 AND WAS ON THE AIR FOR 27 YEARS!

THEME SONG: "SEEMS LIKE OLD TIMES"

TALENT SCOUT GODFREY HELPED THE CAREERS OF PAT BOONE, THE McGUIRE SISTERS, JULIUS LA ROSA, CARMEL QUINN AND THE CHORDETTES

RADIO'S GOLDEN YEARS.©

by FRANK BRESEE & BOBB LYNES

THE GOLDEN DAYS OF RADIO WENT ON THE AIR IN AUGUST 1949, AND HAS CONTINUED FOR THE BETTER PART OF HALF A CENTURY... OVER THE YEARS IT HAS BEEN HEARD ON THE LIBERTY BROADCASTING SYSTEM, MUTUAL AND FOR 29 YEARS ON THE ARMED FORCES RADIO SERVICE. IT WAS ALSO HEARD IN SOUTHERN CALIFORNIA ON KFI, KMPC, KGIL & KPCC

GOLDEN DAYS OF RADIO

GOLDEN DAYS FEATURES EXCERPTS FROM FRANK BRESEE'S VAST COLLECTION OF GREAT RADIO PROGRAMS OF THE PAST: THE SHADOW, THE LONE RANGER, JACK ARMSTRONG, SAM SPADE, AMOS 'N' ANDY, LIGHTS OUT, HENRY ALDRICH & MORE

HOST IS RADIO HISTORIAN FRANK BRESEE

THESE RADIO STARS HAVE APPEARED IN PERSON: BOB HOPE, BING CROSBY, JACK BENNY, GEORGE BURNS, BERGEN & McCARTHY, FIBBER McGEE AND MANY MORE!

ANNOUNCERS: GENE BAKER, BILL BALDWIN, ART GILMORE

RADIO'S GOLDEN YEARS.©
by FRANK BRESEE & BOBB LYNES

CATCH PHRASE: "YOO-HOO! IS ANYBODY?"

THE RISE OF THE GOLDBERGS

THE GOLDBERGS WAS ONE OF RADIO'S FIRST SOAP OPERAS (SERIALS) BEGINNING ON NBC IN 1929 AND RUNNING UNTIL 1950..

THE SHOW TOOK PLACE IN THE NEW YORK-BRONX AREA, WHERE MOLLY LIVED WITH HUSBAND JAKE AND THEIR 2 CHILDREN, SAMMY & ROSALIE

IT WAS A HOME-SPUN PROGRAM WITH MOLLY ALWAYS WORRIED OVER HER KIDS' PROBLEMS AND HER STRUGGLE TO KEEP JAKE'S BLOOD PRESSURE DOWN!

MOLLY GOLDBERG WAS PLAYED BY GERTRUDE BERG WHO ALSO CREATED & WROTE THE SERIES

THE SERIES BEGAN ON NBC NOV. 20, 1929, MOVED TO CBS AND MBS, BACK TO NBC IN 1941, ENDING ON CBS IN 1950

CAST REGULARS: JAMES WATERS, ROSLYN SILBER, ALFRED RYDER, EVERETT SLOANE AND MENASHA SKULNIK....

SPONSORS: PEPSODENT, COLGATE, OXYDOL AND GENERAL FOODS

THE SERIES WAS ALSO VERY POPULAR WHEN MOVED TO TV

RADIO'S GOLDEN YEARS. ©

by FRANK BRESEE & BOBB LYNES

GOOD NEWS

GOOD NEWS OF 1938 WAS THE FIRST RADIO SHOW TO JOIN HANDS WITH THE MOTION PICTURE STUDIOS TO PRODUCE A VARIETY SERIES

METRO-GOLDWYN-MAYER PRODUCED THE WEEKLY ONE HOUR SHOW "LIVE" COAST-TO-COAST ON NBC FROM THEIR STUDIOS...

MAXWELL HOUSE COFFEE PRESENTS A NEW AND BRILLIANT RADIO SHOW PRODUCED BY METRO-GOLDWYN-MAYER CLARK GABLE

PREMIER BROADCAST NEXT THURSDAY, NOV. 4TH COAST-TO-COAST NBC RED NETWORK

HOST-M.C.'S WERE YOUNG MGM STARS JAMES STEWART ROBERT TAYLOR ROBERT YOUNG

THE SHOW FEATURED COMEDY, MUSIC, DRAMATIC STORIES & INTERVIEWS WITH MOVIE STARS. EACH WEEK A NEW M-G-M MOVIE WAS PREVIEWED WITH THE CAST APPEARING IN PERSON. MOST MGM STARS (EXCEPT GARBO) APPEARED INCLUDING: CLARK GABLE, JUDY GARLAND, MICKEY ROONEY, SPENCER TRACY, ETC.

SPONSOR: MAXWELL HOUSE COFFEE

ANNOUNCERS: WARREN HULL, JOHN CONTE

MUSIC: MEREDITH WILLSON ORCH.

FANNY BRICE APPEARED AS BABY SNOOKS AND LOVEABLE FRANK MORGAN DID COMEDY ROUTINES

RADIO'S GOLDEN YEARS ©
by FRANK BRESEE & BOBB LYNES

GRAND OLE OPRY

THE LONGEST CONTINUING RADIO SHOW IN AMERICA, THE GRAND OLE OPRY BEGAN ON NOVEMBER 28, 1925 ON WSM-NASHVILLE. STATION MANAGER GEORGE D. HAY, WHO A YEAR EARLIER HELPED LAUNCH THE WLS BARN DANCE, CREATED THE WSM BARN DANCE AND ONE NIGHT CALLED THE MUSIC "GRAND OLE OPRY"...

IN 1939 NBC PICKED UP 30 MINUTES OF THE 4-HOUR HILLBILLY-FOLK-COUNTRY MUSIC MARATHON AND CARRIED IT NATION-WIDE ON SATURDAY NIGHTS UNTIL 1957

SPONSOR:
PRINCE ALBERT TOBACCO

STARS OVER THE YEARS: UNCLE JIMMY THOMPSON, DAVE MACON, DEFORD BAILEY, ROY ACUFF, BILL MONROE, ERNEST TUBB, HANK WILLIAMS, HANK SNOW, RED FOLEY, MINNIE PEARL, KITTY WELLS, WEBB PIERCE, JIM REEVES, FARON YOUNG, CARL SMITH, MARTY ROBBINS, JOHNNY CASH, FERLIN HUSKY, CONNIE SMITH, PORTER WAGONER, DOLLY PARTON, PATSY CLINE, EDDY ARNOLD, GEORGE JONES, LORETTA LYNN & MORE!

RADIO'S GOLDEN YEARS ©

by FRANK BRESEE & BOBB LYNES

THE GREAT GILDERSLEEVE

THE GREAT GILDERSLEEVE WENT ON THE AIR AS A WEEKLY HALF HOUR NBC SHOW ON AUGUST 31, 1941......

THE COMEDY SERIES WAS RADIO'S FIRST "SPIN-OFF"; THE CHARACTER OF THROCKMORTON P. GILDERSLEEVE WAS ORIGINATED ON THE FIBBER McGEE & MOLLY SHOW IN 1937

DURING ITS HEYDAY (1941-1950) HAROLD PEARY PLAYED "GILDY"

CAST REGULARS: WALTER TETLEY, ARTHUR Q. BRYAN, LILLIAN RANDOLPH, EARLE ROSS, RICHARD LeGRAND LURENE TUTTLE, MARY LEE ROBB, LOUISE ERICKSON & SHIRLEY MITCHELL

HAL PEARY SAID IN AN INTERVIEW THE FIRST NAME AND INITIAL OF THE GILDERSLEEVE CHARACTER WAS DERIVED FROM PEARY'S CHICAGO ADDRESS: THROCKMORTON PLACE

SPONSOR: KRAFT FOODS

NATIONAL BROADCASTING COMPANY, INC.
HOLLYWOOD STUDIOS
SUNSET AND VINE

NBC Wed. Dec. **11**

N B C Presents
"THE GREAT GILDERSLEEVE"
Starring
WILLARD WATERMAN

STUDIO **B**
Doors Close 7:50 P.M.

ADMITTED ★

FOR ITS LAST 7 YEARS ON THE AIR (1950-1957) WILLARD WATERMAN WAS GILDERSLEEVE

RADIO'S GOLDEN YEARS ©
by FRANK BRESEE & BOBB LYNES

GREAT RADIO COMEDIANS

DURING THE GREAT RADIO DAYS, FOUR COMEDIANS DOMINATED THE AIRWAVES.........

GEORGE BURNS

GEORGE BURNS (WITH GRACIE ALLEN) HAD ONE OF THE MOST POPULAR SHOWS ON TV; BURNS CONTINUED PERFORMING IN NIGHT CLUBS & IN LAS VEGAS DURING HIS 99TH YEAR!

JACK BENNY

JACK BENNY CONTINUED HIS CAREER IN RADIO & EVENTUALLY MOVED INTO TELEVISION

EDDIE CANTOR

EDDIE CANTOR DISCOVERED TALENTED NEWCOMERS ON HIS RADIO SHOW INCLUDING DINAH SHORE, EDDIE FISHER. CANTOR MOVED INTO TV ON THE COLGATE COMEDY HOUR

GEORGE JESSEL

GEORGE JESSEL LATER BECAME A MOTION PICTURE PRODUCER AT 20TH CENTURY-FOX & WAS CALLED "TOAST-MASTER GENERAL OF THE UNITED STATES"

FOR THE MOST PART, JACK BENNY WAS HEARD ON SUNDAY, EDDIE CANTOR ON WEDNESDAY, GEORGE AND GRACIE ON THURSDAY AND GEORGE JESSEL ON FRIDAY.....

RADIO'S GOLDEN YEARS©

by FRANK BRESEE & BOBB LYNES

The Green Hornet

THE GREEN HORNET HAD A LONG AND SUCCESSFUL CAREER ON RADIO.... BEGINNING IN JANUARY 1936, IT WAS HEARD UNTIL DECEMBER 1952, CONTINUING IN SYNDICATION FOR ANOTHER FORTY-PLUS YEARS!

"HE HUNTS THE BIGGEST GAME OF ALL.....PUBLIC ENEMIES WHO TRY TO DESTROY OUR AMERICA!

BRITT REID (SON OF THE LONE RANGER'S NEPHEW, DAN) PUBLISHER OF THE DAILY SENTINAL NEWSPAPER, BECAME THE MASKED CRIME-FIGHTER WHO.... "WITH HIS FAITHFUL VALET KATO, MATCHES WITS WITH THE UNDER-WORLD.....RISKING HIS LIFE THAT CRIMINALS & RACKETEERS, WITHIN THE LAW, CAN FEEL THE STING OF THE GREEN HORNET!"

THE HORNET/BRITT REID WAS PLAYED BY:
AL HODGE (1936-43)
BOB HALL (1943-46)
JACK McCARTHY (1946-52)

MOST OF THE YEARS ON THE AIR THE ADVENTURE WAS HEARD WEEKLY ON TUESDAYS & THURSDAYS

THEME: "FLIGHT OF THE BUMBLEBEE" BY RIMSKY-KORSAKOV

REGULAR CAST:
RAYMOND TOYO, MIKE TOLAN, ROLLON PARKER........"KATO"
LEONORE ALLMAN....:"CASEY"
JIM IRWIN, GILLY SHEA ......:"MICHAEL AXFORD"
JOHN TODD..."DAN REID"

THE HORNET USED A SOUPED-UP CAR CALLED "THE BLACK BEAUTY"

ANNOUNCERS:
CHARLES WOOD, MIKE WALLACE FIELDEN FARRINGTON & BOB HITE

THE HORNET WAS CREATED/WRITTEN BY LONE RANGER CREATOR FRAN STRIKER & WAS BROADCAST FROM GEORGE W. TRENDLE'S WXYZ IN DETROIT.

Cheerios
WHEATIES
Puffed Flakes
Kix
BREAKFAST OF CHAMPIONS
Orange-Crush Company Bottle

SPONSORS: GENERAL MILLS, ORANGE CRUSH

RADIO'S GOLDEN YEARS©

by FRANK BRESEE & BOBB LYNES

The Guiding Light

THE GUIDING LIGHT IS THE LONGEST RUNNING DAYTIME DRAMA OF ALL TIME. THE FIRST BROADCAST WAS HEARD ON NBC ON JANUARY 25, 1937. COLLECTIVELY, ON RADIO AND TELEVISION, THE DAILY SERIAL HAS AIRED FOR OVER 60 YEARS!!

CREATOR IRNA PHILLIPS

WRITER-CREATOR OF MANY FAMOUS "SOAP OPERAS":
- "PAINTED DREAMS" ('30)
- "TODAY'S CHILDREN" ('33)
- "ROAD OF LIFE" ('37)
- "RIGHT TO HAPPINESS" ('39)
- "WOMAN IN WHITE" ('43)
- "THE BRIGHTER DAY" ('48)
  AND OTHERS

THEME: "APHRODITE" BY GOETZL

THE SERIES WAS AIRED ON NBC FOR OVER TEN YEARS, THEN MOVED TO CBS; IN JULY, 1952 IT WAS HEARD AND SEEN ON BOTH RADIO AND TV. (ITS FINAL YEAR ON RADIO WAS 1956)

THE CAST INCLUDED: ED PRENTISS, ARTHUR PETERSON, MERCEDES McCAMBRIDGE, MARVIN MILLER, BRET MORRISON, RAYMOND EDWARD JOHNSON, WILLARD WATERMAN, SAM WANAMAKER, BETTY LOU GERSON, CHARITA BAUER, NED LeFEVRE, JOHN BARCLAY, MORE!

SPONSORS: GENERAL MILLS, DUZ SOAP & WHITE NAPTHA SOAP

ANNOUNCERS: FORT PEARSON, BUD COLLYER, HERB ALLEN

RADIO'S GOLDEN YEARS.©
by FRANK BRESEE & BOBB LYNES

GUNSMOKE

"AROUND DODGE CITY AND THE TERRITORY ON WEST, THERE'S JUST ONE WAY TO HANDLE THE KILLERS AND SPOILERS...THAT'S WITH A U.S. MARSHALL AND THE SMELL OF....GUNSMOKE!

GUNSMOKE, CREATED BY NORMAN MACDONNELL & JOHN MESTON, WAS KNOWN AS RADIO'S ADULT WESTERN...

EACH WEEK THE PROGRAM OPENED WITH MATT DILLON SAYING: "I'M THAT MAN, MATT DILLON, U.S. MARSHALL.. THE FIRST MAN THEY LOOK FOR.. AND THE LAST ONE THEY WANNA MEET....

THE SHOW BEGAN ON CBS RADIO IN 1952, RAN UNTIL 1961 AND WAS SO POPULAR THAT IT ALSO BEGAN A LONG TV RUN IN 1955..

NORM MACDONNELL JOHN MESTON

SPONSOR: CHESTERFIELD

MATT DILLON, U.S. MARSHALL WAS PLAYED BY LEGENDARY RADIO ACTOR WILLIAM CONRAD

ANNOUNCERS: ROY ROWAN KEN PETERS, GEORGE WALSH

GUNSMOKE WAS KNOWN FOR AWARD-WINNING SOUND PATTERNS BY RAY KEMPER, BILL JAMES AND TOM HANLEY

MUSIC BY REX KOURY

HOWARD McNEAR WAS "DR. CHARLES ADAMS"

GEORGIA ELLIS WAS "KITTY RUSSELL"

PARLEY BAER WAS "DEPUTY CHESTER PROOFOOT"

RADIO'S GOLDEN YEARS. ©

by FRANK BRESEE & BOBB LYNES

THE HALLS OF IVY

THE HALLS OF IVY FEATURED FILM STAR RONALD COLMAN AND HIS WIFE BENITA HUME AS THEY RELATED TO INCIDENTS THAT BEFELL THE MYTHICAL IVY LEAGUE COLLEGE, ITS STUDENTS AND FACULTY.... COLMAN PLAYED WILLIAM TODHUNTER HALL, PRESIDENT OF IVY COLLEGE AND BENITA WAS WIFE, VICKY, THE FORMER VICTORIA CROMWELL OF THE ENGLISH THEATRE

THE HEART-WARMING SERIES RAN ON NBC FROM JANUARY 6, 1950 TO JUNE, 1952

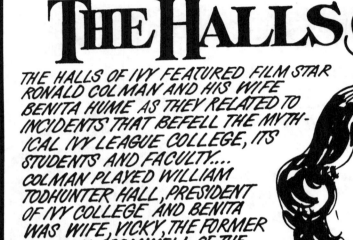

RONALD COLMAN ALSO APPEARED ON OTHER SHOWS: LUX RADIO THEATRE, SUSPENSE, JACK BENNY SHOW, THE CIRCLE AND HOSTED EVERYTHING FOR THE BOYS & FAVORITE STORY....

ANNOUNCER: KEN CARPENTER

THE SERIES WAS CREATED & WRITTEN BY DON QUINN (CREATOR OF FIBBER McGEE AND MOLLY)

SPONSOR: SCHLITZ BREWING COMPANY

MUSIC: HENRY RUSSELL ORCH.

CAST MEMBERS: GALE GORDON, ARTHUR Q. BRYAN, ALAN REED, WILLARD WATERMAN AND HERB BUTTERFIELD

RADIO'S GOLDEN YEARS©
by FRANK BRESEE & BOBB LYNES

THE HAPPINESS BOYS
BILLY JONES & ERNIE HARE

BILLY JONES AND ERNIE HARE WERE SINGERS AND COMEDIANS WHO APPEARED ON RADIO IN 1921

THEY WERE ONE OF THE FIRST TEAMS TO BECOME RADIO STARS, LASTING FOR 18 YEARS. THEY JOINED NBC IN 1926!

NAMED FOR THEIR MANY SPONSORS, JONES AND HARE WERE KNOWN AS "THE HAPPINESS BOYS" (HAPPINESS CANDY) AND "THE INTERWOVEN PAIR" (INTERWOVEN SOCKS)

THEIR THEME SONG:
HOW DO YOU DO, EVERYBODY, HOW DO YOU DO?
GEE, IT'S GREAT TO SAY HELLO TO ALL OF YOU
I'M BILLY JONES
I'M ERNIE HARE
AND WE'RE A SILLY-LOOKIN' PAIR
HOW DO YOU DOODLE-DOODLE-DOODLE-DOODLE-DO?

THEY ALSO MADE PHONOGRAPH RECORDS AND WERE FEATURED IN MOVIE SHORT SUBJECTS

RADIO'S GOLDEN YEARS ©

by FRANK BRESEE & BOBB LYNES

The HARDY FAMILY

THE HARDY FAMILY STARRING MICKEY ROONEY WAS BASED ON THE VERY POPULAR M-G-M MOTION PICTURE SERIES

THE PROGRAM WAS SYNDICATED AND ALSO HEARD COAST-TO-COAST ON THE MUTUAL BROADCASTING SYSTEM FROM JANUARY UNTIL DECEMBER, 1952......

MICKEY ROONEY

STONE

MBS

HOLDEN

ORCHESTRA: JERRY FIELDING

DIRECTOR: THOMAS McAVITY

OPENING: "WE'RE PROUD TO PRESENT THE HARDY FAMILY, BASED ON THE FAMOUS METRO-GOLDWYN-MAYER MOTION PICTURE SERIES WHICH BROUGHT TO LIFE TO MILLIONS AND REFLECTED THE COMMON JOYS AND TRIBULATIONS OF THE AVERAGE AMERICAN FAMILY"

JUST LIKE THE MOVIE SERIES, THE WEEKLY SHOW STARRED MICKEY ROONEY (ANDY HARDY) LEWIS STONE (JUDGE HARDY) AND FAY HOLDEN (MRS. HARDY) DICK CRENNA (ANDY'S PAL, BEASEY)

THE SHOW WAS RECORDED AT NBC STUDIOS AT SUNSET & VINE IN HOLLYWOOD......

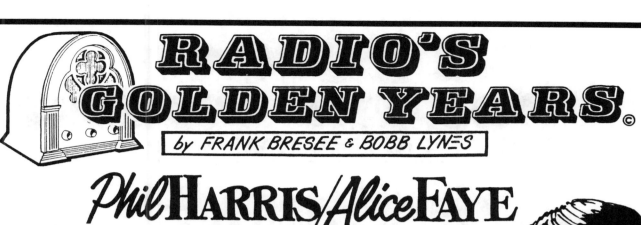

RADIO'S GOLDEN YEARS ©

by FRANK BRESEE & BOBB LYNES

Phil HARRIS / Alice FAYE

PHIL HARRIS AND ALICE FAYE HAD ONE OF THE MOST POPULAR COMEDY SHOWS... THEY FIRST CO-STARRED ON NBC'S "FITCH BANDWAGON" (FOLLOWING JACK BENNY SUNDAY EVENINGS DEBUTING ON SEPT. 29, 1946. THE REAL-LIFE MARRIED COUPLE BEGAN THEIR OWN HARRIS-FAYE SHOW ON NBC OCT. 3, 1948

THE FUNNY ENSEMBLE CAST INCLUDED: ELLIOTT LEWIS (FRANK REMLEY), WALTER TETLEY (JULIUS ABBRUZIO), ROBERT NORTH (WILLIE), THE HARRIS DAUGHTERS WERE PLAYED BY JEANINE ROOSE & ANNE WHITFIELD, MR. SCOTT (REXALL BOSS) WAS GALE GORDON

ANNOUNCER: BILL FORMAN

SPONSORS: FITCH SHAMPOO, REXALL DRUGS, NBC AND RCA

FITCH DANDRUFF REMOVER SHAMPOO

NBC

RCA

Rexall DRUG STORE

RADIO'S GOLDEN YEARS ©
by FRANK BRESEE & BOBB LYNES

HAVE GUN WILL TRAVEL
WIRE PALADIN — SAN FRANCISCO

CREATED & WRITTEN BY HERB MEADOW & SAM ROLFE (SOME SCRIPTS BY GENE RODDENBERRY) HAVE GUN, WILL TRAVEL WAS ONE THE FEW SHOWS THAT BEGAN ON TV, THEN MOVED ALSO TO RADIO DEBUTING ON CBS NOVEMBER 23, 1958 AND RUNNING UNTIL NOVEMBER 27, 1960.
BETWEEN ADVENTURES, PALADIN LIVED AT SAN FRANCISCO'S CARLTON HOTEL, WHERE CHINESE SERVANTS "HEYBOY" & "MISS WONG" WORKED

ANNOUNCER: HUGH DOUGLAS

THE WESTERN STARRED JOHN DEHNER AS "PALADIN," A SOLDIER OF FORTUNE WHOSE FAST GUN WAS FOR HIRE; A LONER WITH FEW FRIENDS AND A GUNMAN'S REPUTATION.

HOLLYWOOD'S BEST RADIO ACTORS APPEARED ON THE SHOW: LARRY DOBKIN, HELEN KLEEB, HOWARD McNEAR, SAM EDWARDS, JEANETTE NOLAN, HARRY BARTELL & VIC PERRIN
DIRECTED BY NORMAN MacDONNELL

BEN WRIGHT WAS "HEYBOY"

VIRGINIA GREGG WAS "MISS WONG"

TV TO RADIO

RADIO'S GOLDEN YEARS ©
by FRANK BRESEE & BOBB LYNES

HAWTHORNE!

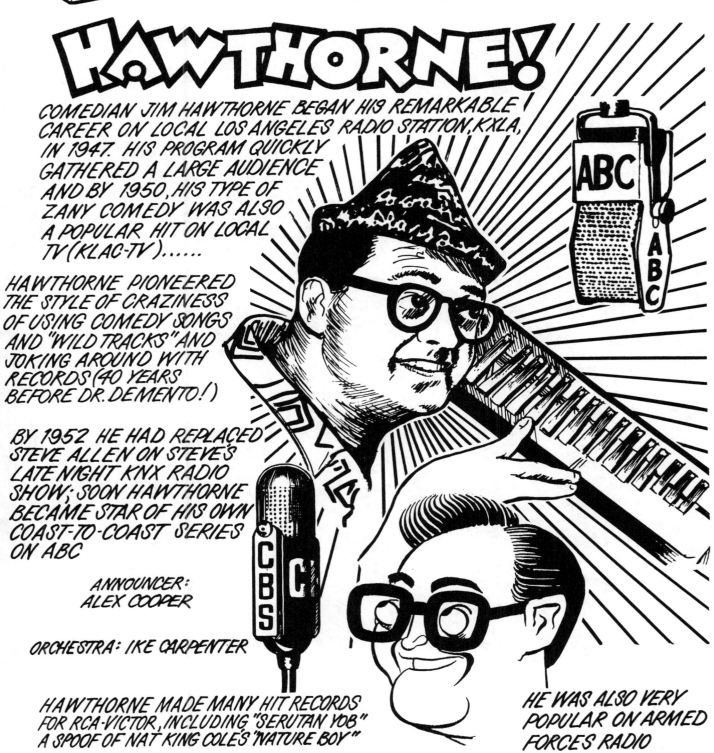

COMEDIAN JIM HAWTHORNE BEGAN HIS REMARKABLE CAREER ON LOCAL LOS ANGELES RADIO STATION, KXLA, IN 1947. HIS PROGRAM QUICKLY GATHERED A LARGE AUDIENCE AND BY 1950, HIS TYPE OF ZANY COMEDY WAS ALSO A POPULAR HIT ON LOCAL TV (KLAC-TV)......

HAWTHORNE PIONEERED THE STYLE OF CRAZINESS OF USING COMEDY SONGS AND "WILD TRACKS" AND JOKING AROUND WITH RECORDS (40 YEARS BEFORE DR. DEMENTO!)

BY 1952 HE HAD REPLACED STEVE ALLEN ON STEVE'S LATE NIGHT KNX RADIO SHOW; SOON HAWTHORNE BECAME STAR OF HIS OWN COAST-TO-COAST SERIES ON ABC

ANNOUNCER: ALEX COOPER

ORCHESTRA: IKE CARPENTER

HAWTHORNE MADE MANY HIT RECORDS FOR RCA-VICTOR, INCLUDING "SERUTAN YOB" A SPOOF OF NAT KING COLE'S "NATURE BOY"

HE WAS ALSO VERY POPULAR ON ARMED FORCES RADIO

RADIO'S GOLDEN YEARS ©

by FRANK BRESEE & BOBB LYNES

THE HERMIT'S CAVE WAS ONE OF THE SCARIEST HORROR AND SUSPENSE-FILLED PROGRAMS OF RADIO'S EARLY YEARS....

HERMIT'S CAVE

WITH ITS GHOST STORIES AND EERIE SOUND EFFECTS, THE SHOW KEPT LISTENERS FRIGHTENED AND AWAKE LONG AFTER THEIR BEDTIME VICTIMS WERE SHOT, SLASHED, GASHED AND BASHED.....ANYTHING THAT WOULD CREATE NEW & TERRIFYING SOUNDS ON RADIO

OPENING (HERMIT'S VOICE): "GHOST STORIES.....WEIRD STORIES.... AND MURDERS TOO! THE HERMIT KNOWS OF THEM ALL! TURN OUT YOUR LIGHTS! TURN THEM OUT! HAVE YOU HEARD TONIGHT'S STORY? THEN LISTEN WHILE THE HERMIT TELLS YOU...."

The cast of HERMIT'S CAVE

THE HERMIT WAS PLAYED BY MEL JOHNSON

DIRECTOR: WILLIAM CONRAD

MUSIC BY REX KOURY

WRITERS: LOU HUSTON, HERBERT O'CONNOR

THE SERIES ORIGINATED AT KMPC-BEVERLY HILLS, CALIF. AND INTRODUCED THESE NEWCOMERS TO RADIO: WILLIAM CONRAD, BILL FORMAN, REX KOURY & JOHN DEHNER

THE SHOW WAS HEARD BY SYNDICATED TRANSCRIPTION AROUND THE U.S.

RADIO'S GOLDEN YEARS.©
by FRANK BRESEE & BOBB LYNES

HERB MORRISON
HINDENBURG DISASTER

THE MOST FAMOUS ON-THE-SPOT NEWSCAST OF ALL TIME TOOK PLACE ON MAY 6, 1937 AT LAKEHURST, NEW JERSEY.....

"....IT BURST INTO FLAMES!!.... GET THIS, CHARLIE... GET THIS..... OH, THE HUMANITY..."

HERB MORRISON

CHARLES NEHLSEN, ENGINEER

HERB MORRISON OF CHICAGO STATION WLS WAS ON HAND WITH SPECIAL RECORDING EQUIPMENT AT THE U.S. NAVAL AIR STATION TO DESCRIBE THE ARRIVAL OF THE GERMAN DIRIGIBLE, HINDENBURG.....

THE GIGANTIC AIRSHIP SUDDENLY EXPLODED, DROPPED TO THE GROUND AND BURNED, KILLING 35 PEOPLE.......

MORRISON WAS IN TEARS AS HE DESCRIBED TO HIS LISTENERS ONE OF THE MOST DRAMATIC EYEWITNESS REPORTS EVER BROADCAST.......

RADIO'S GOLDEN YEARS©

by FRANK BRESEE & BOBB LYNES

"CX-4 CALLING CONTROL TOWER, CX-4 CALLING CONTROL TOWER..... THIS IS HOP HARRIGAN COMING IN!..

HOP HARRIGAN!

HOP HARRIGAN, AMERICA'S ACE OF THE AIRWAYS WAS ONE OF THE MORE POPULAR AFTERNOON ADVENTURE PROGRAMS. THE RADIO SERIES WAS ORIGINALLY BASED ON THE ADVENTURE COMIC STRIP, BUT THE RADIO VERSION ACHIEVED GREATER FAME..

HOP AND HIS MECHANIC-PAL TANK TINKER SURVIVED MANY FLYING MISSIONS BEHIND THE ENEMY LINES IN WORLD WAR II AND FOUGHT DUELS IN THE AIR WITH MANY OF AMERICA'S ADVERSARIES.....

HOP HARRIGAN: CHESTER STRATTON LATER, ALBERT ALEY

ALEY

STRATTON

TANK TINKER: KEN LYNCH

FOLLOWING THE WAR, HOP & TANK RETURNED TO THE UNITED STATES AND SET UP THEIR OWN FLYING FIELD. HOP WAS SUPPOSED TO MERELY FLY CARGO AND GIVE FLYING LESSONS, BUT HE HAD COUNTLESS ADVENTURES IN HIS BATTLES WITH SPIES, SMUGGLERS & GANGSTERS...

OTHER CAST MEMBERS: MITZI GOULD, JACKSON BECK, MATT CROWLEY

ANNOUNCER: GLENN RIGGS

THE MONDAY-FRIDAY DAILY 15-MINUTE SHOW DEBUTED IN 1942 ON THE BLUE (ABC) NETWORK, FROM 1946 ON MUTUAL, ENDING IN 1948

SPONSORS: GRAPE NUTS FLAKES, LEVER BROTHERS & TAYLOR-REED PRODUCTS

Post's GRAPE: NUTS

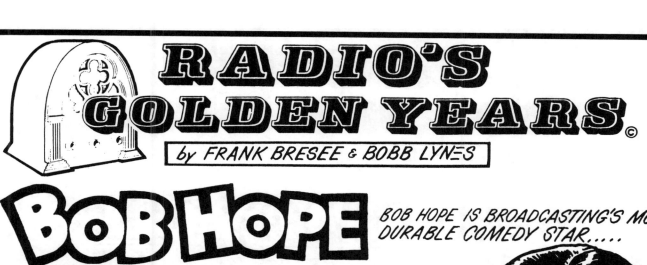

RADIO'S GOLDEN YEARS ©
by FRANK BRESEE & BOBB LYNES

BOB HOPE

BOB HOPE IS BROADCASTING'S MOST DURABLE COMEDY STAR.....

HE BEGAN ON THE NBC-BLUE NETWORK IN JANUARY, 1935 AND CONTINUED ON THE NBC RADIO AND TV NETWORKS FOR 60 YEARS!

SPONSORS: PEPSODENT TOOTH PASTE, SWAN SOAP AND CHESTERFIELD CIGARETTES

A TICKET TO THE BOB HOPE SHOW WAS TREASURED BY ALL WHO WERE LUCKY ENOUGH TO OBTAIN ONE....

ANNOUNCERS: BILL GOODWIN, WENDELL NILES, HY AVERBACK

BOB HOPE'S FAMOUS THEME SONG IS "THANKS FOR THE MEMORY"

THE BOB HOPE SHOW WAS AIRED FROM HOLLYWOOD UNTIL THE BEGINNING OF WORLD WAR II. FROM THAT TIME & FOR THE DURATION, HIS SHOW WAS BROADCAST FROM MILITARY BASES ALL OVER THE WORLD.

MANY GUEST STARS APPEARED ON HIS SHOW, BUT HIS FAVORITE FOIL.... BING CROSBY

MUSIC BY: SKINNAY ENNIS, LATER LES BROWN

REGULARS ON THE SHOW WERE JERRY COLONNA, FRANCES LANGFORD, VERA VAGUE, BRENDA AND COBINA AND DORIS DAY

RADIO'S GOLDEN YEARS ©

by FRANK BRESEE & BOBB LYNES

HOLLYWOOD HOTEL

HOLLYWOOD HOTEL WAS THE FIRST IMPORTANT NETWORK RADIO SHOW TO ORIGINATE COAST-TO-COAST FROM HOLLYWOOD AND WAS HEARD ON CBS FROM 1934 THROUGH 1938. MASTER OF CEREMONIES OF THE VARIETY HOUR WAS DICK POWELL LATER FRED MacMURRAY, HERBERT MARSHALL AND WILLIAM POWELL HOSTED

DICK POWELL SANG AND INTRODUCED WEEKLY DRAMATIC PLAYS WHICH WERE AN IMPORTANT, POPULAR PART OF THE PROGRAM

VOCALISTS: ANNE JAMISON, FRANCES LANGFORD

FAMED GOSSIP COLUMNIST LOUELLA PARSONS WAS A REGULAR ON THE SHOW, INTERVIEWING HOLLYWOOD STARS

GUEST STARS: MARGARET SULLAVAN, LOUISE RAINER, CAROLE LOMBARD, MIRIAM HOPKINS

Campbell's
Quality

SPONSOR: CAMPBELL SOUPS

ANNOUNCER: KEN NILES

MUSIC: RAYMOND PAIGE ORC.

118

RADIO'S GOLDEN YEARS ©

by FRANK BRESEE & BOBB LYNES

HOPALONG CASSIDY

THE PROGRAM DEBUTED ON MUTUAL JANUARY 1, 1950, WHERE IT REMAINED FOR TWO YEARS BEFORE GOING INTO SYNDICATION...

MBS

"HOPALONG CASSIDY" STARRED WILLIAM BOYD AS "HOPPY" AND ANDY CLYDE AS HIS SIDEKICK "CALIFORNIA"

OPENING:
"TO THE RING OF SILVER SPURS, IT'S HOPALONG CASSIDY..! WITH HIS COMPANION, THE SAME CALIFORNIA YOU'VE LAUGHED AT A MILLION TIMES...".

A TRUE AMERICAN SUCCESS STORY, WILLIAM BOYD PLAYED "HOPPY" IN THE MOVIES IN THE 1930s & 1940s. AFTER THE SUCCESS OF OLD MOVIES ON EARLY TV, BOYD HOCKED EVERYTHING HE OWNED TO ACQUIRE THE RIGHTS TO HIS OLD FILMS. IT PAID OFF, AND HOPALONG CASSIDY BECAME THE KIDS' HERO ON TV.
LATER HE PRODUCED BRAND NEW SHOWS FOR TV AND THEN TOOK HIS ADVENTURES TO RADIO. WILLIAM BOYD WAS ON TOP OF THE WORLD, AND THE "HOPPY CRAZE" MEANT MILLIONS IN SALES FOR HIS HOPPY MERCHANDISE: BOOKS, COMICS, CLOTHES, GUN SETS, FURNITURE AND MORE....

Post
GRAPE-NUTS
Post TOASTIES
Post SUGAR CRISP
Post 40% BRAN FLAKES

Barbara Ann
All BUTTER

SPONSORS: GENERAL FOODS (POST CEREALS), BARBARA ANN BREAD

TV TO RADIO

BOYD DEVOTED HIS LIFE TO BEING A HUMANITARIAN WHO FELT IT WAS HIS RESPONSIBILITY TEACHING KIDS THE RIGHT WAY TO LIVE

RADIO'S GOLDEN YEARS.©

by FRANK BRESEE & BOBB LYNES

HEDDA HOPPER & LOUELLA PARSONS

TWO OF THE MOTION PICTURE COLONY'S MOST OUTSPOKEN GOSSIP COLUMNISTS WERE HEDDA HOPPER & LOUELLA PARSONS WHO EACH ALSO HAD THEIR OWN NATIONAL RADIO SHOW BROADCAST WEEKLY FROM HOLLYWOOD....

LOUELLA WAS HEARD IN THE FORTIES & FIFTIES ON ABC, FOLLOWING WALTER WINCHELL ON SUNDAY EVENINGS

HEDDA & LOUELLA HAD MANY FEUDS OVER THE YEARS: SOMETIMES IN PRINT AND ON THE AIR

HEDDA WAS ON CBS THREE TIMES A WEEK, TAKING SOME STARS TO TASK ON-THE-AIR FOR THEIR MISBE-HAVING WAYS.

SPONSORS INCLUDED: PROCTER & GAMBLE, ARMOUR & COMPANY JERGENS LOTION, & WOODBURY SOAP

Armour and Company

LOUELLA'S ANNOUNCER: MARVIN MILLER

HEDDA'S ANNOUNCER: WENDELL NILES

OTHER POPULAR RADIO HOLLYWOOD COLUMNISTS WERE JIMMY FIDLER, GEORGE FISHER & SHEILAH GRAHAM

RADIO'S GOLDEN YEARS ©

by FRANK BRESEE & BOBB LYNES

HOUSE PARTY

HOUSE PARTY STARRING ART LINKLETTER BEGAN ON CBS ON JANUARY 15, 1945 AND CONTINUED ON RADIO FOR AN AMAZING 22 YEARS, RUNNING UNTIL OCTOBER 13, 1967...

IT WAS A DAILY 30-MINUTE AUDIENCE PARTICIPATION SHOW, WITH LINKLETTER INTERVIEWING ON THE STAGE AND IN THE AUDIENCE. ART LINKLETTER'S BRILLIANT SKILL AT AD-LIBBING WITH PEOPLE MADE THIS THE MOST LISTENED-TO DAYTIME RADIO SHOW OF ALL TIME!

A FAVORITE PORTION OF HOUSE PARTY WAS THE "KIDS SAY THE DARNDEST THINGS" SEGMENT, IN WHICH THE KIDS WOULD OFTEN RESPOND WITH EMBARRASSING ANSWERS....

ART LINKLETTER LATER WROTE BOOKS & PRODUCED A RECORD ALBUM TITLED "KIDS SAY THE DARNDEST THINGS"

ANNOUNCER: JACK SLATTERY

MUSIC: MUZZY MARCELLINO TRIO

PRODUCER/DIRECTOR: JOHN GUEDEL

KIDS SAY THE DARNDEST THINGS!
by Art Linkletter
PEANUTS
INTRODUCTION BY WALT DISNEY

Rinso
LIFEBUOY HEALTH SOAP
Pillsbury BEST XXXX
GE

SPONSORS: GENERAL ELECTRIC, LEVER BROTHERS & PILLSBURY

AFTER RADIO, HOUSE PARTY CONTINUED ON TELEVISION FOR ANOTHER DOZEN YEARS

RADIO'S GOLDEN YEARS.©

by FRANK BRESEE & BOBB LYNES

I LOVE A MYSTERY!

CARLTON E. MORSE'S "I LOVE A MYSTERY" DEBUTED ON NBC-PACIFIC OUTLETS JANUARY 16, 1939, WAS SO POPULAR IT MOVED TO THE FULL NBC-BLUE 9 MONTHS LATER. JACK PACKARD, DOC LONG & REGGIE YORKE RAN THE A-1 DETECTIVE AGENCY & TRAVELLED THE WORLD LOOKING FOR ADVENTURE...

DURING THE EARLY RUN, PROGRAM WAS 15 MINUTES FIVE-A-WEEK SERIAL; FROM 1940-42 WAS A 30 MINUTE MONDAY SHOW; 1943-44 : 15 MINUTE SERIAL ON CBS. OFF THE AIR FIVE YEARS, "I.L.A.M." WAS REVIVED IN 1949 ON MBS & RAN TO 1952

CAST, 1939-44:
JACK-MICHAEL RAFFETTO
DOC-BARTON YARBOROUGH
REGGIE-WALTER PATTERSON
JERRY-GLORIA BLONDELL

SPONSORS: FLEISCHMANN'S YEAST, PROCTER & GAMBLE

FLEISCHMANN'S YEAST

IVORY SNOW
Brand of IVORY
NEW! SUDS IN COLD WATER TOO
...and woolens

CAST 1949-52:
JACK-RUSSELL THORSON
DOC-JIM BOLES
REGGIE-TONY RANDALL

LATER CAST REGULARS:
MERCEDES McCAMBRIDGE, LUIS VAN ROOTEN & SARAH FUSSELL

RADIO'S GOLDEN YEARS ©
by FRANK BRESEE & BOBB LYNES

Information PLEASE

ORIGINATED BY & PRODUCED BY DAN GOLANPAUL INFORMATION PLEASE WAS THE PRESTIGE QUIZ SHOW OF RADIO THE SHOW DEBUTED ON NBC-BLUE IN MAY, 1938 AND LASTED UNTIL 1951. IT FEATURED QUESTIONS SENT IN BY LISTENERS, WHO TRIED TO STUMP THE EXPERT PANEL (THE EXPERTS WERE: JOHN KIERAN, FRANKLIN P. ADAMS AND OSCAR LEVANT)

LEVANT

KIERAN

ADAMS

HOST-MODERATOR WAS CLIFTON FADIMAN

A LISTENER WHO STUMPED THE EXPERTS WOULD RECEIVE CASH AND A SET OF THE ENCYCLOPEDIA BRITANNICA

OVER THE YEARS FAMOUS "GUEST EXPERTS" INCLUDED: JOHN GUNTHER, DEEMS TAYLOR, WENDELL WILKIE, FRED ALLEN, ORSON WELLES, GRACIE ALLEN & ALFRED HITCHCOCK!

WAKE UP, AMERICA! IT'S TIME TO STUMP THE EXPERTS!

ANNOUNCERS: MILTON CROSS, BEN GRAUER, ED HERLIHY

SPONSORS: CANADA DRY, LUCKY STRIKE, PARKER PEN CO., HEINZ 57 VARIETIES & MOBIL GAS

Mobilgas

CANADA DRY

HEINZ 57 VARIETI

LUCKY STRIKE

Parker

THE PROGRAM WAS HEARD ON NBC-RED & BLUE NETWORKS, CBS AND MUTUAL

RADIO'S GOLDEN YEARS ©

by FRANK BRESEE & BOBB LYNES

"GOOD EVENING, FRIENDS OF THE INNER SANCTUM... THIS IS YOUR HOST INVITING YOU THROUGH THE SQUEAKING DOOR.... FOR ANOTHER STORY OF MYSTERY AND HORROR..."

INNER SANCTUM MYSTERIES

CREATED BY THE PRODUCER-DIRECTOR HIMAN BROWN, INNER SANCTUM MYSTERIES DEBUTED ON NBC-BLUE JANUARY 7, 1941 AND "SCARED THE YELL" OUT OF LISTENERS UNTIL OCTOBER 5, 1952...

THE HORROR SHOW WAS HEARD OVER THE YEARS ON CBS AND ABC

"RAYMOND, YOUR HOST" WAS PLAYED EERILY BY RAYMOND EDWARD JOHNSON

STARS IN VARIOUS STORIES WERE: BORIS KARLOFF, RAYMOND MASSEY, LES TREMAYNE, MERCEDES McCAMBRIDGE, MASON ADAMS, EVERETT SLOANE, LARRY HAINES, JOSEPH JULIAN, ANN SHEPHERD AND RICHARD WIDMARK

SPONSORS: COLGATE TOOTHPASTE, LIPTON TEA AND SOUP, BROMO-SELTZER & MARS CANDY

IN 1945, PAUL McGRATH BECAME "YOUR HOST..."

ANNOUNCERS:

ED HERLIHY   DWIGHT WEIST

& ALLEN C. ANTHONY

RADIO'S GOLDEN YEARS©
by FRANK BRESEE & BOBB LYNES

IT PAYS TO BE IGNORANT

THE GREAT COMEDY "QUIZ" SHOW OF RADIO STARRED TOM HOWARD, GEORGE SHELTON, HARRY McNAUGHTON & LULU McCONNELL. HOWARD WAS THE EMCEE AND THE THREE ZANIES MADE A SHAMBLES OF THE SHOW WITH THEIR INSULTS & JOKES:

McNAUGHTON: "FUNNY, I HAD FISH FOR DINNER... IT WAS FRIED AMATTA"

SHELTON: "AMATTA.... WHAT'S AMATTA?"

McNAUGHTON: "NOTHING... WHAT'S AMATTA WITH YOU?"

QUESTIONS INCLUDED:
"WHAT COLOR IS A WHITE HORSE?"
"IN WHAT SPORT IS A FOOTBALL USED?"
"WHAT MATERIAL IS A SILK DRESS MADE OF?"

THE SHOW WAS HEARD ON BOTH CBS & MUTUAL FROM JUNE 25, 1942 TO SEPT. 26, 1951

HARRY McNAUGHTON: "I HAVE A POEM, MR. HOWARD"

LULU McCONNELL: "WHAT'S YOUR NAME, HONEY?"

TOM HOWARD

GEORGE SHELTON: "I USED TO WORK IN THAT TOWN!"

KEN ROBERTS   DICK STARK

ANNOUNCERS:

SPONSORS:
PHILIP MORRIS CIGARETTES & DODGE-PLYMOUTH AUTOMOBILES

THEME SONG:
"IT PAYS TO BE IGNORANT, TO BE DUMB, TO BE DENSE, TO BE IGNORANT.
IT PAYS TO BE IGNORANT JUST LIKE ME!
EACH WEEK I EARN 6 DOLLARS MY BRAIN IS TERRIBLY LAX.
BUT WHEN THERE AIN'T NO INCOME.....THERE AIN'T NO INCOME TAX.
SO YOU SEE IT PAYS TO BE IGNORANT JUST LIKE ME!"

RADIO'S GOLDEN YEARS©
by FRANK BRESEE & BOBB LYNES

JACK ARMSTRONG! JACK ARMSTRONG!

JACK WAS PLAYED BY ACTORS JIM AMECHE, STANLEY (STACY) HARRIS AND RYE BILLSBURY....

JACK ARMSTRONG, THE ALL-AMERICAN BOY, WAS ONE OF THE LONGEST-RUNNING AFTERNOON ADVENTURE SHOWS, STARTING ON JULY 31, 1933 ON WBBM, CHICAGO & LASTING UNTIL 1951

THE LONGTIME ANNOUCER WAS FRANKLYN MacCORMACK

JIM AMECHE

THE SHOW FEATURED MANY RADIO PREMIUMS WHICH WERE SENT FOR A DIME AND A WHEATIES BOX-TOP. INCLUDING:

SECRET DE-CODER MANUALS
LAPEL PINS
MAGIC LIE DETECTOR BOX

THE SPONSOR OVER THE YEARS WAS WHEATIES, BREAKFAST OF CHAMPIONS

THE MOST FAMOUS WAS CHARLES FLYNN, WHO HAD THE ROLE LONGER THAN ANYONE (1939 -1951)

JACK ARMSTRONG'S THEME SONG:
"WAVE THE FLAG FOR HUDSON HIGH, BOYS; SHOW THEM HOW WE STAND; EVER SHALL OUR TEAM BE CHAMPIONS, KNOWN THROUGH-OUT THE LAND!"

THE MOST FAMOUS JACK ARMSTRONG PREMIUM WAS THE HIKE-O-METER.....THOUSANDS WERE SENT TO LISTENERS!

RADIO'S GOLDEN YEARS ©

by FRANK BRESEE & BOBB LYNES

THE AIR ADVENTURES OF Jimmie Allen

THE FIRST OF THE AFTERNOON ADVENTURE SHOWS...

THE STORY OF A YOUNG DAREDEVIL PILOT IN 1933 DURING THE EARLY DAYS OF AVIATION.

THE PROGRAM ATTRACTED MORE THAN THREE MILLION KIDS INTO THE JIMMIE ALLEN FLYING CLUB.

THE LONGTIME SPONSOR OF THE PROGRAM WAS RICHFIELD GAS & OIL

LISTENERS COULD VISIT THEIR LOCAL RICHFIELD SERVICE STATION AND RECEIVE A JIMMIE ALLEN FLYING CLUB STAMP ALBUM. EACH WEEK, RICHFIELD WOULD ISSUE A NEW STAMP FOR THE ALBUM.

THE PROGRAM'S POPULARITY LED TO A PARAMOUNT MOVIE "THE SKY PARADE"

THE PROGRAM WAS HEARD FOR MANY YEARS IN SYNDICATION

COPIES OF THE ORIGINAL 16 INCH RADIO TRANSCRIPTIONS ARE HIGHLY PRIZED BY COLLECTORS.....

RADIO'S GOLDEN YEARS ©

by FRANK BRESEE & BOBB LYNES

Yours Truly.... JOHNNY DOLLAR

JOHNNY DOLLAR, "THE INSURANCE INVESTIGATOR WITH THE ACTION-PACKED EXPENSE ACCOUNT" BEGAN ON CBS FEBRUARY 18, 1949

CHARLES RUSSELL FIRST PLAYED JOHNNY DOLLAR, THEN EDMOND O'BRIEN, JOHN LUND, BOB BAILEY, BOB READICK & MANDEL KRAMER

BAILEY

DICK POWELL STARRED IN THE AUDITION SHOW

O'BRIEN

LUND

KRAMER

READICK

DIRECTORS: RICHARD SANVILLE, JACK JOHNSTONE, JAIME DEL VALLE, FRED HENDRICKSON & BRUNO ZIRATO, JR.

THE SERIES FEATURED THE FINEST CHARACTER ACTORS: VIRGINIA GREGG, JOHN DEHNER, MARVIN MILLER, VIC PERRIN, HARRY BARTELL, PEGGY WEBBER, FORREST LEWIS, BOB DRYDEN, RALPH BELL, JIM BOLES & MORE....

THE SHOW WAS A FIVE-A-WEEK SERIAL DURING 1955-56..... OTHERWISE IT WAS A WEEKLY 30-MINUTE PROGRAM

ANNOUNCER: ROY ROWAN

"JOHNNY DOLLAR" & "SUSPENSE" WERE THE LAST NETWORK DRAMA SERIES, ENDING ON THE SAME NIGHT...SUNDAY SEPT. 30. 1962

RADIO'S GOLDEN YEARS.©
by FRANK BRESEE & BOBB LYNES

AL JOLSON

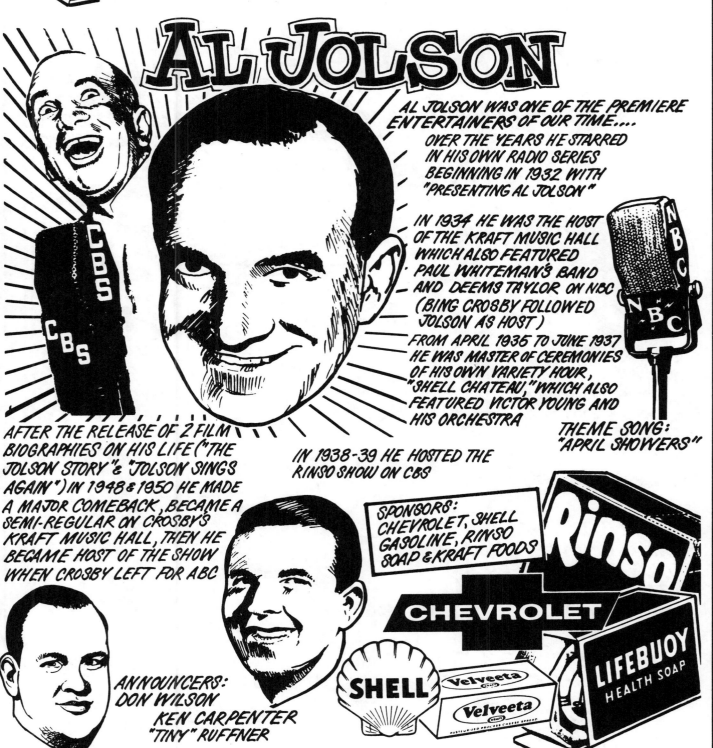

AL JOLSON WAS ONE OF THE PREMIERE ENTERTAINERS OF OUR TIME....

OVER THE YEARS HE STARRED IN HIS OWN RADIO SERIES BEGINNING IN 1932 WITH "PRESENTING AL JOLSON"

IN 1934 HE WAS THE HOST OF THE KRAFT MUSIC HALL WHICH ALSO FEATURED PAUL WHITEMAN'S BAND AND DEEMS TAYLOR ON NBC (BING CROSBY FOLLOWED JOLSON AS HOST)

FROM APRIL 1935 TO JUNE 1937 HE WAS MASTER OF CEREMONIES OF HIS OWN VARIETY HOUR, "SHELL CHATEAU," WHICH ALSO FEATURED VICTOR YOUNG AND HIS ORCHESTRA

THEME SONG: "APRIL SHOWERS"

AFTER THE RELEASE OF 2 FILM BIOGRAPHIES ON HIS LIFE ("THE JOLSON STORY" & "JOLSON SINGS AGAIN") IN 1948 & 1950 HE MADE A MAJOR COMEBACK, BECAME A SEMI-REGULAR ON CROSBY'S KRAFT MUSIC HALL, THEN HE BECAME HOST OF THE SHOW WHEN CROSBY LEFT FOR ABC

IN 1938-39 HE HOSTED THE RINSO SHOW ON CBS

SPONSORS: CHEVROLET, SHELL GASOLINE, RINSO SOAP & KRAFT FOODS

ANNOUNCERS: DON WILSON KEN CARPENTER "TINY" RUFFNER

RINSO

CHEVROLET

SHELL

Velveeta

LIFEBUOY HEALTH SOAP

129

RADIO'S GOLDEN YEARS ©
by FRANK BRESEE & BOBB LYNES

JUNGLE JIM

THE ADVENTURES OF JUNGLE JIM WERE BASED ON THE EXPLOITS OF COMIC STRIP CHARACTER, JUNGLE JIM BRADLEY, DRAWN BY FLASH GORDON CREATOR, ALEX RAYMOND

SYNDICATED BY HEARST, PROGRAM CAME TO RADIO IN 1941 AND LASTED THROUGH MOST OF WORLD WAR II

THE TITLE ROLE WAS PLAYED BY MATT CROWLEY (ALSO RADIO'S BUCK ROGERS, BATMAN & LATER MARK TRAIL)

ANNOUNCERS: GLENN RIGGS, ROGER KRUPP

SPONSOR: HEARST NEWSPAPERS' COMIC WEEKLY

RIGGS

OTHER CAST MEMBERS: VICKI VOLA, ARTHUR HUGHES AND KENNY DELMAR

RADIO'S GOLDEN YEARS ©
by FRANK BRESEE & BOBB LYNES

JUNIOR MISS

JUNIOR MISS HAD A LONG ALBEIT CHECKERED CAREER ON RADIO BASED ON SALLY BENSON'S NEW YORKER MAGAZINE STORIES ABOUT TEENAGER JUDY GRAVES AND HER MISS-ADVENTURES, THE SERIES STARRING SHIRLEY TEMPLE, DEBUTED ON CBS MARCH 4, 1942

IT WAS SOON CANCELLED BECAUSE OF THE TOO-HIGH WEEKLY BUDGET.....

A 1946 SERIES ALSO FAILED

WHEN JUNIOR MISS WAS REVIVED IN 1948 AS A SATURDAY MORNING SHOW, IT BECAME SO POPULAR IT LASTED UNTIL 1954

SHIRLEY TEMPLE

BARBARA WHITING (MARGARET'S SISTER) PLAYED "JUDY"

LIFEBUOY EALTH SOAP

Rinso

CAST: BEVERLY WILLS (JOAN DAVIS' DAUGHTER) WAS "FUFFY ADAMS"
PEGGY KNUDSEN WAS "LOIS GRAVES"
GALE GORDON WAS "HARRY GRAVES"
SARAH SELBY WAS "MOTHER GRAVES"

ANNOUNCER: JOHNNY JACOBS

SPONSOR: LEVER BROTHERS

RADIO'S GOLDEN YEARS

by FRANK BRESEE & BOBB LYNES

KAY KYSER's KOLLEGE OF MUSICAL KNOWLEDGE

THEME SONG: "THINKING OF YOU"

BANDLEADER KAY KYSER WENT ON THE NBC NETWORK IN 1938 WITH HIS VERY POPULAR MUSICAL QUIZ SHOW.... THE PROGRAM HAD A COLLEGE FORMAT, WITH VARIOUS QUIZ SEGMENTS CALLED "MID-TERMS" AND "FINAL EXAMS"

ONE SEGMENT WAS A TRUE OR FALSE QUIZ USING THE WORDS "RIGHT" OR "WRONG" AS ANSWERS: WHEN A CONTESTANT ANSWERED INCORRECTLY, KAY KYSER WOULD YELL "THAT'S RIGHT, YOU'RE WRONG!" IF THE ANSWER WAS CORRECT, KYSER WOULD SHOUT "THAT'S RIGHT, YOU'RE RIGHT!"

KAY TOOK THE SHOW TO MILITARY POSTS DURING WWII, FEATURED SERVICEMEN AS CONTESTANTS AND WAS VERY POPULAR AS A MORALE BOOSTER.....

ANNOUNCERS: VERNE SMITH JOHN HIESTAND

KAY WAS "THE OLD PROFESSOR ON THE SHOW AND THE CAST, INCLUDING ANNOUNCER, WORE CAPS AND GOWNS

SPONSORS: LUCKY STRIKE CIGARETTES, COLGATE & PILLSBURY

FEATURED PERFORMERS: ISH KABIBBLE, GEORGIA CARROLL, GINNY SIMMS, HARRY BABBITT, TRUDY ERWIN, SULLY MASON, THE TOWN CRIERS, KING SISTERS & SHIRLEY MITCHELL

RADIO'S GOLDEN YEARS ©
by FRANK BRESEE & BOBB LYNES

JACK KIRKWOOD

COMEDIAN JACK KIRKWOOD BEGAN HIS RADIO CAREER IN 1943 ON HIS OWN SHOW "MIRTH & MADNESS" ON NBC. IN 1944 HE MOVED TO THE CBS NETWORK WITH HIS OWN "JACK KIRKWOOD SHOW" HEARD COAST-TO-COAST FIVE DAYS A WEEK FOLLOWING LOWELL THOMAS' NEWSCAST

"THE KIRKWOOD CORNER STORE" WAS HEARD IN 1949 ON ABC

DURING THE FORTIES AND FIFTIES HE WAS A REGULAR ON BOB HOPE'S RADIO SHOW

HIS HELLO TO HOPE: "PUT SOMETHING IN THE POT, BOY"

THE SHOW FEATURED OLD VAUDEVILLE JOKES AND COMIC SKETCHES THAT KEPT AUDIENCES LAUGHING

IN 1950 KIRKWOOD WENT TO MUTUAL, ENDING HIS SHOW IN 1953

JACK KIRKWOOD'S REAL LIFE WIFE, LILLIAN LEIGH WAS PERMANENT SHOW CAST MEMBER OVER THE YEARS...

ANNOUNCERS: JIMMY WALLINGTON, BILL BALDWIN, STEVE DUNNE

SPONSOR: PROCTOR & GAMBLE

NATIONAL BROADCASTING CO., Inc.
RCA BUILDING RADIO CITY STUDIOS NEW YORK
ENTRANCE ON 49th OR 50th STS., BETWEEN 5th & 6th AVES.

FRI.
21
JAN. '44
8:55 AM

Mirth and Madness

COLUMBIA BROADCASTING SYSTEM
COLUMBIA SQUARE PLAYHOUSE
6121 SUNSET BOULEVARD — HOLLYWOOD

STUDIO
C
CBS

IVORY SOAP
presents
THE JACK KIRKWOOD SHOW

CHILDREN UNDER TWELVE WILL NOT BE ADMITTED

THURSC
JAN
3
1946
8:00 p.m
Doors Clo
at 7:45 p.r

by FRANK BRESEE & BOBB LYNES

LASSIE

OPENING:
"FROM HOLLYWOOD......THREE FLAVORED RED HEART DOG FOOD, AMERICA'S FAVORITE DOG FOOD, PRESENTS METRO-GOLDWYN-MAYER'S FAVORITE MOTION PICTURE STAR....LASSIE!"

LASSIE, THE WONDER DOG, CAME TO RADIO FOLLOWING THE SUCCESSFUL M-G-M FILM "LASSIE COME HOME", WHICH WAS BASED ON THE POPULAR NOVEL BY ERIC KNIGHT....

LASSIE COME HOME

RODDY McDOWALL · DONALD CRISP
DAME MAY WHITTY
EDMUND GWENN
NIGEL BRUCE
ELSA LANCHESTER
LASSIE

PRODUCER: FRANK FERRIN

LASSIE

ABC

ON RADIO, LASSIE (WHO WAS A MALE COLLIE) PLAYED MANY DIFFERENT BREEDS OF DOGS!

DIRECTOR: HARRY STEWART
WRITER: HOBART DONAVAN

ANNOUNCER: CHARLIE LYON

SPONSOR: RED HEART DOG FOOD

RED HEART

THE PROGRAM WAS NARRATED BY LASSIE'S OWNER-TRAINER RUDD WEATHERWAX, AND WAS PERFORMED "LIVE" BEFORE A STUDIO AUDIENCE OF BOYS AND GIRLS, WHO WERE FASCINATED BY THE ON-CUE BARKING BY LASSIE AND OTHER ANIMAL SOUNDS MADE BY EARL KEEN

THE 15-MINUTE WEEKLY SERIES DEBUTED ON ABC ON JUNE 8, 1947, MOVED TO NBC IN 1948 AND RAN UNTIL 1950

RADIO'S GOLDEN YEARS ©

by FRANK BRESEE & BOBB LYNES

LET GEORGE DO IT

LET GEORGE DO IT WAS ONE OF RADIO'S POPULAR MYSTERY-DETECTIVE PROGRAMS

IT WAS HEARD ON THE WEST COAST MUTUAL-DON LEE NETWORK BEGINNING IN 1946; A LATER SYNDICATED VERSION WAS HEARD NATIONWIDE....

THIS SERIES REVOLVED AROUND SPECIAL INVESTIGATOR GEORGE VALENTINE WHO SOLVED MYSTERIES & HELPED ARREST CRIMINALS

HE GOT HIS CASES FROM HIS NEWSPAPER AD: "PERSONAL NOTICE: DANGER IS MY STOCK-IN-TRADE. IF THE JOB IS TOO TOUGH FOR YOU TO HANDLE, YOU'VE GOT A JOB FOR ME, GEORGE VALENTINE. WRITE FULL DETAILS"

THE SERIES ORIGINATED FROM THE KHJ-MUTUAL-DON LEE STUDIOS ON MELROSE IN HOLLYWOOD....

A PRE-"JOHNNY DOLLAR" ROBERT BAILEY WAS GEORGE VALENTINE

MUTUAL—DON LEE BROADCASTING SYSTEM
DON LEE PLAYHOUSE
5515 Melrose Ave.   Hollywood, Calif.

CHEVRON GASOLINE
Presents
"LET GEORGE DO IT"
A Comedy-Mystery Drama
Starring ROBERT BAILEY, FRANCES ROBINSON, EDDIE FIRESTONE, JR.

CHILDREN UNDER 12 WILL NOT BE ADMITTED

FRIDAY
MAY
23
1947
8:30 P.M.
DOORS CLOS
7:50 P.M.
Admit O

ANNOUNCER: JOHN HIESTAND

WRITERS: POLLY HOPKINS, DAVID VICTOR & JACKSON GILLIS

REGULAR CAST: "BROOKSIE"–FRANCES ROBINSON; LATER VIRGINIA GREGG OLAN SOULÉ, EDDIE FIRESTONE, JR., AND JOSEPH KEARNS

MUSIC: EDDIE DUNSTEDTER

SPONSOR: CHEVRON GASOLINE

CHEVRON SUPREME GASOLINE

RADIO'S GOLDEN YEARS.©

by FRANK BRESEE & BOBB LYNES

Let's Pretend

NILA MACK

PRODUCED AND DIRECTED BY NILA MACK, LET'S PRETEND FEATURED CHILD ACTORS IN FAVORITE FAIRY TALES DRAMATIZED FOR KIDS IN THE RADIO AUDIENCE....

IT WAS PURE FANTASY WITH KINGS & QUEENS, WITCHES, PRINCESSES & ENCHANTED FORESTS.....

THE KIDS SHOW WAS USUALLY HEARD AT 11:05 -11:30 AM (E.S.T.) SATURDAYS

THE HOST WAS "UNCLE BILL" ADAMS, WHO EACH WEEK WOULD TRANSPORT THE CAST TO THE LAND OF MAKE-BELIEVE VIA SOME UNIQUE WAY OF TRAVEL

ANNOUNCERS: JACKSON WHEELER, GEORGE BRYAN

THE SERIES EVOLVED FROM "THE ADVENTURES OF HELEN & MARY" WHICH BEGAN IN 1929 IT HAD AN AMAZING 20 YEAR RUN ON CBS FROM MARCH 24, 1934 TO OCTOBER 23, 1954....

CBS RADIO THEATRE NO. 4
24 WEST 64th STREET, NEW YORK 19, NEW YORK
FEBRUARY 23 Sat. Morn. 11:05 AM.
The Cream of Wheat Corporation PRESENTS NILA MACK'S "LET'S PRETEND"
782

THE CREAM OF WHEAT/THEME:
"CREAM OF WHEAT IS SO GOOD TO EAT YES, WE HAVE IT EVERY DAY; WE SING THIS SONG, IT WILL MAKE US STRONG AND IT MAKES US SHOUT "HOORAY!" IT'S GOOD FOR GROWING BABIES AND GROWN-UPS TOO TO EAT FOR ALL THE FAMILY'S BREAKFAST YOU CAN'T BEAT CREAM OF WHEAT!"

SPONSOR: CREAM OF WHEAT CEREAL

REGULAR CAST MEMBERS OVER THE YEARS: PATRICIA RYAN, SYBIL TRENT, GWEN DAVIES, MICHAEL O'DAY, MIRIAM WOLFE, JACK GRIMES, ALBERT ALEY, ARTHUR ANDERSON, BILL LIPTON, PATSY O'SHEA, EVIE JUSTER, DAISY ALDEN, EDDIE RYAN, BOBBY READICK, SANDRA GOULD AND MORE!

RADIO'S GOLDEN YEARS©

by FRANK BRESEE & BOBB LYNES

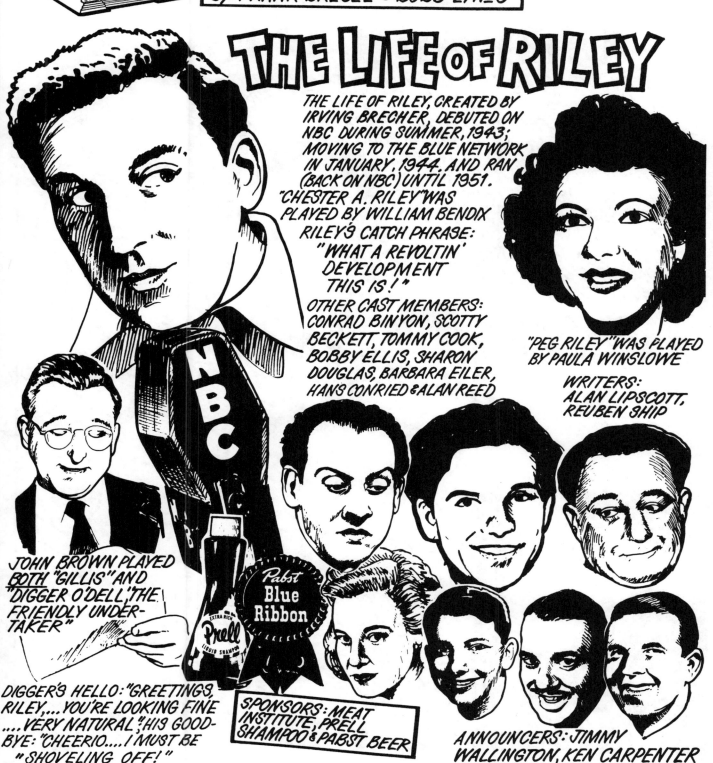

THE LIFE OF RILEY

THE LIFE OF RILEY, CREATED BY IRVING BRECHER, DEBUTED ON NBC DURING SUMMER, 1943; MOVING TO THE BLUE NETWORK IN JANUARY, 1944. AND RAN (BACK ON NBC) UNTIL 1951. "CHESTER A. RILEY" WAS PLAYED BY WILLIAM BENDIX RILEY'S CATCH PHRASE:

"WHAT A REVOLTIN' DEVELOPMENT THIS IS!"

OTHER CAST MEMBERS: CONRAD BINYON, SCOTTY BECKETT, TOMMY COOK, BOBBY ELLIS, SHARON DOUGLAS, BARBARA EILER, HANS CONRIED & ALAN REED

"PEG RILEY" WAS PLAYED BY PAULA WINSLOWE

WRITERS: ALAN LIPSCOTT, REUBEN SHIP

JOHN BROWN PLAYED BOTH "GILLIS" AND "DIGGER O'DELL", THE FRIENDLY UNDERTAKER"

DIGGER'S HELLO: "GREETINGS, RILEY,...YOU'RE LOOKING FINE ....VERY NATURAL", HIS GOODBYE: "CHEERIO.....I MUST BE "SHOVELING OFF!"

SPONSORS: MEAT INSTITUTE, PRELL SHAMPOO & PABST BEER

ANNOUNCERS: JIMMY WALLINGTON, KEN CARPENTER

RADIO'S GOLDEN YEARS ©
by FRANK BRESEE & BOBB LYNES

LIFE WITH LUIGI

LIFE WITH LUIGI STARRED J. CARROLL NAISH IN THE TITLE ROLE, LUIGI BASCO, AN ITALIAN IMMIGRANT AND HIS PALS

LUIGI'S CLOSE FRIEND PASQUALE HAD A DAUGHTER, ROSA, WHO HE WAS ALWAYS TRYING TO MARRY OFF... HOPEFULLY TO LUIGI. HER 300 LB. FRAME SQUEAKY VOICE AND HIGH, SHRILL LAUGH KEPT THE TWO APART FOR 5 YEARS! BUT THE LAUGHS KEPT COMING AND THE AUDIENCE LOVED IT.....

CREATED BY CY HOWARD THE SHOW WAS ON CBS FROM 1948 TO 1953

ANNOUNCERS: CHARLES LYON, BOB LEMOND

PASQUALE: ALAN REED

LUIGI: J. CARROLL NAISH

ROSA: JODY GILBERT

CAST MEMBERS: MARY SHIPP, JOE FORTE, HANS CONRIED, GIL STRATTON, JR., KEN PETERS AND SANDRA GOULD....

SPONSOR: WRIGLEY'S SPEARMINT GUM

WRIGLEY'S SPEARMINT CHEWING GUM

MUSIC: LYN MURRAY, LUD GLUSKIN

RADIO'S GOLDEN YEARS©

by FRANK BRESEE & BOBB LYNES

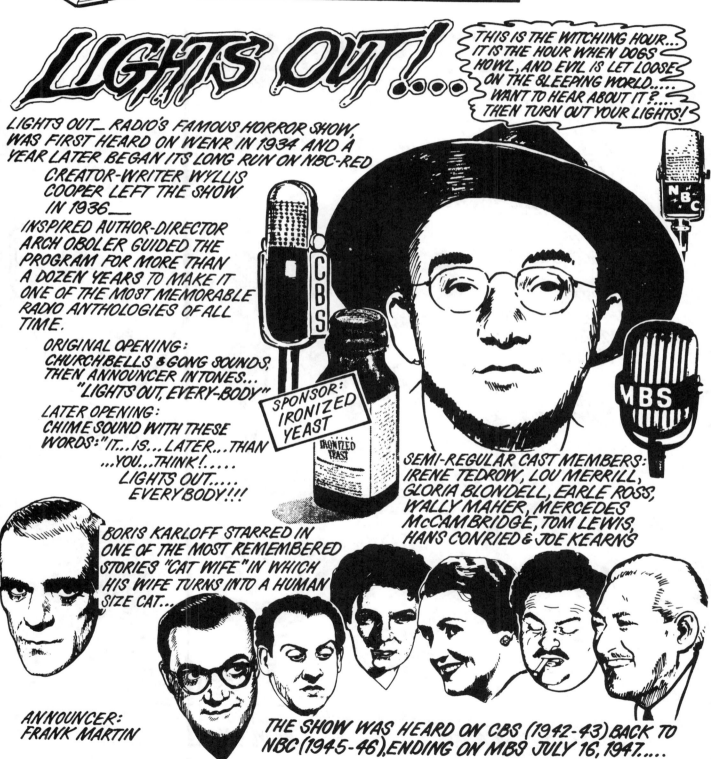

LIGHTS OUT!...

THIS IS THE WITCHING HOUR... IT IS THE HOUR WHEN DOGS HOWL, AND EVIL IS LET LOOSE ON THE SLEEPING WORLD..... WANT TO HEAR ABOUT IT?.... THEN TURN OUT YOUR LIGHTS!

LIGHTS OUT_ RADIO'S FAMOUS HORROR SHOW, WAS FIRST HEARD ON WENR IN 1934 AND A YEAR LATER BEGAN ITS LONG RUN ON NBC-RED

CREATOR-WRITER WYLLIS COOPER LEFT THE SHOW IN 1936_

INSPIRED AUTHOR-DIRECTOR ARCH OBOLER GUIDED THE PROGRAM FOR MORE THAN A DOZEN YEARS TO MAKE IT ONE OF THE MOST MEMORABLE RADIO ANTHOLOGIES OF ALL TIME.

ORIGINAL OPENING: CHURCHBELLS & GONG SOUNDS, THEN ANNOUNCER INTONES... "LIGHTS OUT, EVERY-BODY"

LATER OPENING: CHIME SOUND WITH THESE WORDS:"IT...IS...LATER...THAN ...YOU...THINK!..... LIGHTS OUT..... EVERYBODY!!!

SPONSOR: IRONIZED YEAST

SEMI-REGULAR CAST MEMBERS: IRENE TEDROW, LOU MERRILL, GLORIA BLONDELL, EARLE ROSS, WALLY MAHER, MERCEDES McCAMBRIDGE, TOM LEWIS, HANS CONRIED & JOE KEARNS

BORIS KARLOFF STARRED IN ONE OF THE MOST REMEMBERED STORIES "CAT WIFE" IN WHICH HIS WIFE TURNS INTO A HUMAN SIZE CAT...

ANNOUNCER: FRANK MARTIN

THE SHOW WAS HEARD ON CBS (1942-43) BACK TO NBC (1945-46), ENDING ON MBS JULY 16, 1947.....

RADIO'S GOLDEN YEARS.©

by FRANK BRESEE & BOBB LYNES

THE LINE·UP

THE LINE-UP WAS A WEEKLY DRAMATIC PROGRAM WHICH TOOK LISTENERS "BEHIND THE SCENES OF A POLICE HEADQUARTERS IN A GREAT AMERICAN CITY (SAN FRANCISCO) WHERE THE COLD, GLARING LIGHTS PASS THE INNOCENT, THE VAGRANT, THE THIEF, THE MURDERER".....

THE SHOW WAS CBS' ANSWER TO NBC'S DRAGNET WITH REALISTIC STORIES, ACTING & SOUND-EFFECTS

WRITERS:
BLAKE EDWARDS; LATER MORTON FINE & DAVID FRIEDKIN

WALLY MAHER WAS "SGT. MATT GREBB"

BILL JOHNSTONE STARRED AS "LT. BEN GUTHRIE"

HOLLYWOOD RADIO ACTORS WHO APPEARED:
HOWARD McNEAR, RAYMOND BURR, JEANETTE NOLAN & SHELDON LEONARD

DE SOTO APPROVED SERVICE PLYMOUTH

WRIGLEY'S SPEARMINT CHEWING GUM

THE LINE-UP DEBUTED ON CBS ON JULY 6, 1950, RAN FOR THREE YEARS AND, LIKE DRAGNET, WAS LATER A POPULAR TV SERIES.....

SPONSORS: WRIGLEYS GUM AND PLYMOUTH

140

RADIO'S GOLDEN YEARS.©
by FRANK BRESEE & BOBB LYNES

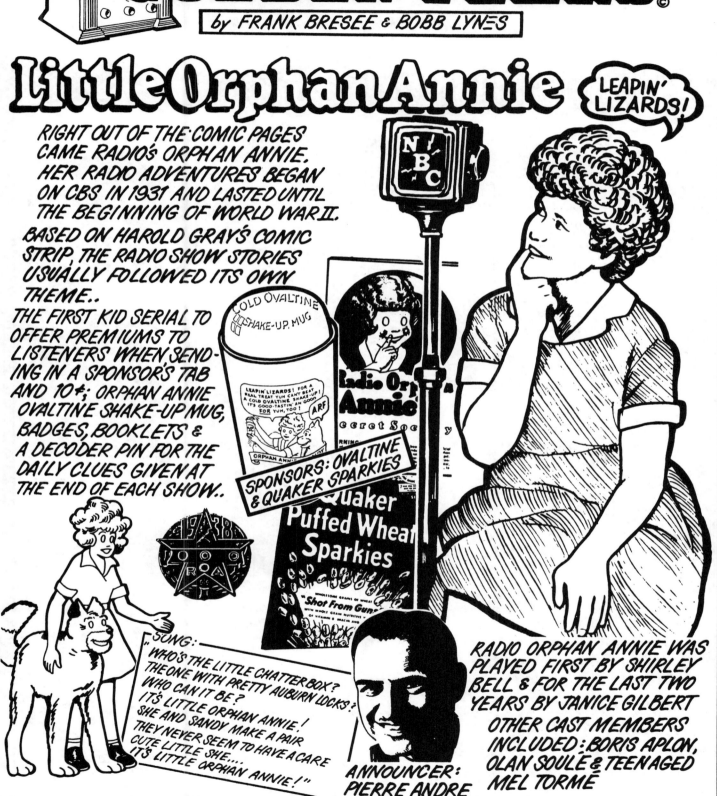

Little Orphan Annie

LEAPIN' LIZARDS!

RIGHT OUT OF THE COMIC PAGES CAME RADIO'S ORPHAN ANNIE. HER RADIO ADVENTURES BEGAN ON CBS IN 1931 AND LASTED UNTIL THE BEGINNING OF WORLD WAR II.

BASED ON HAROLD GRAY'S COMIC STRIP, THE RADIO SHOW STORIES USUALLY FOLLOWED ITS OWN THEME..

THE FIRST KID SERIAL TO OFFER PREMIUMS TO LISTENERS WHEN SENDING IN A SPONSOR'S TAB AND 10¢; ORPHAN ANNIE OVALTINE SHAKE-UP MUG, BADGES, BOOKLETS & A DECODER PIN FOR THE DAILY CLUES GIVEN AT THE END OF EACH SHOW..

SPONSORS: OVALTINE & QUAKER SPARKIES

SONG:
"WHO'S THE LITTLE CHATTERBOX?
THE ONE WITH PRETTY AUBURN LOCKS?
WHO CAN IT BE?
IT'S LITTLE ORPHAN ANNIE!
SHE AND SANDY MAKE A PAIR
THEY NEVER SEEM TO HAVE A CARE
CUTE LITTLE SHE,....
IT'S LITTLE ORPHAN ANNIE!"

ANNOUNCER: PIERRE ANDRE

RADIO ORPHAN ANNIE WAS PLAYED FIRST BY SHIRLEY BELL & FOR THE LAST TWO YEARS BY JANICE GILBERT OTHER CAST MEMBERS INCLUDED: BORIS APLON, OLAN SOULE & TEENAGED MEL TORMÉ

RADIO'S GOLDEN YEARS

by FRANK BRESEE & BOBB LYNES

THE LONE RANGER

THE LONE RANGER WAS ONE OF THE EARLIEST AND MOST POPULAR RADIO SHOWS OF ALL TIME...

CREATED BY GEORGE W. TRENDLE, BEGINNING IN JANUARY, 1933 THE WESTERN ADVENTURE WAS BROADCAST FROM THE STUDIOS OF DETROIT, MICHIGANS WXYZ. IT SOON WAS ALSO HEARD ON WOR-NEW YORK AND WGN-CHICAGO WHICH WAS THE BASIS FOR THE MUTUAL BROADCASTING SYSTEM....

SPONSORS: SILVERCUP BREAD, MERITA BREAD, GENERAL MILLS

EARL GRASER WAS THE RANGER FOR EIGHT YEARS

ANNOUNCER FRED FOY IS REMEMBERED BY MOST AS THE SHOW'S NARRATOR

THE RANGER'S HORSE, WAS "SILVER", TONTO'S HORSE WAS "SCOUT"

ROSSINI'S "WILLIAM TELL OVERTURE" WAS THE SHOW'S MEMORABLE THEME

SCRIPTS WERE EDITED BY FRAN STRIKER

"THE LONE RANGER" WAS PLAYED BY BRACE BEEMER DURING MOST OF THE RADIO DAYS

THE RANGER AND TONTO CALLED EACH OTHER "KEMO SABE" (FAITHFUL FRIEND)

"TONTO" WAS PLAYED BY SHAKESPEARIAN ACTOR JOHN TODD

ALSO FAMOUS FOR MOTION PICTURES, SERIALS, COMICS, NOVELS AND TV SERIES, THE PROGRAM CONTINUES TO BE HEARD ON RADIO IN RE-RUNS

RADIO'S GOLDEN YEARS ©

by FRANK BRESEE & BOBB LYNES

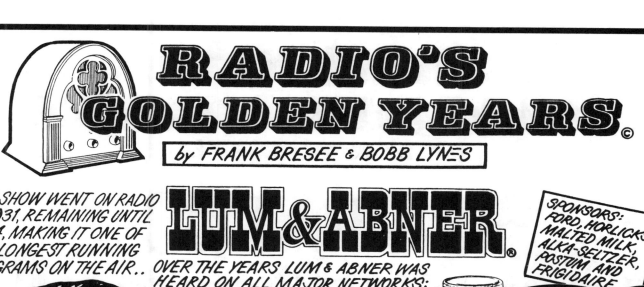

LUM & ABNER ®

THE SHOW WENT ON RADIO IN 1931, REMAINING UNTIL 1954, MAKING IT ONE OF THE LONGEST RUNNING PROGRAMS ON THE AIR..

OVER THE YEARS LUM & ABNER WAS HEARD ON ALL MAJOR NETWORKS: NBC, CBS, ABC AND KEYSTONE...

SPONSORS: FORD, HORLICK'S MALTED MILK, ALKA-SELTZER, POSTUM AND FRIGIDAIRE

ANNOUNCERS:

GENE BAKER   LOU CROSBY   WENDELL NILES

THE SERIES TOOK PLACE IN THE MYTHICAL TOWN OF "PINE RIDGE, ARKANSAS" AND LUM & ABNER BECAME SO POPULAR THAT AS A TRIBUTE, IN 1936 THE TOWN OF WATERS, ARKANSAS ACTUALLY CHANGED ITS NAME TO "PINE RIDGE."...

CHET LAUCK WAS "LUM EDWARDS" (AND "CEDRIC" & "GRANDPAPPY SPEARS")

NORRIS GOFF WAS "ABNER PEABODY" (AND "SQUIRE SKIMP," "MOUSEY GREY" & "DICK HUDDLESTON")

THE NATIONAL LUM & ABNER SOCIETY HONORS THEIR MEMORY AND HAS OVER 1000 MEMBERS.....

THE NATIONAL LUM & ABNER SOCIETY ®

DESIGNED BY THIS ARTIST 5

143

RADIO'S GOLDEN YEARS ©

by FRANK BRESEE & BOBB LYNES

Lux RADIO Theatre

MOVIE ADAPTATIONS ON RADIO BROADCAST FROM HOLLYWOOD FROM JUNE 1, 1936 TO JUNE 7, 1955, IT WAS KNOWN AS THE LUX RADIO THEATRE BECAUSE ITS ONLY SPONSOR FOR ALL THOSE YEARS WAS LUX SOAP PRODUCTS

THE BEST-REMEMBERED HOST OF THE PROGRAM WAS THE FAMOUS MOTION PICTURE DIRECTOR, CECIL B. DeMILLE

MOST OF HOLLYWOOD'S GREAT STARS APPEARED ON THE PROGRAM: GARY COOPER, CARY GRANT, BARBARA STANWYCK, AL JOLSON, RONALD COLMAN, JOAN CRAWFORD, CLARK GABLE, MARLENE DIETRICH, JAMES STEWART, ROBERT TAYLOR, LIONEL BARRYMORE, MARILYN MONROE LIZABETH SCOTT & MARGARET O'BRIEN

THE SHOW WAS BROADCAST EVERY MONDAY NIGHT 9-10 PM (EASTERN TIME) ON CBS.

STARS WERE PAID $5,000.00 FOR THE ONE HOUR APPEARANCE....

LONGTIME ANNOUNCER WAS JOHN MILTON KENNEDY

TICKETS WERE HARD TO GET & REQUESTS TOOK AS LONG AS 6 MONTHS TO FILL!

RADIO'S GOLDEN YEARS.©

by FRANK BRESEE & BOBB LYNES

MAIL CALL

MAIL CALL WAS ANOTHER PROGRAM BROADCAST ONLY FOR U.S./ALLIED SERVICEMEN, AND WAS HEARD AROUND THE WORLD ON ARMED FORCES RADIO SERVICE

THE 30-MINUTE WEEKLY VARIETY SERIES DEBUTED ON AUGUST 11, 1942 AND RAN UNTIL 1950.... AS WITH COMMAND PERFORMANCE IT FEATURED THE TOP STARS IN SHOW BUSINESS WITH SONGS AND COMEDY SKETCHES DIRECTLY FOR SERVICE PERSONNEL WORLDWIDE

MOST OF HOLLYWOOD'S TOP STARS APPEARED: BOB HOPE, BING CROSBY, JACK BENNY, ORSON WELLES, FRANCES LANGFORD, DINAH SHORE, ROCHESTER, KAY KYSER, EDDIE CANTOR LINA ROMAY AND MORE!

ANNOUNCER: DON WILSON

MEL BLANC

ARTHUR Q. BRYAN

REGULARS: MEL (SAD SACK) BLANC AND ARTHUR Q. (WAYMOND WADCWIFF) BRYAN

MAIL CALL WAS RECORDED AT NBC'S HOLLYWOOD STUDIOS AT SUNSET & VINE

RADIO'S GOLDEN YEARS.©

by FRANK BRESEE & BOBB LYNES

MAISIE

ANN SOTHERN STARRED IN THE RADIO SHOW "MAISIE" BASED ON HER POPULAR M·G·M MOVIE SERIES OF THE SAME NAME. THE COMEDY BEGAN ON CBS IN JULY, 1945 AND RAN FOR SEVEN YEARS.....

MISS SOTHERN WAS MAISIE REVERE, A BROOKLYN BEAUTY WHO ALWAYS LOOKED AT THE BRIGHT SIDE OF LIFE WHILE HELPING FRIENDS AND NEIGHBORS OUT OF THEIR TROUBLES.

REGULAR ACTORS IN THE CAST OVER THE YEARS: MARVIN MILLER, HANS CONRIED, PETER LEEDS, LURENE TUTTLE, SHELDON LEONARD AND FRANK NELSON

ANNOUNCER: JACK McCOY

SPONSOR: EVERSHARP

EVERSHARP

RADIO'S GOLDEN YEARS©
by FRANK BRESEE & BOBB LYNES

The March of Time

Every Thursday Night
HE MARCH OF TIME
over 111 stations of the NBC Blue Network
P.M. E.S.T. Rebroadcast on 0 P.M. P.S.T.

STATION   TIME
WAKR ..8 P.M. E.S.
rque..KOB...6 P.M. M.S
wn....WSAN..8 P.M. C.S.
WIIMA..7 P.M. E.S

THE MARCH OF TIME WAS ONE OF THE PRESTIGE PROGRAMS ON RADIO. IT WENT ON THE AIR IN 1931, AND WAS A POPULAR FEATURE UNTIL THE END OF WORLD WAR 2...

MARCH OF TIME FEATURED THE NEWS OF WEEK IN DOCUMENTARY STYLE. EACH PROGRAM PRESENTED NEW YORK'S BEST RADIO ACTORS RECREATING IMPORTANT EVENTS FROM THE PAGES OF AMERICA'S NEWSPAPER & TIME MAGAZINE

"TIME MARCHES ON!"

NARRATORS: HARRY VON ZELL   WESTBROOK VAN VOORHIS   TED HUSING

CAST MEMBERS: AGNES MOOREHEAD, ORSON WELLES, ELLIOTT REID, JEANETTE NOLAN, JOHN McINTIRE, MARTIN GABEL, KARL SWENSON, GARY MERRILL, EVERETT SLOANE, KENNY DELMAR, STAATS COTSWORTH, ETC.

SPONSORS: TIME MAGAZINE, REMINGTON RAND, ELECTROLUX AND WRIGLEY'S GUM

MUSIC BY: DONALD VOORHEES, HOWARD BARLOW

OVER THE YEARS MARCH OF TIME WAS HEARD ON CBS AND NBC-BLUE NETWORKS

147

GENE AHERN.

MAJOR HOOPLE

MAJOR HOOPLE WAS RIGHT OUT OF THE PAGES OF THE COMIC STRIPS; IT WENT ON THE NBC BLUE NETWORK IN JUNE 1942 AND LASTED FOR THE BETTER PART OF ONE YEAR....

MAJOR HOOPLE WAS A SITUATION COMEDY BASED ON THE ONE-PANEL NEWSPAPER STRIP "OUR BOARDING HOUSE." ON THE RADIO SHOW, THE MAJOR & HIS WIFE MARTHA, RAN THE HOOPLE BOARDING HOUSE

"MAJOR HOOPLE" WAS PLAYED BY ARTHUR Q. BRYAN, "MARTHA" BY PATSY MORAN & "TIFFANY TWIGGS" (THEIR STAR BOARDER) BY MEL BLANC. "LITTLE ALVIN" WAS PLAYED BY CONRAD BINYON & FRANKLIN BRESEE

THE SHOW'S WRITER WAS PHIL LESLIE

NOTE: ARTHUR Q. BRYAN WAS ALSO THE VOICE OF "ELMER FUDD" IN WARNER BROS. CARTOONS, IN ADDITION TO RUNNING PARTS IN FIBBER McGEE & GREAT GILDERSLEEVE SHOWS

RADIO'S GOLDEN YEARS ©

by FRANK BRESEE & BOBB LYNES

MAKE-BELIEVE BALLROOM

TWO OF THE GREATEST DISC JOCKEYS (RECORD SPINNERS) ON RADIO DURING THE 1930s, 40s AND 50s WERE MARTIN BLOCK AND AL JARVIS, HOSTS OF "THE MAKE-BELIEVE BALLROOM" WHICH FEATURED THE TOP RECORDS AND MUSICAL PERSONALITIES OF THE DAY......

MARTIN BLOCK
MARTIN BLOCK HOSTED ON NEW YORK'S WNEW

AL JARVIS
AL JARVIS HOSTED ON WEST COAST (LOS ANGELES) STATIONS KLAC & KFWB

EACH OF THE MUSICAL PROGRAMS WERE TOP RATED IN THEIR MARKETS AND WERE HEARD FOR MANY YEARS......

OTHER POPULAR LOCAL D.J.s OVER THE YEARS:
JOHN GAMBLING (WOR-NY)
ALAN FREED (CLEVELAND)
BARRY GRAY (NY)
FRED ROBBINS (NY)
FRANKLIN MacCORMICK (CHICAGO)
GENE NELSON (HOLLYWOOD)
JIM AMECHE (SYND.)
PETER POTTER (HOLLYWOOD)

RADIO'S GOLDEN YEARS ©

TED MALONE
BETWEEN the BOOKENDS

TED MALONE (REAL NAME, FRANK RUSSELL) CAME TO RADIO IN THE LATE 1920S AND BY 1935, HAD HIS OWN COAST-TO COAST PROGRAM ON CBS.

DURING THE SUMMER OF 1945, TED MALONE HAD A REGULAR 15 MINUTE DAILY SHOW ON ABC — WHICH RAN FOR 10 MORE YEARS......

BETWEEN the BOOKENDS

re new poems worth reading— some old ones, worth remembering

By TED MALONE

Be sure to listen to Ted Malone's morning program Monday, Wednesday, Friday at 11:45 EST, over ABC

ANNIVERSARY

IT WAS REPORTED THAT DURING HIS RADIO DAYS HE RECEIVED 15,000 LETTERS A MONTH, USED CONTRIBUTED STORIES AND POEMS FROM HIS MANY LISTENERS, AND DREW UPON HIS HUGE PERSONAL LIBRARY OF TIDBITS AND POETRY.....

Sungold on a tennis court,
Swinging at a ball,
Buying tickets for the game,
A shadow in a hall,
Climbing in a cock-pit
Whistling down a street,
Dancing in a corner,
Always the strange and fleet
Familiar look of eye or hand,
The half-glimpse of a shoulder,
The way we think that he might look
A long, war year older.
Light steps precede us as we go,
Light steps follow after,
We are walking out again,
Listening for his laughter.
— Gladys McKee

THE FACE

As a beauty I'm not a great star,
There are others more handsome by far,
But my face I don't mind it,
Because I'm behind it —
'Tis the folks in the front that I jar.
— Anthony Euwer
(Woodrow Wilson's favorite limerick)

BEFORE SLEEPING

Matthew, Mark, Luke and John
Bless the bed that I lie on!
Four corners to my
Four angels round
One at head and
And two to guard

HE WAS ALSO POETRY EDITOR OF GOOD HOUSEKEEPING MAGAZINE WROTE A 2 PAGE FEATURE EACH MONTH IN RADIO MIRROR MAGAZINE

SPONSOR: WESTINGHOUSE

RADIO'S GOLDEN YEARS.©
by FRANK BRESEE & BOBB LYNES

THE MAN CALLED X

THE MAN CALLED X DEBUTED ON CBS JULY 10, 1944. IT FEATURED THE GLOBE-TROTTING ADVENTURES OF AMERICAN SECRET AGENT KEN THURSTON (CODE NAME "X") AND HIS SLIGHTLY LARCENOUS SIDE-KICK, PAGAN ZELDSCHMIDT...

THE SERIES WAS HEARD ON BLUE-ABC, THEN NBC, LATER CBS; ENDING ON NBC IN 1952.

MUSIC: GORDON JENKINS, LATER CLAUDE SWEETEN, FELIX MILLS & JOHN GREEN

LEON BELASCO WAS PAGAN

SUAVE BRITISH MOVIE STAR HERBERT MARSHALL PLAYED KEN THURSTON

WENDELL NILES
ANNOUNCERS: JOHN McINTIRE

HERBERT MARSHALL

PEGGY WEBBER

LOCKHEED
Pepsodent
TOOTH PASTE · CONTAINS IRIUM

SPONSORS: LOCKHEED AIRCRAFT, FRIGIDAIRE AND PEPSODENT

JACK JOHNSTONE

DIRECTORS: WILLIAM N. ROBSON, JACK JOHNSTONE, DEE ENGLEBACH

RADIO'S GOLDEN YEARS ©

by FRANK BRESEE & BOBB LYNES

MA PERKINS

MA PERKINS WAS RADIO'S DEFINITIVE SOAP OPERA

THIS DAYTIME SERIAL DRAMA WAS SET IN THE MYTHICAL TOWN OF RUSHVILLE CENTER NEAR CHICAGO. MA OPERATED THE TOWN'S LUMBER YARD.

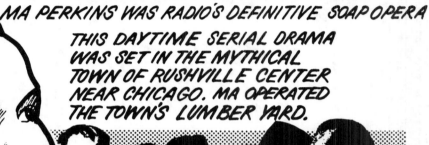

MA PERKINS WAS PLAYED BY 21-YEAR-OLD (WHEN SHE BEGAN THE SHOW) VIRGINIA PAYNE. SHE WAS MA FOR THE ENTIRE 27-YEAR RUN (7065 BROADCASTS!)

MA PERKINS BEGAN ON NBC, AND FOR A TIME WAS HEARD DAILY ON BOTH NBC AND CBS.....

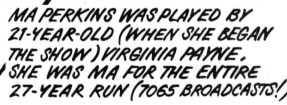

THE SPONSOR FOR MANY YEARS WAS OXYDOL SOAP IT WAS SO CLOSELY ASSOCIATED THAT THE PROGRAM WAS KNOWN AS "OXYDOL'S OWN MA PERKINS."......

MARVIN MILLER WAS THE ANNOUNCER FOR MUCH OF THE TIME THE PROGRAM ORIGINATED FROM CHICAGO......

RADIO'S GOLDEN YEARS.©

by FRANK BRESEE & BOBB LYNES

DEAN MARTIN & JERRY LEWIS

DEAN MARTIN AND JERRY LEWIS BEGAN THEIR RADIO SHOW ON NBC IN 1949 AT THE SAME TIME THEIR STARS WERE RISING IN NIGHTCLUBS & PARAMOUNT MOTION PICTURES...

DEAN MARTIN WAS THE HANDSOME SINGER AND JERRY LEWIS WAS HIS YOUNG (CRAZY) FRIEND EACH WEEK A POPULAR GUEST STAR WAS FEATURED, SUCH AS LUCILLE BALL, BOB HOPE OR BING CROSBY....

THE RADIO SHOW WAS WRITTEN BY ED SIMMONS AND NORMAN LEAR

SPONSORS INCLUDED ANACIN AND CHESTERFIELD CIGARETTES

ANACIN

Chesterfield CIGARETTES

ORCHESTRA LEADER: DICK STABILE

MARTIN & LEWIS MOVED TO TV IN 1950 AND A POPULAR FEATURE OF "THE COLGATE COMEDY HOUR" FROM HOLLYWOOD

RADIO'S GOLDEN YEARS.©

by FRANK BRESEE & BOBB LYNES

THE ONE... THE ONLY....
Groucho Marx

CBS

GROUCHO MARX FOUND RADIO SUCCESS AFTER A FEW FAILURES ("FLYWHEEL, SHYSTER & FLYWHEEL" AND "BLUE RIBBON TOWN") WHEN HE BEGAN THE QUIZ SHOW "YOU BET YOUR LIFE" ON ABC, OCTOBER 27, 1947.... IN 1949 THE SHOW MOVED TO CBS FOR ONE SEASON, THEN ON TO NBC, WHERE IT RAN UNTIL THE FINAL BROADCAST IN 1959 GROUCHO WAS AT HIS BEST AD-LIBBING WITH CONTESTANTS ON THE SHOW......

ABC

ANNOUNCER: GEORGE FENNEMAN

NBC

PRODUCER-CREATOR: JOHN GUEDEL

DIRECTOR: BOB DWAN

WHEN THE SHOW DEBUTED ON NBC-TV (VERY SUCCESSFULLY) IT WAS REALLY THE RADIO SHOW ON FILM..

ALWAYS IN THE TOP TEN IN RATINGS, GROUCHO ALSO WON A PEABODY AWARD

SPONSORS: ELGIN-AMERICAN COMPACTS & DE SOTO-PLYMOUTH

DE SOTO APPROVED SERVICE PLYMOUTH

RADIO'S GOLDEN YEARS.©

by FRANK BRESEE & BOBB LYNES

MAYOR OF THE TOWN

MAYOR OF THE TOWN WAS A WARM, HEARTFELT SERIES OF HUMAN DRAMAS SET IN THE MYTHICAL SMALL VILLAGE OF SPRINGDALE. IT DEBUTED ON NBC SEPTEMBER 6, 1942 AND RAN ON CBS, ABC AND ENDED ON MUTUAL IN 1949

STAGE & MOTION PICTURE VETERAN LIONEL BARRYMORE PLAYED THE GRUFF BUT LOVEABLE MAYOR

MARILLY, THE MAYOR'S MAID WAS AGNES MOOREHEAD

BUTCH, THE MAYOR'S WARD WAS PLAYED BY CONRAD BINYON

WRITERS: HOWARD BRESLIN AND CHARLES TAZEWELL

PRODUCERS: MURRAY BOLEN AND KNOWLES ENTRIKIN

MUSIC: GORDON JENKINS, LATER BERNARD KATZ

SPONSORS: LEVER BROS., NOXZEMA

RADIO'S GOLDEN YEARS©

by FRANK BRESEE & BOBB LYNES

Meet Me at PARKY'S

MEET ME AT PARKY'S WAS ONE OF THE POPULAR SITUATION COMEDIES OF THE MID-1940s. IT WAS ON THE AIR FROM JUNE 1945 TO JULY 1948. IT STARRED POPULAR COMEDIAN HARRY EINSTEIN AS "PARKYAKARKUS," OWNER OF A GREEK RESTAURANT AND THE MANY ADVENTURES IN WHICH HE WAS INVOLVED......

HIS RADIO DEBUT AS "PARKYAKARKUS" WAS ON A BOSTON STATION IN 1932, WHICH WAS THE SAME YEAR HE APPEARED ON THE EDDIE CANTOR SHOW, WHERE HE BECAME A REGULAR.

BY 1938 HARRY EINSTEIN HAD MOVED TO AL JOLSON'S LIFEBOUY SHOW.

WITH THE CHARACTER FIRMLY ESTABLISHED, HE BEGAN HIS OWN SHOW ON NBC IN 1945.....
LATER, THE SERIES WAS ON MBS.

"PARKY'S" REGULAR CAST INCLUDED: BETTY JANE RHODES & DAVID STREET

SPONSOR: OLD GOLD CIGARETTES

MUSIC BY OPIE CATES

ANNOUNCER: ART GILMORE

HARRY EINSTEIN'S SONS ARE COMEDIANS BOB EINSTEIN AND ALBERT (EINSTEIN) BROOKS.....

RADIO'S GOLDEN YEARS©

by FRANK BRESEE & BOBB LYNES

Mercury Theatre on the Air

THIS POPULAR RADIO SHOW BEGAN IN 1938 ON THE CBS NETWORK AFTER A SPECTACULAR SEASON ON THE NEW YORK STAGE. ORSON WELLES PRODUCED, DIRECTED AND STARRED IN THIS WEEKLY ANTHOLOGY PROGRAM, AS HE AND HIS CAST PRESENTED FAMOUS STORIES FROM LITERATURE.

THE FIRST SHOW WAS "DRACULA" FOLLOWED BY: "A TALE OF TWO CITIES" "THE 39 STEPS" "ABRAHAM LINCOLN" "COUNT OF MONTE CRISTO" "JULIUS CAESAR" "SHERLOCK HOLMES" "TREASURE ISLAND"....

BY THE TIME THE SHOW WAS FOUR MONTHS OLD, WELLES PRESENTED HIS FAMOUS "WAR OF THE WORLDS" BROADCAST (OCT. 30, 1938) WHICH SENT IT ON ITS WAY TO RADIO IMMORTALITY.... AND TO A SPONSOR; THE NAME WAS SOON CHANGED TO THE CAMPBELL PLAYHOUSE

CAST: AGNES MOOREHEAD, JOHN McINTIRE, RAY COLLINS, ALICE FROST, MERCEDES McCAMBRIDGE, PAUL STEWART, EVERETT SLOANE, KARL SWENSON, FRANK READICK AND KENNY DELMAR

ANNOUNCER: DAN SEYMOUR

SPONSOR: CAMPBELL SOUPS; LATER LADY ESTHER & PABST BLUE RIBBON BEER

THEME: TCHAIKOVSKY'S "PIANO CONCERTO #1 IN B-FLAT MINOR"

RADIO'S GOLDEN YEARS ©

by FRANK BRESEE & BOBB LYNES

MICHAEL SHAYNE   PRIVATE DETECTIVE

MICHAEL SHAYNE WAS FEATURED IN DETECTIVE NOVELS BY BRETT HALLIDAY. SHAYNE, "THE RECKLESS RED-HEADED IRISHMAN" WAS A PRIVATE INVESTIGATOR WHO WAS INVOLVED IN CASES OF MURDER AND MAYHEM WORKING OUT OF HIS NEW YORK OFFICE.

THE SERIES DEBUTED ON WEST COAST RADIO IN 1944 ON THE DON LEE NETWORK AND TWO YEARS LATER, MOVED TO THE COAST-TO-COAST MUTUAL BROADCASTING SYSTEM.

ORIGINALLY WALLY MAHER PLAYED SHAYNE, LATER JEFF CHANDLER.

WALLY MAHER

JEFF CHANDLER

INSPECTOR: JOE FORTE

CAST: HARRY LANG, CHARLIE LUNG, GEGE PEARSON, CATHY LEWIS, LOUISE ARTHUR, BILL CONRAD & ANN STONE

THE SHOW WAS HEARD ON MUTUAL, THEN ABC BEFORE GOING INTO SYNDICATION....

ANOTHER MICHAEL SHAYNE SERIES WAS HEARD ON MUTUAL IN 1952 STARRING ROBERT STERLING

Mickey Mouse ©
w.d.p.
THEATRÈ OF THE AIR

THE MICKEY MOUSE THEATRE OF THE AIR BROUGHT THE MASTER CARTOON PRODUCER, WALT DISNEY AND HIS VERY POPULAR CREATION MICKEY MOUSE TO THE NATION'S AIRWAVES FOR THE FIRST TIME IN JANUARY, 1938....

CAST MEMBERS: STUART BUCHANAN, FLORENCE GILL AND THELMA BOARDMAN

ANNOUNCER: JOHN "BUD" HIESTAND

MUSIC: FELIX MILLS & HIS ORCHESTRA

THE WEEKLY PROGRAM WAS AIRED SUNDAY EVENINGS ON NBC

MICKEY MOUSE
THEATRE OF THE AIR

8:00-8:30 PM EST

SUNDAY - JANUARY 2, 1938

MUSIC: OPENING FANFARE AND THEME - FADE FOR:

PEPSODENT PRESENTS THE MICKEY MOUSE THEATRE OF THE AIR ---- FEATURING STUART BUCHANAN, FLORENCE GILL AND THELMA BOARDMAN --- WITH MUSIC BY FELIX MILLS AND HIS ORCHESTRA. ALL BROUGHT TO YOU BY PEPSODENT TOOTH PASTE, THE FINEST DENTIFERACE YOU CAN BUY. AND NOW, HERE IS THE HOST OF THE SHOW, ALONG WITH HIS GOOD FRIEND, MICKEY MOUSE --- WALT DISNEY.

UP TO END

MUSIC: (APPLAUSE)

WALT DISNEY WAS THE VOICE OF MICKEY MOUSE ON THE SHOW
CLARENCE NASH WAS DONALD DUCK'S VOICE

SPONSOR: PEPSODENT TOOTHPASTE

Pepsodent

RADIO'S GOLDEN YEARS ©
by FRANK BRESEE & BOBB LYNES

GLENN MILLER'S
Moonlight Serenade

GLENN MILLER'S MOONLIGHT SERENADE
BEGAN IN 1939 FEATURING THE TOP
BIG BAND OF THE DAY. THE MILLER
BAND WAS ALSO HEARD ON MANY REMOTES
FROM: THE MEADOWBROOK, GLEN ISLAND
CASINO, THE CAFE ROUGE & THE PALLADIUM

THEME:
"MOONLIGHT
SERENADE"

DURING THE EARLY
PART OF 1942, HE
BROADCAST HIS
MOONLIGHT
SERENADE FROM
HOLLYWOOD....

COLUMBIA BROADCASTING SYSTEM
CBS RADIO PLAYHOUSE
1615 NORTH VINE — HOLLYWOOD
CHESTERFIELD
presents
GLENN MILLER'S Moonlight Serenade
and the motion picture
TOBACCOLAND, U.S.A., by March of Time
CHILDREN UNDER 12 YEARS WILL NOT BE ADMITTED

Tuesday
MAY
12
1942
Doors Close
p.m.

SPONSOR:
CHESTERFIELD
CIGARETTES

ANNOUNCER:
PAUL DOUGLAS

GLENN MILLER ENTERTAINED THE NATION
ON RECORDS, IN FILMS AND ON STAGE, THEN
JOINED THE U.S. AIR CORPS DURING WORLD
WAR II, LEADING AN AIR FORCE BAND
WHICH WAS HEARD ON ARMED FORCES RADIO

RADIO'S GOLDEN YEARS ©

by FRANK BRESEE & BOBB LYNES

MISTER CHAMELEON

MR. CHAMELEON WAS A LATE ENTRY ON RADIO AS AN INTERESTING MYSTERY-DETECTIVE SHOW

CREATED BY FRANK AND ANNE HUMMERT (CREATORS OF SOAP OPERAS & MR. KEEN, TRACER OF LOST PERSONS) THIS SERIES FEATURED A DETECTIVE WHO USED DISGUISES TO TRACK DOWN CRIMINALS AND BRING THEM TO JUSTICE....

RICHARD KEITH WAS COMMISSIONER

DAVE BUTLER WAS DET. DAVE ARNOLD

KARL SWENSON WAS MR. CHAMELEON

MUSIC: VICTOR ARDEN ORCH.

ANNOUNCERS: ROGER KRUPP, HOWARD CLANEY

THE PROGRAM AIRED ON CBS FROM JULY 14, 1948 TO JANUARY 9, 1953

SPONSORS: GENERAL FOODS, BAYER ASPIRIN AND WRIGLEY'S GUM

RADIO'S GOLDEN YEARS ©
by FRANK BRESEE & BOBB LYNES

MOLASSES & JANUARY

"MOLASSES N'JANUARY" PLAYED BY COMEDIANS PICK MALONE AND PAT PADGETT, WERE ALSO KNOWN DURING THE EARLY DAYS OF RADIO AS "PICK N'PAT"......

FAMOUS CATCH-PHRASE "HOPE TO KISS A CRIPPLE CRICKET I'M RIGHT!"

THEIR MINSTREL ROUTINES WERE VERY AMUSING AND KEPT THE NATIONAL AUDIENCE IN STITCHES.....

ONE OF THE FIRST RADIO COMEDY TEAMS (A LA "AMOS N'ANDY") THEY APPEARED ON NBC'S SHOWBOAT MUSICAL VARIETY SERIES BEGINNING IN 1932.....

SHOWBOAT CAST

LATER, THEY HAD THEIR OWN COAST-TO-COAST SYNDICATED PROGRAM

RADIO'S GOLDEN YEARS.©

by FRANK BRESEE & BOBB LYNES

FRANK MORGAN

FRANK MORGAN IS BEST REMEMBERED AS "THE WIZARD" IN THE FAMOUS MGM CLASSIC MOVIE "THE WIZARD OF OZ"...

FRANK MORGAN

IN ADDITION TO HIS FILM CAREER, HE WAS ALSO A VERY POPULAR RADIO STAR, APPEARING ON THESE SHOWS: GOOD NEWS, MAXWELL HOUSE COFFEE TIME, KRAFT MUSIC HALL, OLD GOLD SHOW, THE FRANK MORGAN SHOW AND FABULOUS DOCTOR TWEEDY

CO-STARS AND CAST MEMBERS OVER THE YEARS: FANNY BRICE, ROBERT YOUNG, HANLEY STAFFORD, JOHN CONTE, FRANCES LANGFORD, DON AMECHE, CASS DALEY, FRANK NELSON, ERIC BLORE & MORE

IN 1945, ON A VERY SPECIAL AFRS COMMAND PERFORMANCE, FRANK MORGAN PLAYED "VITAMIN FLINTHEART" IN AN ALL-STAR DICK TRACY SATIRE

THE BREAD SPREAD
KRAFT
Miracle Whip
Salad Dressing

FOR GLASS COFFEE-MAKERS
MAXWELL HOUSE Coffee

Old Gold CIGARETTES

SPONSORS: OLD GOLD, KRAFT FOODS & MAXWELL HOUSE

RADIO'S GOLDEN YEARS.©

by FRANK BRESEE & BOBB LYNES

HENRY MORGAN

OPENING: "HELLO, ANYBODY, HERE'S MORGAN"

COMEDIAN HENRY MORGAN WAS A PRODUCT OF RADIO AND HIS SHOW, HEARD IN THE FORTIES AND FIFTIES, WAS ONE OF THE MOST POPULAR COMEDY PROGRAMS ON THE AIR

HE KIDDED HIS SPONSORS, WHICH CAUSED THEM TO CANCEL HIS SHOWS FROM TIME TO TIME!

HIS BRILLIANTLY HUMOROUS CAST, WITH THEIR PARODIES OF THE POPULAR RADIO SHOWS OF THE DAY, MADE HIS NAME A HOUSEHOLD WORD

CAST INCLUDED: ARNOLD STANG, FLORENCE HALOP, MINERVA PIOUS & DURWARD KIRBY

ANNOUNCERS: CHARLES IRVING, DAN SEYMOUR, DAVID ROSS, ED HERLIHY & BILL BALDWIN

MUSIC: BERNIE GREEN

EVERSHARP-SCHICK INJECTOR RAZOR

SPONSORS: BRISTOL MYERS, CAMEL CIGARETTES AND EVERSHARP

OVER THE YEARS, MORGAN WAS HEARD ON NBC, ABC & MUTUAL....

HIS PROGRAM WAS SO POPULAR THAT IN 1946, HENRY MORGAN WENT TO HOLLYWOOD TO STAR IN A MOTION PICTURE: "SO THIS IS NEW YORK"

MR. DISTRICT ATTORNEY

MR. DISTRICT ATTORNEY! CHAMPION OF THE POEPLE.... GUARDIAN OF OUR FUNDAMENTAL RIGHTS; TO LIFE, LIBERTY AND THE PURSUIT OF HAPPINESS!

MR. DISTRICT ATTORNEY WAS INSPIRED BY THE NEW YORK RACKET-BUSTING D.A. OF 1938-39, THOMAS E. DEWEY, AND WAS HEARD FROM APRIL 3, 1939 TO JUNE 13, 1952

"AND IT SHALL BE MY DUTY AS DISTRICT ATTORNEY, NOT ONLY TO PROSECUTE TO THE LIMIT OF THE LAW ALL PERSONS ACCUSED OF CRIMES PERPETRATED WITHIN THIS COUNTY, BUT TO DEFEND WITH EQUAL VIGOR THE RIGHTS AND PRIVILEGES OF ALL ITS CITIZENS"

SPONSOR: BRISTOL-MYERS PRODUCTS

OTHER CAST MEMBERS INCLUDED: DWIGHT WEIST, RAYMOND EDWARD JOHNSON, FRANK LOVEJOY, PAUL STEWART AND ARLENE FRANCIS

THE SHOW STARRED JAY JOSTYN AS MR. D.A.
WITH LEN DOYLE AS HARRINGTON, VICKI VOLA AS MISS MILLER

ANNOUNCERS: ED HERLIHY, FRED UTTAL

RADIO'S GOLDEN YEARS ©
by FRANK BRESEE & BOBB LYNES

MR. KEEN
TRACER of LOST PERSONS

ONE OF THE EARLIEST RADIO DETECTIVE PROGRAMS ON THE AIR FROM OCTOBER, 12, 1937 TO APRIL 19, 1955....

THE SHOW'S THEME SONG: "SOMEDAY I'LL FIND YOU"

DURING THE EARLY DAYS, MR. KEEN ACTUALLY TRACED LOST PERSONS ON THIS CBS NETWORK MYSTERY SHOW.

SPONSORS: KOLYNOS TOOTHPASTE, CHESTERFIELD CIGARETTES, PROCTOR AND GAMBLE & ANACIN

BENNETT KILPACK PLAYED MR. KEEN FOR MOST OF THE BROADCAST YEARS

CLARKE   HUGHES

LATER, PHILIP CLARKE AND ARTHUR HUGHES STARRED

THE DIALOGUE WAS CAMPY AND UNREAL, BUT IT WAS VERY ENTERTAINING

JAMES KELLY PLAYED KEEN'S SIDEKICK "MIKE CLANCY"

RADIO'S GOLDEN YEARS.©
by FRANK BRESEE & BOBB LYNES

Mr. & Mrs. North

MR. & MRS. NORTH WAS ONE OF THE MOST POPULAR RADIO CRIME DRAMAS, BASED ON THE BOOKS BY FRANCES AND RICHARD LOCKRIDGE......
PAM & JERRY NORTH, THO THEY WEREN'T TRAINED DETECTIVES, WOULD SOLVE MURDERS AND CRIMES DURING THEIR WEEKLY ADVENTURES

JOSEPH CURTIN PLAYED JERRY NORTH

ALICE FROST WAS PAM NORTH

FIRST PLAYED BY PEGGY CONKLIN & CARL EASTMAN, THE SERIES BEGAN ON CBS IN 1941 AND MOVED TO NBC IN 1942, THEN BACK CBS UNTIL THE END IN 1954.....

SPONSORS: WOODBURY SOAP, HALO SHAMPOO & COLGATE-PALMOLIVE

HALO SHAMPOO

WOODBURY FACIAL SOAP

COL DENTAL CR

ANNOUNCER: JOSEPH KING

LATER, THE STARS WERE RICHARD DENNING AND BARBARA BRITTON

RADIO'S GOLDEN YEARS©

by FRANK BRESEE & BOBB LYNES

MR. PRESIDENT

MR. PRESIDENT WAS A WEEKLY DRAMATIZED HISTORY LESSON, WITH LITTLE-KNOWN STORIES OF U.S. PRESIDENTS DURING THEIR WHITE HOUSE YEARS. WELL RESEARCHED & WRITTEN, THE DRAMAS TOLD OF THE HUMAN SIDE OF MR. PRESIDENT...

THE CHIEF EXECUTIVE WAS NEVER IDENTIFIED DURING THE STORY; LISTENERS WERE TO GUESS HIS IDENTITY, WHICH WOULD BE REVEALED AT THE END OF THE DRAMA

ANNOUNCER: TED DE CORSIA (SOMETIMES BILL CONRAD)

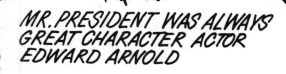

MR. PRESIDENT WAS ALWAYS GREAT CHARACTER ACTOR EDWARD ARNOLD

BETTY LOU GERSON WAS PRESIDENTIAL SECRETARY, ALWAYS CALLED "MISS SARAH"

HOLLYWOOD'S BEST ACTORS SUPPORTED: WILLIAM CONRAD, HOWARD McNEAR, HERB BUTTERFIELD, LOU MERRILL VIRGINIA GREGG, GRIFF BARNETT & PARLEY BAER

CREATED BY ROBERT G. JENNINGS, THE SERIES WAS SUSTAINED BY ABC FROM JUNE 26, 1947 TO 1953

PRODUCER-DIRECTOR: DICK WOOLEN

WRITERS: JEAN HOLLOWAY, IRA MARION & BERNARD DOUGALL

RADIO'S GOLDEN YEARS ©
by FRANK BRESEE & BOBB LYNES

MUTUAL/SEARS RADIO THEATRE

MUTUAL RADIO THEATRE BEGAN AIRING ON FEBRUARY 5, 1979 AND RAN UNTIL DECEMBER 19, 1981. AS SEARS RADIO THEATRE IT WAS HEARD ON CBS FOR 6 MONTHS IN 1979

ARCH OBOLER

FLETCHER MARKLE

ELLIOTT LEWIS

HOLLYWOOD'S BEST RADIO TALENT WAS FEATURED: VIRGINIA GREGG, BYRON KANE, VIC PERRIN, LURENE TUTTLE, HANS CONRIED, PAT BUTTRAM, WILLIAM CONRAD, PARLEY BAER, FRANK BRESEE, MARY JANE CROFT, JANET WALDO, LES TREMAYNE, PEGGY WEBBER, HERB VIGRAN, FRANK NELSON, SHEP MENKEN, BARNEY PHILLIPS, ELLIOTT LEWIS, PETER LEEDS, MORE...

THE HOUR-LONG SERIES WAS HEARD MONDAY THRU FRIDAY WITH A DIFFERENT HOST ON EACH DAY.... ANDY GRIFFITH, VINCENT PRICE, LORNE GREENE, LEONARD NIMOY, RICHARD WIDMARK AND LATER CECILY TYSON..

SPONSOR: SEARS AND VARIOUS PRODUCTS

DIRECTORS: ELLIOTT LEWIS, FLETCHER MARKLE & ARCH OBOLER

MUSIC: NELSON RIDDLE

ART GILMORE

JOHN HARLAN

ANNOUNCERS:

RADIO'S GOLDEN YEARS ©
by FRANK BRESEE & BOBB LYNES

MY *FAVORITE* HUSBAND

"TWO PEOPLE WHO LIVE TOGETHER AND LIKE IT!"

MY FAVORITE HUSBAND WAS THE FIRST RADIO SERIES TO STAR MOTION PICTURE MUSICAL COMEDY PERFORMER LUCILLE BALL. HER CO-STAR ON THE CBS COMEDY SHOW WAS RICHARD DENNING

BALL AND DENNING WERE LIZ AND GEORGE COOPER, A HAPPY COUPLE WHO WOULD GET THEMSELVES INTO ALL KINDS OF DOMESTIC SCRAPES

IT WAS A SORT OF FORE-RUNNER OF TV'S "I LOVE LUCY" BEING WRITTEN BY JESS OPPENHEIMER, MADELYN PUGH AND BOB CARROLL, JR. WHO LATER DID THE "LUCY" SCRIPTS

THEIR BEST FRIENDS WERE RUDOLPH ATTERBURY (GALE GORDON) AND HIS WIFE, IRIS (BEA BENADERET)

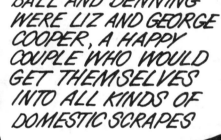

SPONSOR: GENERAL FOODS

ANNOUNCER: BOB LEMOND

MUSIC BY WILBUR HATCH

SERIES DEBUTED IN 1948 AND RAN UNTIL 1951; LATER LUCILLE BALL AND HUSBAND DESI ARNAZ MOVED TO TV WITH "I LOVE LUCY."...

RADIO'S GOLDEN YEARS ©

by FRANK BRESEE & BOBB LYNES

My Friend IRMA

CREATED BY CY HOWARD, ONE OF THE RADIO SITUATION COMEDIES TO FEATURE A MOTION PICTURE PERSONALITY MARIE WILSON STARRED AS THE CLASSIC "DUMB BLONDE" WHO GOT INTO TROUBLE EVERY DAY OF HER LIFE & LIVED WITH A GIRL FRIEND WHO ALWAYS GAVE HER GOOD ADVICE, BUT HER BOY FRIEND AL WAS NO HELP....

THE WEEKLY SHOW WAS BROADCAST "LIVE" WITH AN AUDIENCE FROM HOLLYWOOD'S CBS-COLUMBIA SQUARE

SPONSORS: PEPSODENT TOOTHPASTE, CAMEL CIGARETTES, AND TONI PERMANENTS

CATHY LEWIS

ORCHESTRA: LUD GLUSKIN

VOCAL GROUP WHICH SANG THE THEME SONG "FRIENDSHIP" WAS THE SPORTSMEN QUARTET

JOHN BROWN

ALAN REED

MANY OF RADIO'S BEST ACTORS WERE FEATURED INCLUDING: CATHY LEWIS, ALAN REED, JOHN BROWN, JOAN BANKS, GLORIA GORDON, HANS CONRIED, MARY SHIPP, LEIF ERICKSON AND SANDRA GOULD....

THE COMEDY WAS HEARD FROM 1947 TO 1954....

RADIO'S GOLDEN YEARS©

by FRANK BRESEE & BOBB LYNES

MY LITTLE MARGIE RAN ON THE CBS RADIO NETWORK FROM DECEMBER 1952 TO JUNE 1955; IT WAS ONE OF A HANDFULL OF SERIES THAT BEGAN ON TV AND MOVED OVER TO RADIO! FILM STAR GALE STORM PLAYED MARGIE ALBRIGHT (A NATURAL DO-GOODER) WHO LIVED WITH HER DOTING FATHER VERNE, (HONEYWELL INDUSTRIES EXECUTIVE) PLAYED BY FORMER SILENT SCREEN STAR CHARLES FARRELL

My Little MARGIE

EACH WEEK MARGIE WOULD GET INTO ALL KINDS OF SCAPES AND HER DAD WOULD SPEND THE HALF HOUR RESOLVING HER PROBLEMS.....

SUPPORT CAST: VERNA FELTON, GIL STRATTON, JR. & WILL WRIGHT

GALE STORM

SPONSOR: PHILIP MORRIS CIGARETTES

CHARLES FARRELL

PRODUCER-DIRECTOR GORDON T. HUGHES

TV TO RADIO

CHARLES FARRELL WAS THE FOUNDER & OWNER OF PALM SPRINGS RACQUET CLUB

RADIO'S GOLDEN YEARS©

by FRANK BRESEE & BOBB LYNES

THE STORY OF Myrt&Marge

THE STORY OF MYRT AND MARGE DEBUTED AS A 15-MINUTE DAILY EARLY-EVENING SERIAL ON CBS NOVEMBER 2, 1931. THE SHOW WAS CREATED AND WRITTEN BY CO-STAR MYRTLE VAIL, AT THAT TIME A 43 YEAR-OLD STAGE VETERAN. IT TOLD OF THE HARDSHIPS AND TRIUMPHS OF TWO BROADWAY SHOWGIRLS IN THEIR SEARCH FOR STARDOM

WHEN, TRAGICALLY, DONNA DIED IN CHILDBIRTH IN 1941, HELEN MACK TOOK THE PART OF MARGE

IN 1946, A SYNDICATED VERSION OF THE SERIAL WAS HEARD, CO-STARRING ALICE YOURMAN & ALICE GOODKIN

MYTLE VAIL WAS "MYRTLE SPEAR"

VAIL'S REAL-LIFE DAUGHTER DONNA DAMAREL CO-STARRED AS "MARGE MINTER"

ALICE YOURMAN As "MYRT"

ALICE GOODKIN As "MARGE"

ANDRE BARUCH

HARLOW WILCOX

ANNOUNCERS:

OVER THE YEARS CAST INCLUDED: VINTON HAYWORTH, HELEN CHOAT, REGINALD KNORR, RAY HEDGE, ED BEGLEY & RICHARD KEITH

VINTON HAYWORTH As "JACK ARNOLD"

RICHARD KEITH As "RAY HUNT"

HELEN CHOAT As "BILLIE DEVERE"

ED BEGLEY As "FRANCIS HAYFIELD"

RAY HEDGE As "CLARENCE TIFFINGTUFFER"

THEME: "POOR BUTTERFLY"

SPONSOR: WRIGLEY'S CHEWING GUM

WRIGLEY'S DOUBLEMINT CHEWING GUM®

174

RADIO'S GOLDEN YEARS ©

by FRANK BRESEE & BOBB LYNES

THE MYSTERIOUS TRAVELER

THE MYSTERIOUS TRAVELER DEBUTED ON MBS IN 1943 AND RAN (SUSTAINED) UNTIL 1952.....

OPENING:
"THIS IS THE MYSTERIOUS TRAVELER, INVITING YOU TO JOIN ME ON ANOTHER JOURNEY INTO THE STRANGE AND TERRIFYING. I HOPE YOU ENJOY THE TRIP, THAT IT WILL THRILL YOU A LITTLE AND CHILL YOU A LITTLE. SO SETTLE BACK, GET A GOOD GRIP ON YOUR NERVES AND BE COMFORTABLE.....IF YOU CAN."

THE SCARY SERIES ANTHOLOGY WAS MUTUAL'S VERSION OF THE WHISTLER, WITH "THE TRAVELER" TELLING US STORIES OF HORROR, MYSTERY AND FANTASY.....

THE TRAVELER WAS ALWAYS PLAYED BY MAURICE TARPLIN

NEW YORK'S BEST ACTORS WERE FEATURED: LAWSON ZERBE, RALPH BELL, LARRY HAINES, SANTOS ORTEGA & MORE

WRITTEN, PRODUCED & DIRECTED BY ROBERT A. ARTHUR & DAVID KOGAN

RADIO'S GOLDEN YEARS

by FRANK BRESEE & BOBB LYNES

A SERIES THAT COULD BE CALLED SON OF INNER SANCTUM, THE CBS RADIO MYSTERY THEATRE WAS THE MOST AMBITIOUS ATTEMPT TO BRING BACK TO LIFE THE ALMOST-DEAD ART OF AUDIO DRAMA. CREATED, PRODUCED & DIRECTED BY RADIO VETERAN HIMAN BROWN, THIS 1-HOUR HORROR SERIES DEBUTED ON THE CBS NETWORK JANUARY 6, 1974 AND RAN 7 DAYS A WEEK UNTIL DECEMBER 31, 1982

CBS RADIO

mystery theater

HOST: E.G. MARSHALL LATER, TAMMY GRIMES

HIMAN BROWN

BROWN USED ACTORS FROM THE OLD DAYS: AGNES MOOREHEAD, MANDEL KRAMER, LARRY HAINES, LES TREMAYNE, ANNE SEYMOUR, SANTOS ORTEGA, BRET MORRISON, MERCEDES McCAMBRIDGE AND MORE.....

MERCEDES McCAMBRIDGE

SOME NEW-TO-RADIO ACTORS: KIM HUNTER, LOIS NETTLETON, FRED GWYNNE & TONY ROBERTS

USING NEW SCRIPTS, SOME SHOWS WERE BASED ON CLASSICS.... DRACULA, BLACK CAT, SHERLOCK HOLMES AND MORE

SOME CBS AFFILIATES REFUSED TO BREAK FORMAT (MUSIC, NEWS, ETC.) AND CARRY THE SATELLITED SERIES, SO MANY INDEPENDENTS PICKED IT UP. KOA-NBC, DENVER PLAYED IT....KNX-CBS, HOLLYWOOD RECEIVED ITS HIGHEST RATINGS FROM 9-10 PM AND THE AUDIENCE DEMANDED MORE DRAMA WHEN MYSTERY THEATRE ENDED!

RADIO'S GOLDEN YEARS ©

by FRANK BRESEE & BOBB LYNES

KEN MURRAY

KEN MURRAY, AN EARLY VAUDEVILLE STAR FIRST CAME TO RADIO IN 1932 WITH HIS OWN CBS PROGRAM

BY 1938 HE WAS ON TOP, AND A REGULAR ON "HOLLYWOOD HOTEL" WITH HIS SIDE-KICK OSWALD (TONY LABRIOLA). IN 1939 HE WAS THE HOST OF THE TEXACO STAR THEATRE AND BY 1944, WAS QUIZ-MASTER FOR A POPULAR GAME SHOW:(WHICH IS WHICH?)

SPONSORS:
OLD GOLD CIGARETTES,
TEXACO GAS,
LIFEBOUY SOAP

THE FAMOUS CATCH PHRASE:
MURRAY: "ISN'T THAT RIGHT, OSWALD?"
OSWALD: "OH, YEAH!"

IN THE MID-FORTIES KEN MURRAY BEGAN THE LONG-RUNNING HOLLYWOOD STAGE SHOW "BLACKOUTS." IN 1950 MURRAY MOVED TO CBS-TV WITH HIS OWN VARIETY SHOW WHICH LASTED FOR MANY YEARS

RADIO'S GOLDEN YEARS ©

by FRANK BRESEE & BOBB LYNES

ADVENTURES OF NERO WOLFE

THE ADVENTURES OF NERO WOLFE DEBUTED ON THE NBC-BLUE NETWORK IN JULY 1943....

THE WEEKLY DETECTIVE PROGRAM WAS BASED ON THE MYSTERY NOVELS OF REX STOUT. NERO WOLFE WAS AN ORCHID FANCIER FIRST CLASS AND A PONDEROUS GENIUS WHOSE EYE FOR DETAIL SOLVED MANY "PERFECT" MURDERS.

ANNOUNCER: DON STANLEY

SPONSOR: JERGENS LOTION

HIS "LEG-MAN," ARCHIE GOODWIN WAS PLAYED BY GERALD MOHR, WALLY MAHER, HARRY BARTELL & LARRY DOBKIN

DURING THE EARLY YEARS, WOLFE WAS PLAYED BY SANTOS ORTEGA AND LUIS VAN ROOTEN. BY 1945 THE SERIES MOVED TO NBC-HOLLYWOOD AND FORMER SILENT-FILM STAR FRANCIS X. BUSHMAN STARRED AS WOLFE. IN THE '50s ON NBC, WOLFE WAS PLAYED BY FILM ACTOR SIDNEY GREENSTREET

RADIO'S GOLDEN YEARS ©
by FRANK BRESEE & BOBB LYNES

NICK CARTER
MASTER DETECTIVE

NICK CARTER, MASTER DETECTIVE BEGAN AS A PULP FICTION HERO IN 1886 IN STREET & SMITH'S NEW YORK WEEKLY AND SUCCESSFULLY DEBUTED ON RADIO — MBS ON APRIL 11, 1943 & RAN 'TIL 1955...

FAMOUS OPENING:
(KNOCKING ON DOOR)
BANG-BANG-BANG!
BANG-BANG-BANG!
BANG-BANG-BANG!
"WHAT'S THE MATTER?...
WHAT IS IT?"
"ANOTHER CASE FOR NICK CARTER, MASTER DETECTIVE!"

LON CLARK WAS NICK CARTER

HELEN CHOAT

ANNOUNCER: MICHAEL FITZMAURICE

GIRLFRIEND PATSY BOWEN WAS PLAYED BY HELEN CHOAT AND CHARLOTTE MANSON

CUDAHY
Plus Product
VALUE TESTED AND PR...

SPONSORS: OLD DUTCH CLEANSER, LIN-X AND CUDAHY MEATS

WRITTEN, DIRECTED & PRODUCED BY JOCK MacGREGOR

RADIO'S GOLDEN YEARS.©

by FRANK BRESEE & BOBB LYNES

NIGHTBEAT

NIGHTBEAT FEATURED THE ADVENTURES OF REPORTER RANDY STONE OF THE MYTHICAL CHICAGO STAR NEWSPAPER, WHO ROAMED THE STREETS AT NIGHT LOOKING FOR HUMAN INTEREST STORIES AND HELP PEOPLE OUT OF TROUBLE. THE WEEKLY SERIES BEGAN ON NBC ON FEBRUARY 6, 1950 AND RAN UNTIL 1952....

HOLLYWOOD'S BEST SUPPORT ACTORS APPEARED: WILLIAM CONRAD, JOAN BANKS (MRS. LOVEJOY), PETER LEEDS LURENE TUTTLE, HERB BUTTERFIELD AND MORE....

FRANK LOVEJOY STARRED AS RANDY STONE

STONE ENDED EACH STORY WITH "COPY BOY!"

PRODUCER/DIRECTOR: WARREN LEWIS

SPONSORS: SUSTAINED BY NBC, WHEATIES (SUMMER OF 1950)

NBC

WHEATIES
Breakfast of Champions

BREAKFAST OF CHAMPIONS

RADIO'S GOLDEN YEARS

by FRANK BRESEE & BOBB LYNES

One Man's Family

CREATED & WRITTEN BY CARLTON E. MORSE, ONE MAN'S FAMILY WAS RADIO'S LONGEST RUNNING SERIAL DRAMA, BEGINNING IN APRIL, 1932 & LASTING UNTIL 1959

THE SERIES BEGAN AT NBC-SAN FRANCISCO, LATER MOVED TO NBC-HOLLYWOOD STUDIOS AS A 30-MINUTE WEEKLY FEATURE, BUT IN 1950 STARTED AIRING AS A 15-MINUTE 5-DAYS A WEEK SHOW.....

FATHER BARBOUR WAS PLAYED ALL 27 YEARS BY J. ANTHONY SMYTHE, MOTHER BARBOUR: (A REAL-LIFE BACHELOR!) MINETTA ELLEN

CARLTON E. MORSE

CAST REGULARS: MICHAEL RAFFETTO, BERNICE BERWIN, BARTON YARBOROUGH, PAGE GILMAN, JEAN ROUVEROL

SPONSORS: WESSON OIL, ROYAL GELATIN, TENDERLEAF TEA & MILES LABORATORIES

ANNOUNCERS: BILL ANDREWS, KEN CARPENTER & FRANK BARTON

OTHERS OVER THE YEARS: CONRAD BINYON, BARBARA FULLER, WALTER PATTERSON, TOM COLLINS, ANNE WHITFIELD, DAWN BENDER, GEO. PIRRONE, MARVIN MILLER, JANET WALDO, TYLER McVEY, ETC..

RADIO'S GOLDEN YEARS.©

by FRANK BRESEE & BOBB LYNES

Our Miss Brooks

CREATED BY CY HOWARD, OUR MISS BROOKS DEBUTED ON CBS JULY 19, 1948 AND WAS ONE OF THE MOST POPULAR SITUATION COMEDIES FOR 9 YEARS. IT WAS ALSO CONCURRENTLY SEEN ON CBS-TV FROM 1952 TO 1956 WITH ALMOST THE SAME CAST FROM THE RADIO SERIES

CONNIE BROOKS, MADISON HIGH'S ENGLISH TEACHER, WAS PLAYED BY EVE ARDEN

REGULAR CAST: GALE GORDON (OSGOOD CONKLIN), JEFF CHANDLER (PHILIP BOYNTON), RICHARD CRENNA (WALTER DENTON), JANE MORGAN (MRS. DAVIS), GLORIA McMILLAN (HARRIET CONKLIN) & LEONARD SMITH (STRETCH)

WRITER: AL LEWIS

MUSIC BY WILBUR HATCH

ANNOUNCER: BOB LEMOND

SPONSORS: COLGATE & TONI HOME PERMANENT

The Adventures of OZZIE & HARRIET

OSWALD NELSON FORMED HIS OWN BAND AT AGE 14 & PEGGY LOU SNYDER (HARRIET HILLIARD) JOINED HIM IN 1932 AS HIS SINGER; THEY MARRIED OCT. 8, 1935. THE COUPLE LATER APPEARED ON JOE PENNER, ROBERT RIPLEY & RED SKELTON SHOWS. WHEN RED WAS DRAFTED, THEY GOT THEIR OWN SERIES....

THE ADVENTURES OF OZZIE & HARRIET BEGAN ON CBS ON OCTOBER 8, 1944 AND RAN LATER ON NBC AND ABC UNTIL 1954

SPONSORS: INTERNATIONAL SILVER, HEINZ FOODS, HOTPOINT & LISTERINE

LISTERINE
ANTISEPTIC
KILLS GERMS BY MILLIONS ON CONTACT

HEINZ 57 VARIETIES

1847 ROGERS BROS. for 102 years America's Finest Silverplate

Hotpoint ELECTRIC REFRIGERATOR

LONGTIME ANNOUNCER: VERNE SMITH

JOHN BROWN

LURENE TUTTLE

RADIO CAST INCLUDED: JOHN BROWN, LURENE TUTTLE, JANET WALDO & BEA BENADERET; SONS RICKY & DAVID NELSON WERE PLAYED BY TOMMY BERNARD & HENRY BLAIR UNTIL MARCH, 1949 WHEN THE BOYS BEGAN PLAYING THEMSELVES

RADIO'S GOLDEN YEARS ©

by FRANK BRESEE & BOBB LYNES

BERT PARKS

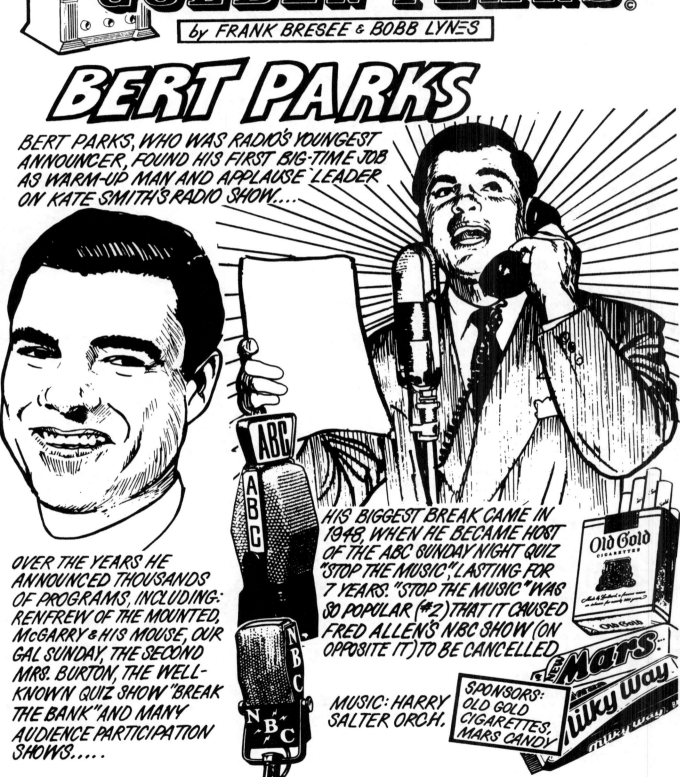

BERT PARKS, WHO WAS RADIO'S YOUNGEST ANNOUNCER, FOUND HIS FIRST BIG-TIME JOB AS WARM-UP MAN AND APPLAUSE LEADER ON KATE SMITH'S RADIO SHOW.....

OVER THE YEARS HE ANNOUNCED THOUSANDS OF PROGRAMS, INCLUDING: RENFREW OF THE MOUNTED, McGARRY & HIS MOUSE, OUR GAL SUNDAY, THE SECOND MRS. BURTON, THE WELL-KNOWN QUIZ SHOW "BREAK THE BANK" AND MANY AUDIENCE PARTICIPATION SHOWS.....

HIS BIGGEST BREAK CAME IN 1948, WHEN HE BECAME HOST OF THE ABC SUNDAY NIGHT QUIZ "STOP THE MUSIC", LASTING FOR 7 YEARS. "STOP THE MUSIC" WAS SO POPULAR (#2) THAT IT CAUSED FRED ALLEN'S NBC SHOW (ON OPPOSITE IT) TO BE CANCELLED

MUSIC: HARRY SALTER ORCH.

SPONSORS: OLD GOLD CIGARETTES, MARS CANDY

184

RADIO'S GOLDEN YEARS©

by FRANK BRESEE & BOBB LYNES

THE PASSING PARADE

HOST JOHN NESBITT PRESENTED "THE PASSING PARADE" WITH THE SAME DELIVERY AND EXCITEMENT HE USED IN HIS POPULAR M·G·M SHORT SUBJECTS OF THE SAME NAME....

THE SERIES BEGAN ON RADIO IN 1937 AND CONTINUED IN VARIOUS FORMATS UNTIL 1949

OPENING: "HERE IS YOUR PASSING PARADE.... FAVORITE STORIES AS TOLD BY YOUR FAVORITE STORYTELLER, JOHN NESBITT"

DURING EACH PROGRAM, HOST-NARRATOR JOHN NESBITT WOULD VERY DRAMATICALLY RELATE ADVENTURE TALES, MYSTERY & HISTORIC STORIES AND UNIQUE, WEIRD, UNEXPLAINED ACCOUNTS....

OVER THE YEARS THE SHOW WAS HEARD ON CBS, NBC AND MUTUAL

SPONSORS: CREME OF MILK FACIAL CREME, UNION OIL COMPANY, GULF OIL, JOHNSON'S WAX & WESTINGHOUSE

ORCHESTRA: MEREDITH WILLSON CARMEN DRAGON VICTOR YOUNG

HOST-NARRATOR JOHN NESBITT

CHARLES LYON

KEN CARPENTER

HARLOW WILCOX

ANNOUNCERS:

PAT NOVAK FOR HIRE

PAT NOVAK: FOR HIRE WAS ONE OF THE FIRST RADIO SHOWS TO STAR JACK WEBB. THE SERIES BEGAN IN SAN FRANCISCO WHERE THE STORIES TOOK PLACE: PAT NOVAK WOULD BE HIRED FOR A SIMPLE JOB... DELIVER A PACKAGE, MEET SOMEONE FROM OUT OF TOWN OR TAIL A BLONDE. IT USUALLY LED TO MURDER WITH NOVAK ACCUSED. HE CLEARED HIMSELF BY FINDING THE MURDERER.

PAT NOVAK, FOR HIRE... THAT'S WHAT THE SIGN OUTSIDE MY OFFICE SAYS. DOWN HERE ON THE WATERFRONT YOU DON'T GET PRIZES FOR BEING SUBTLE. YOU WANT TO MAKE A LIVING, YOU GET YOUR HAND IN THE TILL ANYWAY YOU CAN. IT'S A HAPPY LIFE, IF YOU DON'T MIND LOOKING UP AT A HEADSTONE... BECAUSE SOONER OR LATER YOU DRAW TROUBLE A SIZE TOO BIG!

NOVAK WAS PLAYED BY BEN MORRIS WHEN WEBB WENT TO HOLLYWOOD TO STAR AS JOHNNY MODERO (ALSO WRITTEN BY NOVAK CREATOR, RICHARD BREEN) WEBB ENDED THE SERIES IN 1949, MOVING ON TO DRAGNET

PAT NOVAK HAD AN ASSISTANT, JOCKO MADIGAN PLAYED BY TUDOR OWEN, WITH RAYMOND BURR AS POLICE INSPECTOR HELLMAN

THE SERIES BEGAN IN 1946 ON ABC'S WEST COAST NETWORK, ENDING ON ABC IN 1949

ANNOUNCER: GEORGE FENNEMAN

RADIO'S GOLDEN YEARS ©
by FRANK BRESEE & BOBB LYNES

AL PEARCE

THE AL PEARCE SHOW WAS HEARD ON THE NBC, CBS AND BLUE NETWORKS (JAN. 13, 1934 TO OCT. 25, 1947) COMEDIAN AL PEARCE DEBUTED ON KFRC, SAN FRANCISCO IN THE HAPPY-GO-LUCKY HOUR IN 1929

AL PEARCE AND HIS GANG WENT TO THE NBC NETWORK FROM NEW YORK IN 1935; LATER ON CBS, ABC-BLUE, ENDING ON ABC

HIS MOST POPULAR CHARACTER WAS "ELMER BLURT," A SELF-CONSCIOUS SALESMAN, WHO ALWAYS HOPED NO ONE WOULD ANSWER THE DOOR WHEN HE KNOCKED _ EACH SHOW BEGAN WITH ELMER KNOCKING ON A DOOR AND SAYING: "NOBODY'S AT HOME... I HOPE, I HOPE, I HOPE"

HIS REGULAR COMEDY CAST: ARLENE HARRIS, MOREY AMSTERDAM, KITTY O'NEIL, BILL COMSTOCK (AS "TIZZIE LISH," A WOMAN COOKING EXPERT), ARTHUR Q. BRYAN, ARTIE AUERBACH AND HARRY STEWART

ANNOUNCERS: KEN ROBERTS (N.Y.) WENDELL NILES (HOLLYWOOD)

MUSIC: CARL HOFF ORCHESTRA

SPONSORS: PEPSODENT, FORD, GRAPE-NUTS, DOLE PINEAPPLE, DR. PEPPER & CAMEL CIGARETTES

ARLENE HARRIS

ELMER BLURP
ORIGINAL NAME

"TIZZIE LISH" BILL COMSTOCK (1934)

MOREY AMSTERDAM

Post's GRAPE-NUTS
DOLE
Ford
CAMEL
Pepsodent

RADIO'S GOLDEN YEARS ©

by FRANK BRESEE & BOBB LYNES

JACK PEARL
"BARON MUNCHAUSEN"

JACK PEARL HAD ONE OF THE POPULAR COMEDY VARIETY SHOWS OF THE DEPRESSION ERA. HIS COMEDY LINES AND TIMING KEPT AMERICA IN STITCHES DURING THE EARLY 1930s...

HIS STRAIGHT MAN, CLIFF HALL (ALSO A MASTER OF COMEDY), WAS CALLED "SHARLIE" BY JACK PEARL WHEN PEARL WAS "BARON M UNCHAUSEN"

CHARLIE: "I THOUGHT YOUR COUSIN HUGO WAS A MUSICIAN"
BARON: "HE VAS, HE VAS. YOU KNOW HE HAS OVER 200 WHYOLINS IN THAT....."
CHARLIE: "I HATE TO CORRECT YOU, BUT IT'S NOT WHYOLINS. VIOLINS, VI....VI..."
BARON: "BECAUSE HE LIKED THEM, THAT'S WHY...HE HAS 200 WHYOLINS.....AND HE'S GOT 20 HOBOS...."
CHARLIE: "OBOES!"
BARON: "BUMS, HE'S GOT IN THAT BAND"
CHARLIE: "OH, NO, BARON...THAT IS UNBELIEVABLE.....THAT IS PREPOSTEROUS!"
BARON: "VAS YOU DERE, SHARLIE?"

EVERY MONDAY NIGHT AT 9:30 ON NBC, PEARL'S "WORLD-WIDE INFORMATION BUREAU" WAS ON THE AIR! MILLIONS TUNED IN TO HEAR THE BARON POUR OUT SIDE-SPLITTING MIS-IN-FORMATION.....

SPONSORS: ROYAL GELATIN, RALEIGH, LUCKY STRIKE AND VICEROY CIGARETTES

OVER THE YEARS PEARL WAS HEARD ON NBC RED AND BLUE NETWORKS.....

"VAS YOU DERE SHARLIE?"
THE BARON'S FAMOUS CATCH PHRASE

RADIO'S GOLDEN YEARS ©

by FRANK BRESEE & BOBB LYNES

COMEDIAN JOE PENNER WAS A GUEST ON THE RUDY VALLEÉ HOUR AND WAS SUCH A HIT, HE WAS GIVEN HIS OWN HALF-HOUR SHOW.....

JOE PENNER

HIS SHOW WAS BROADCAST FROM CBS' NEW MILLION DOLLAR STUDIOS ON HOLLYWOOD'S SUNSET BLVD.

JOE PENNER'S HEAD WRITER WAS CARROLL CARROLL, WHO LATER WROTE ALL OF BING CROSBY'S MATERIAL

ON THE PROGRAM (AND IN MOVIES) JOE HAD A DUCK NAMED "GOO-GOO" (ON RADIO VOICED BY MEL BLANC)

FAMOUS PHRASES:
"WANNA BUY A DUCK?"
"YOU NAHHSTY MAN!
"DON'T EVER DOOO THAT!"

FROM 1933 TO 1940 ON CBS AND NBC-BLUE HIS COMEDY SERIES WAS ONE OF THE MOST POPULAR ON RADIO..

CAST: ROY ATWELL, CLIFF HALL, GAY SEABROOK, TOMMY MACK & DICK RYAN

FLEISCHMANN'S YEAST

SPONSORS: FLEISCHMANN'S, COCOMALT AND WARD BAKING COMPANY

MUSIC BY JIMMY GRIER, BEN POLLACK ORCHESTRAS AND OZZIE NELSON BAND

ANNOUNCER: BILL GOODWIN

VOCALISTS WERE JOY HODGES, GENE AUSTIN AND HARRIET HILLIARD

RADIO'S GOLDEN YEARS ©

by FRANK BRESEE & BOBB LYNES

PEOPLE ARE FUNNY

PEOPLE ARE FUNNY WAS ONE OF THE MOST POPULAR AUDIENCE PARTICIPATION SHOWS ON THE AIR. VARIOUS PEOPLE WERE CHOSEN FROM THE STUDIO AUDIENCE, BROUGHT TO THE STAGE AND ASKED TO PERFORM CRAZY STUNTS AND MAKE FOOLS OF THEMSELVES... IN RETURN, THEY WERE AWARDED MONEY AND PRIZES

THE PROGRAM BEGAN ON NBC ON JULY 3, 1942 AND FOR OVER A YEAR, ART BAKER WAS THE MASTER OF CEREMONIES. IN 1943 A CHARISMATIC PERFORMER JOINED THE SHOW, FOLLOWING HIS SHOW BUSINESS BREAK IN SAN FRANCISCO— FROM THEN ON, ART LINK-LETTER WAS STAR OF THE SHOW!

HOSTS: ART BAKER (78 WEEKS) ART LINKLETTER (17 YEARS!)

THE SHOW WAS BASED ON JOHN GUEDEL'S 1938 GAME SHOW "PULL OVER, NEIGHBOR"

ANNOUNCERS:- ROD O'CONNOR HERB ALLEN TED MEYERS

NATIONAL BROADCASTING COMPANY. IN HOLLYWOOD STUDIOS SUNSET AND VINE

RALEIGH CIGARETTES PRESENT "PEOPLE ARE FUNNY" WITH ART LINKLETTER

★ CHILDREN UNDER 14 WILL NOT BE ADMITTED ★

June 6 See Reverse Side

STUDIO D Doors Close 6:50 P.M.

JOHN GUEDEL

SPONSORS: WINGS, RALEIGH CIGARETTES, MARS CANDY CO. AND TONI PERMANENTS

THE SHOW RAN 18 YEARS ON RADIO (1942-59, NBC AND CBS) AND MOVED TO TELEVISION WITH THE SAME AMAZING RESULTS

RADIO'S GOLDEN YEARS.©
by FRANK BRESEE & BOBB LYNES

PERRY MASON

PERRY MASON, BASED ON THE POPULAR LAWYER-DETECTIVE STORIES BY ERLE STANLEY GARDNER, WAS FIRST HEARD ON CBS IN 1943, AND WAS ON RADIO FOR 12 YEARS.

THIS DAYTIME SERIAL CRIME DRAMA WAS A 15-MINUTE MONDAY THRU FRIDAY SERIES.

SECRETARY DELLA STREET WAS GERTRUDE WARNER, JAN MINER AND JOAN ALEXANDER

LARKIN

ROBINSON

ORTEGA

PERRY MASON WAS PLAYED BY BARTLETT ROBINSON, DONALD BRIGGS, SANTOS ORTEGA & JOHN LARKIN

CAST INCLUDED SOME OF NEW YORK'S BEST ACTORS: MATT CROWLEY, MANDEL KRAMER, BETTY GARDE AND MARY JANE HIGBY

SPONSORS: TIDE, PROCTER AND GAMBLE AND CAMAY SOAP

CAMAY
The "Beauty-Bath" Soap

EXTRA ACTION
Tide
AMERICA'S FAVORITE

LATER, RAYMOND BURR WAS STARRED IN THE POPULAR PERRY MASON TV SERIES

RADIO'S GOLDEN YEARS ©

by FRANK BRESEE & BOBB LYNES

THE ADVENTURES OF PHILIP MARLOWE

THE ADVENTURES OF PHILIP MARLOWE WAS BASED ON NOVELS BY RAYMOND CHANDLER (FAREWELL, MY LOVELY & LADY IN THE LAKE) WHICH FEATURED THE TOUGH, WORLD-WISE LOS ANGELES PRIVATE DETECTIVE. DICK POWELL HAD PLAYED MARLOWE IN THE LUX RADIO THEATRE VERSION OF "MURDER, MY SWEET" MOVIE. HE CAME TO NBC IN 1947 AS A SUMMER SUBSTITUTE FOR BOB HOPE, STARRING VAN HEFLIN; FINALLY GOT A REGULAR SPOT ON CBS IN 1948 AND RAN UNTIL 1950.....

SPONSORS:
PEPSODENT TOOTH PASTE
FORD MOTOR COMPANY AND CBS

VAN HEFLIN

GERALD MOHR WAS A PERFECT RADIO PHILIP MARLOWE

JEFF COREY WAS POLICE LIEUTENANT

WRITERS:
ROBERT MITCHELL
MEL DINELLI AND
GENE LEVITT,

ANNOUNCERS:
ROY ROWAN (CBS)
WENDELL NILES (NBC)

RADIO'S BEST ACTORS SUPPORTED:
VIVI JANISS, LOU KRUGMAN, JOHN DEHNER, GLORIA BLONDELL, VIRGINIA GREGG, PARLEY BAER, JACK MOYLES, HOWARD McNEAR, LAURETTE FILLBRANDT, LARRY DOBKIN, ETC...

RADIO'S GOLDEN YEARS ©

by FRANK BRESEE & BOBB LYNES

PHILIP MORRIS *Playhouse*

"JOHNNY" OF PHILIP MORRIS PRESENTED MANY PROGRAMS DURING RADIO'S GOLDEN AGE. ONE OF THE MOST POPULAR WAS "THE PHILIP MORRIS PLAYHOUSE", WHICH WENT ON CBS IN 1939 AND RAN (LATER ON NBC) UNTIL 1953

THE SERIES FEATURED TOP STARS OF HOLLYWOOD & BROADWAY IN ORIGINAL STORIES, USUALLY MYSTERY & CRIME DRAMAS... STARS INCLUDED: VINCENT PRICE, SUSAN HAYWARD, HOWARD DUFF, MARLENE DIETRICH, GLORIA SWANSON

WRITERS: MORTON FINE & DAVID FRIEDKIN

DIRECTORS: WILLIAM SPIER, CHARLES MARTIN

MUSIC: RAY BLOCH, ELLIOT LAWRENCE

FOUR-FOOT TALL MIDGET JOHNNY ROVENTINI WAS THE ORIGINAL "JOHNNY" AND WAS HEARD ON ALL NEW YORK CITY SERIES FOR PHILIP MORRIS

CALL FOR **PHILIP MORRIS**

ALWAYS BETTER...BETTER ALL WAYS

OTHER "JOHNNYS" WERE HEARD ON HOLLYWOOD & CHICAGO-BASED SHOWS

"JOHNNY" WAS THE ONLY LIVING REGISTERED TRADEMARK

OTHER PHILIP MORRIS-SPONSORED SHOWS: MILTON BERLE, IT PAYS TO BE IGNORANT, QUEEN FOR A DAY, JOHNNY PRESENTS, CRIME DOCTOR

RADIO'S GOLDEN YEARS

by FRANK BRESEE & BOBB LYNES

POINT SUBLIME

POINT SUBLIME, A FICTITIOUS SMALL TOWN ON THE PACIFIC COAST NORTH OF SAN FRANCISCO, WAS THE LOCALE OF THIS HUMAN STORY OF JUST PLAIN PEOPLE.....A DRAMA MIXED WITH COMEDY

THE SERIES REVOLVED AROUND BEN WILLET, TOWN MAYOR & OWNER OF THE LOCAL MERCANTILE STORE & MOTEL

POINT SUBLIME BEGAN ON NBC IN LATE 1940 AND FOR THE NEXT EIGHT YEARS WAS A POPULAR FEATURE, ALSO HEARD ON MUTUAL, LATER ON ABC

CATCH PHRASE: "AIN'T WE THE ONES?"

CLIFF ARQUETTE WAS "BEN WILLET"

HOLLYWOOD'S BEST SUPPORT ACTORS WERE ON THE SHOW: MEL BLANC (AS PORKY PIG SOUND-ALIKE "AUGUST MOON"), VERNA FELTON, LOU MERRILL, JANE MORGAN, EARLE ROSS & LURENE TUTTLE

ART GILMORE
VINCENT PELLETIER
ANNOUNCERS

SPONSORS: JOHN HANCOCK INSURANCE CO. AND UNION OIL CO.

194

RADIO'S GOLDEN YEARS©

by FRANK BRESEE & BOBB LYNES

QUEEN FOR A DAY

"QUEEN FOR A DAY" FIRST ORIGINATED IN NEW YORK ON APRIL 30, 1945 AND WITHIN A FEW MONTHS, MOVED TO HOLLYWOOD WHERE JACK BAILEY BECAME THE TEMPORARY HOST..... A JOB THAT LASTED 20 YEARS!

"Queen for a Day"
Now In Its 19th Year
Starring JACK BAILEY

If I am chosen Queen For a Day, my wish would be

...a word from JACK BAILEY

"WOULD YOU LIKE TO BE ..... QUEEN FOR A DAY?" THEN READ THESE IMPORTANT SUGGESTIONS.

We're looking for interesting and unusual wishes   and the reason for these wishes.

1. Make a wish While we want interesting and unusual wishes it is not necessary that your wish be one involving hardship All interesting and unusual wishes have equal chance. FILL IN YOUR WISH, DON'T LEAVE IT BLANK.

2. If possible, wish for something for yourself, your husband or your children. Don't wish for money. Wish for the thing you want the money for.

3. We cannot accept wishes for operations, medical care or legal services

4. Make the REASON for your wish as complete as possible, and DO NOT attach anything to your ticket.

5. Your story MUST BE TRUE. (An untrue story will cancel out all promises or agreements) ... you must be 18 years or over, unless married.

LADIES WOULD BE CHOSEN FROM THE AUDIENCE, INTERVIEWED ON THE AIR BY JACK BAILEY, AND WERE GIVEN SPECIAL GIFTS IF THEY WERE CHOSEN (BY THE AUDIENCE APPLAUSE METER) TO RECEIVE THEIR WISH....

THE MONDAY THRU FRIDAY 30 MINUTE MUTUAL SHOW WAS ON RADIO FOR 12 YEARS PLUS 8 YEARS ON TV....

OVER 5,000 QUEENS WERE CROWNED DURING THE 20 YEAR HISTORY OF THE PROGRAM... PRIZE AWARDS AMOUNTED TO OVER 16 MILLION DOLLARS!

GENE BAKER

ANNOUNCERS GENE BAKER, FORT PEARSON

SPONSORS: ALKA-SELTZER, OLD GOLD AND PHILIP MORRIS CIGARETTES

MOST POPULAR • WOMEN'S • PROGRAM

Queen for a Day

COAST TO COAST ON 550 RADIO STATIONS
OF THE MUTUAL BROADCASTING SYSTEM
FOR THE MAKERS OF OLD GOLD CIGARETTES

RADIO'S GOLDEN YEARS ©
by FRANK BRESEE & BOBB LYNES

QUIZ KIDS

THE QUIZ KIDS WAS A CHICAGO BASED RADIO SHOW THAT WAS HEARD WEEKLY ON THE NBC NETWORK, LATER ON ABC, THEN CBS UNTIL 1953 FIRST ON JUNE 28, 1940

THE SHOW FEATURED A PANEL OF FIVE YOUNGSTERS AGES 6 TO 16 (SOMETIMES EXTREMELY BRIGHT KIDS AS YOUNG AS 4 WERE ON THE PANEL)..

QUESTIONS RAN THE GAMUT FROM SPELLING, ASTRONOMY, AND SHAKESPEARE....

NATIONAL BROADCASTING CO., Inc.
CHICAGO STUDIOS
MERCHANDISE MART   19th Floor

SUN.
18
MAR.
1951

ALKA-SELTZER
presents
"QUIZ KIDS"

Doors

Close

COMPLIMENTARY TICKET—NOT TO BE SOLD   2:25PM

HOST/QUIZMASTER OF THE SHOW WAS JOE KELLY, AN EARLY MORNING WLS-CHICAGO PERSONALITY WHO ALSO HOSTED THE NATIONAL BARN DANCE....

SOME OF THE MORE FAMOUS QUIZ KIDS WERE: RICHARD WILLIAMS, JOEL KUPPERMAN, HARVE FISHMAN, JOAN BISHOP, VANESSA BROWN & ROBERT EASTON

ANNOUNCERS:
ROGER KRUPP,
FORT PEARSON

ONLY SPONSOR:
ALKA-SELTZER

RADIO'S GOLDEN YEARS.

by FRANK BRESEE & BOBB LYNES

DURING RADIO'S GREAT DAYS, ALL FOUR NETWORKS PRESENTED "LIVE" DANCE BAND MUSIC FROM MOST OF THE TOP NIGHT-CLUBS AROUND THE COUNTRY. THESE "REMOTE" PROGRAMS WERE USUALLY BROADCAST BETWEEN 10:30 P.M. AND 1:00 A.M. SEVEN DAYS A WEEK, RUNNING 15 TO 30 MINUTES EACH....

RADIO DANCE BANDS

SOME OF THE FAMOUS ORCHESTRAS WHICH WERE HEARD ON THESE GREAT BROADCASTS INCLUDE: GLENN MILLER, BENNY GOODMAN, GENE KRUPA, BUDDY ROGERS, HARRY JAMES, TOMMY DORSEY, CAB CALLOWAY, JIMMY DORSEY, XAVIER CUGAT, DUKE ELLINGTON, GUY LOMBARDO, RUSS MORGAN & MORE!

VARIOUS SPONSORS, LOCAL & NATIONAL

A TYPICAL REMOTE HAD THE ANNOUNCER SAYING: "...FROM THE CATALINA CASINO BALLROOM, HIGH ABOVE THE TWINKLING LIGHTS OF ROMANTIC AVALON, CBS RADIO BRINGS YOU THE MUSIC OF THE IDOL OF THE AIRLANES: JAN GARBER & HIS ORCHESTRA"

NOTE: THE FIRST KNOWN DANCE BAND SHOW WAS BROADCAST WITH VINCENT LOPEZ & HIS ORCHESTRA ON NOVEMBER 27, 1921!

RADIO'S GOLDEN YEARS ©

by FRANK BRESEE & BOBB LYNES

RADIO'S GREAT SHOWS

THREE OF THE GREATEST OF ALL RADIO BROADCASTS TOOK PLACE AT THE CBS STUDIOS IN NEW YORK AND HOLLYWOOD

"DICK TRACY in B FLAT"

THE THIRD MOST FAMOUS BROADCAST WAS RECORDED ON FEB. 15, 1945 IN STUDIO A, CBS ON SUNSET BLVD. IN HOLLYWOOD. THE PROGRAM WAS A VERY SPECIAL ONE HOUR AFRS "COMMAND PERFORMANCE" VERSION OF A MUSICAL COMEDY "DICK TRACY IN B FLAT...OR FOR GOODNESS SAKE ISN'T HE EVER GOING TO MARRY TESS TRUEHEART?"

THE SPECIAL FEATURED MOST OF THE TOP COMEDIANS AND SINGERS IN HOLLYWOOD, AN ALL-STAR CAST:

BING CROSBY	DICK TRACY
DINAH SHORE	TESS TRUEHEART
JUDY GARLAND	SNOWFLAKE
BOB HOPE	FLAT-TOP
FRANK SINATRA	SHAKY
JIMMY DURANTE	THE MOLE
FRANK MORGAN	VITAMIN FLINTHEART
CASS DALEY	GRAVEL GERTIE
JERRY COLONNA	POLICE CHIEF
ANDREWS SISTERS	SUMMER SISTERS
HARRY VON ZELL	OLD JUDGE HOOPER

THE SPECIAL WAS NOT AIRED ON ANY U.S. NETWORK, AS IT WAS MEANT ONLY FOR THE ENTERTAINMENT OF G.I.s!

RADIO'S GOLDEN YEARS ©
by FRANK BRESEE & BOBB LYNES

RADIO'S GREAT SHOWS

THREE OF THE GREATEST OF ALL RADIO BROADCASTS TOOK PLACE AT THE CBS STUDIOS IN NEW YORK AND HOLLYWOOD.....

SECOND OF THE GREAT SHOWS HAPPENED THE NIGHT ACTRESS AGNES MOOREHEAD APPEARED ON CBS' SUSPENSE PROGRAM FEATURING "SORRY, WRONG NUMBER" MAY 25, 1943......

SORRY, WRONG NUMBER

THE LUCILLE FLETCHER PLAY WAS SO WELL-RECEIVED, IT WAS REPEATED OVER THE YEARS ON SUSPENSE A TOTAL OF SEVEN TIMES.... IT WAS ALSO MADE INTO A MOVIE STARRING BARBARA STANWYCK

RADIO'S GOLDEN YEARS ©

by FRANK BRESEE & BOBB LYNES

RADIO'S GREAT SHOWS

THREE OF THE GREATEST OF ALL RADIO BROADCASTS TOOK PLACE AT THE CBS STUDIOS IN NEW YORK AND HOLLYWOOD.....

"THE WAR OF THE WORLDS"

FIRST OF THE THREE WAS ORSON WELLES' BROADCAST OF "WAR OF THE WORLDS" ON OCTOBER 30, 1938. WELLES AND HIS MERCURY PLAYERS FRIGHTENED THE NATION OUT OF ITS WITS WITH REPORTS OF A SUPPOSED INVASION BY MEN FROM MARS!

FOR DAYS AFTERWARD THE WHOLE COUNTRY WAS ON EDGE, AS WAS ORSON WELLES HIMSELF, NOT KNOWING IF HE MIGHT BE JAILED FOR THIS RADIO "HOAX."....INSTEAD IT _MADE_ HIS CAREER....

RADIO'S GOLDEN YEARS©

by FRANK BRESEE & BOBB LYNES

RED RYDER

RED RYDER AND HIS INDIAN COMPANION LITTLE BEAVER (CREATED BY FRED HARMAN) CAME TO RADIO FROM THE COMIC PAGES....

RED RYDER AND HIS INDIAN COMPANION LITTLE BEAVER CAME FROM THE COMIC PAGES TO THE RADIO NETWORKS.

Hear the Thrilling Adventures Of

RED RYDER
ON THE RADIO
AMERICA'S FAMOUS FIGHTING COWBOY!

7:30 P.M.

EVERY
TUESDAY
THURSDAY
SATURDAY

BLUE

Tune In Your BLUE NETWORK Station
Presented For Your Enjoyment by The Bakers Of
Langendorf Bread—Judged "America's Finest"

CARLTON KADELL

TOMMY COOK

ANNOUNCER ART GILMORE

RED RYDER WAS PLAYED BY CARLTON KADELL, REED HADLEY AND BROOKE TEMPLE LITTLE BEAVER BY TOMMY COOK, FRANKLIN BRESEE, HENRY BLAIR AND JOHNNY McGOVERN

FOR A TIME THE SHOW WAS HEARD SIX DAYS A WEEK, ON NBC-BLUE AND MUTUAL....

LONGTIME SPONSOR: LANGENDORF BREAD

HORACE "BUCKSKIN" MURPHY

BROOKE TEMPLE

REED HADLEY

RADIO'S GOLDEN YEARS.©
by FRANK BRESEE & BOBB LYNES

RICHARD DIAMOND
PRIVATE DETECTIVE

RICHARD DIAMOND, PRIVATE DETECTIVE STARRED MOTION PICTURE PERSONALITY DICK POWELL. IT CAME TO NBC IN 1949 AND QUICKLY ROSE TO THE TOP OF THE RADIO RATINGS...WITH MANY SCRIPTS

WRITTEN BY BLAKE EDWARDS, THE SERIES WAS A LIGHT-HEARTED RADIO DETECTIVE STORY WITH THE ADDED EXCITEMENT OF GLIB DICK POWELL (WHO ALSO MANAGED TO SING A SONG AT THE CLOSE OF MOST ADVENTURES!

VIRGINIA GREGG

CAST REGULARS:

ARTHUR Q. BRYAN

WILMS HERBERT

ED BEGLEY

CAMEL

Rexall
DRUG STORE

EDDY KING, DON STANLEY, BILL FORMAN ANNOUNCERS

SPONSORS:
REXALL DRUGS AND CAMEL CIGARETTES

THE SHOW MOVED TO ABC IN 1950, LATER TO CBS, LASTING UNTIL 1952

RADIO'S GOLDEN YEARS

by FRANK BRESEE & BOBB LYNES

TOMMY RIGGS & BETTY LOU

TOMMY RIGGS HAD THE AMAZING ABILITY TO ACTUALLY TALK WITH THE VOICE OF A SEVEN YEAR OLD GIRL; HE COULD TALK IN HIS OWN VOICE AND QUICKLY CHANGE HIS SOUND TO THAT OF A CHILD....

TOMMY RIGGS BEGAN HIS CAREER IN 1931 AT KDKA-PITTSBURGH AS A SINGER. HIS BIG NATIONAL BREAK WAS ON THE NBC RUDY VALLEE PROGRAM IN 1937. HE WAS ON ONE SHOW, AND CAME BACK FOR AN AMAZING 49 WEEKS!

IN 1938 HE BEGAN HIS OWN SHOW ON NBC. BY 1942 HE APPEARED ON THE KATE SMITH HOUR, AND IN 1943 HIS SUMMER SHOW REPLACED BURNS & ALLEN

SPONSOR: QUAKER OATS

BILL GOODWIN

ANNOUNCERS

DON WILSON

CAST REGULARS: MEL BLANC, BEA BENADERET, WALLY MAHER AND VERNA FELTON

MUSIC: FRANK DeVOL ORCHESTRA

HIS LAST NETWORK SHOW WAS IN 1946....

RADIO'S GOLDEN YEARS.©

by FRANK BRESEE & BOBB LYNES

Robert Ripley Believe It or Not!®

ROBERT L. RIPLEY'S "BELIEVE IT OR NOT" NEWSPAPER CARTOON APPEARED IN MORE THAN 300 PAPERS IN 38 COUNTRIES! DUE TO ITS GREAT POPULARITY, HE BEGAN HIS OWN NBC RADIO SHOW IN 1930 WHICH LASTED FOR ALMOST TWENTY YEARS

RIPLEY WAS THE FIRST PERSON TO BROADCAST VIA RADIO, TO EVERY NATION IN THE WORLD SIMULTANEOUSLY; HE USED A CORPS OF TRANSLATORS TO ACCOMPLISH THE AMAZING FEAT. BETWEEN HIS RADIO SHOW AND HIS NEWSPAPER FEATURE, HE RECEIVED MORE MAIL THAN ANYONE IN HISTORY! ONE CONTEST ALONE, A MERE 14-DAY PERIOD, NETTED HIM OVER 2,000,000 LETTERS!

ANNOUNCERS: BILL GRIFFIS & DON HANCOCK

HE WAS CALLED THE "MODERN MARCO POLO" BY THE DUKE OF WINDSOR

ON HIS FIRST RADIO SHOW, APRIL 14, 1930, RIPLEY ANNOUNCED TO HIS LISTENERS: "AMERICA HAS NO NATIONAL ANTHEM!" HE WAS RIGHT AND A YEAR LATER, CONGRESS ADOPTED "THE STAR SPANGLED BANNER" AS OUR NATIONAL ANTHEM

SPONSORS: COLONIAL OIL, ESSO OIL CO.

IN 1935 HIS WEEKLY HALF-HOUR PROGRAM FEATURED SINGER HARRIET HILLIARD AND OZZIE NELSON'S ORCHESTRA

RADIO'S GOLDEN YEARS ©

by FRANK BRESEE & BOBB LYNES

ROCKY FORTUNE

THIS PROGRAM FEATURED THE EXPLOITS OF ROCKY FORTUNE, A PRIVATE DETECTIVE WHO EACH WEEK WOULD TACKLE ANY CASE IF THE MONEY WAS RIGHT.....

FRANK SINATRA PLAYED THE TITLE ROLE OF A "FOOT-LOOSE AND FANCY-FREE YOUNG MAN" WHO DRIFTED FROM ONE ADVENTURE TO ANOTHER

FRANK SINATRA IS ONE OF THE GREAT ENTERTAINERS OF OUR TIME, HAVING BEGUN HIS CAREER IN THE LATE 1930s AS VOCALIST WITH HARRY JAMES' BAND. HIS RECORDS HAVE SOLD IN THE MILLIONS AND HIS MOTION PICTURES INCLUDE: "THE MAN WITH A GOLDEN ARM,""FROM HERE TO ETERNITY"(BEST SUPPORT OSCAR), "GUYS AND DOLLS" AND MANY MORE. ON RADIO, HE WAS A REGULAR ON YOUR HIT PARADE AND DURING THE 40s AND 50s STARRED ON HIS OWN MUSICAL VARIETY SHOWS.....

ROCKY FORTUNE: FRANK SINATRA

ANNOUNCER: EDDY KING

CAST MEMBERS: JACK NESTOR, PAUL FREES, MAURICE HART, JACK MATHER, GEORGIA ELLIS, RAYMOND BURR, BARNEY PHILLIPS, ETC.....

THE SERIES WAS HEARD SUSTAINED ON NBC DURING 1953-54

NBC RADIO a service of RCA

RADIO'S GOLDEN YEARS ©
by FRANK BRESEE & BOBB LYNES

Roy Rogers

ROY ROGERS WAS THE NATION'S TOP COWBOY STAR (ALONG WITH GENE AUTRY) IN REPUBLIC PICTURES AND ON THE RADIO.....

HIS RADIO SHOW BEGAN IN 1944 AND WAS HEARD COAST-TO-COAST ON THE MUTUAL BROADCASTING SYSTEM; LATER ON NBC

"HAPPY TRAILS TO YOU UNTIL WE MEET AGAIN"

IN THE MOVIES AND ON RADIO, DALE EVANS PLAYED ROY'S FRIEND AND COMPANION.... THEY WERE MARRIED ON DEC. 31, 1947

HIS SPONSORS WERE GOODYEAR TIRES, MILES LABORATORIES, QUAKER OATS AND GENERAL FOODS

SOME OF ROY'S HIT SONGS OVER THE YEARS INCLUDE: "TUMBLING TUMBLEWEEDS", "COOL WATER", "DON'T FENCE ME IN".....

ROY'S FAMOUS HORSE WAS "TRIGGER"

FOR A WHILE GABBY HAYES WAS A REGULAR IN ROY'S FILMS & RADIO SHOW

THE FAMOUS SINGING GROUP ON THE SHOW: "THE SONS OF THE PIONEERS"

RADIO'S GOLDEN YEARS.©

by FRANK BRESEE & BOBB LYNES

WILL ROGERS

REAL OKLAHOMA COWBOY WILL ROGERS BEGAN HIS SHOW BUSINESS CAREER IN RODEOS, VAUDEVILLE & THE ZIEGFELD FOLLIES; WHEN RADIO CAME ALONG HE SWITCHED TO THAT MEDIUM....

SPONSORED BY GULF OIL, HE BEGAN HIS "WILL ROGERS HEADLINERS" ON NBC IN APRIL, 1933; THEN ON CBS

FAMOUS QUOTES:

"I'M NOT A MEMBER OF ANY ORGANIZED POLITICAL PARTY ....I'M A DEMOCRAT!"

"I NEVER MET A MAN I DIDN'T LIKE"

"ALL I KNOW IS WHAT I READ IN THE PAPERS"

HIS RADIO APPEARANCES ARE LEGENDARY, AND MANY RECORDINGS OF HIS MONOLOGUES CONTINUE TO BE SOLD TODAY.....

WILL ROGERS ALSO STARRED IN MOVIES & HAD A DAILY SYNDICATED NEWSPAPER COLUMN IN LEADING PAPERS ACROSS THE NATION....

HE BEGAN HIS RADIO MONOLOGUES BY SETTING AN ALARM CLOCK TO GO OFF IN 10 MINUTES...WHEN THE ALARM RANG, WILL WOULD END HIS MONOLOGUE.

GULF

SPONSOR: GULF OIL

RADIO'S GOLDEN YEARS.©

by FRANK BRESEE & BOBB LYNES

THE ADVENTURES OF Sam Spade Detective

BASED ON THE CHARACTER IN AUTHOR DASHIELL HAMMETT'S "THE MALTESE FALCON."...THE ADVENTURES OF SAM SPADE WAS FIRST HEARD ON CBS IN JULY, 1946..... THE PROGRAM WAS A HIT RIGHT FROM THE START; IT ROSE IMMEDIATELY TO NATIONAL POPULARITY

SAM SPADE WAS PLAYED BY HANDSOME HOWARD DUFF

DIRECTOR WAS WILLIAM SPIER

SPADE ALWAYS MENTIONED HIS DETECTIVE LICENCE NUMBER.... 137596

ANNOUNCER: DICK JOY

SPONSORED BY WILDROOT HAIR PRODUCTS....

EACH WEEK, SAM SPADE WOULD BEGIN THE SHOW BY DICTATING HIS REPORT OF THE CRIME TO HIS SECRETARY EFFIE.... DURING THE NEXT HALF HOUR THE CAPER WOULD UNFOLD....

EFFIE WAS PLAYED BY LURENE TUTTLE....

COMMERCIAL SONG: "USE WILDROOT CREAM OIL, CHARLIE, IT KEEPS YOUR HAIR IN TRIM. IT'S NON-ALCHOLIC, CHARLIE, IT'S MADE WITH SOOTHIN' LANOLIN."

SAM SPADE 137596 DETECTIVE

SHAKE WELL BEFORE USING
WILDROOT CREAM-OIL FORMULA for the hair
contains LANOLIN

RADIO'S GOLDEN YEARS ©

by FRANK BRESEE & BOBB LYNES

Julia SANDERSON and Frank CRUMIT

JULIA SANDERSON & FRANK CRUMIT WERE THE FIRST HUSBAND AND WIFE TEAM TO BECOME STARS ON RADIO

AFTER MARRIAGE, THEY BECAME WELL-KNOWN AS A MUSICAL COMEDY TEAM IN VAUDEVILLE AND ON RECORDS

THEIR FIRST PROGRAM WAS "BLACKSTONE PLANTATION" ON CBS TUESDAY NIGHTS WHICH BEGAN IN 1929.

OVER THE YEARS, THEIR PROGRAMS WERE HEARD ON CBS, NBC-RED AND BLUE AND MUTUAL

ANNOUNCERS: BEN GRAUER, ALAN KENT

SPONSORS: BOND BREAD, BLACKSTONE CIGARS, NORGE PRODUCTS AND TUMS

IN LATER YEARS THEY STARRED IN OTHER SHOWS, INCLUDING "THE NORGE KITCHEN," "IT'S FLORIDA'S TREAT," (WITH HARRY RICHMAN), "BATTLE OF THE SEXES" AND "THE SINGING SWEET-HEARTS".....

RADIO'S GOLDEN YEARS.©

by FRANK BRESEE & BOBB LYNES

The Screen Guild Theater

THE SCREEN GUILD THEATRE FEATURED TOP HOLLYWOOD STARS IN RADIO ADAPTATIONS OF FAMOUS MOTION PICTURES

THE 30-MINUTE WEEKLY SHOW WAS ON CBS & NBC FOR 13 YEARS, FROM JANUARY 1939 TO JUNE 1952

THE STARS WHO APPEARED ALWAYS DONATED THEIR FEES TO THE MOTION PICTURE RELIEF FUND. THE MONEY WAS USED TO BUILD THE MOTION PICTURE COUNTRY HOME IN WOODLAND HILLS, CALIFORNIA DURING THE FIRST 4 YEARS OF THE SHOW, OVER $800,000 WAS DONATED TO THE FUND....

OVER THE YEARS, SOME OF THE STARS WHO APPEARED WERE ROBERT TAYLOR, BARBARA STANWYCK, GARY COOPER, BING CROSBY, CLARK GABLE, HUMPHREY BOGART & MORE

COLUMBIA BROADCASTING SYSTEM
COLUMBIA SQUARE PLAYHOUSE
BOULEVARD — HOLLYWOOD
LADY ESTHER PRESENTS
SCREEN GUILD PLAYERS
LLOYD NOLAN   WILLIAM LUNDIGAN
in
"THE HOUSE ON 92nd ST."
MONDAY JUNE 10 1946
6-6:30 p.m.
Doors Close at 5:55 p.m.
N° 1144

EARLY HOSTS:
ROGER PRYOR
GEORGE MURPHY

ANNOUNCERS:

JOHN CONTE

TRUMAN BRADLEY

MICHAEL ROY

SPONSORS: GULF OIL, LADY ESTHER, CAMEL CIGARETTES

MUSIC: FRANK TOURS CONDUCTING OSCAR BRADLEY'S ORCHESTRA; LATER, BASIL ADLAM

RADIO'S GOLDEN YEARS.©

by FRANK BRESEE & BOBB LYNES

SGT. PRESTON OF THE YUKON

SERGEANT PRESTON WAS FIRST KNOWN AS "THE CHALLENGE OF THE YUKON" WHEN IT BEGAN ON WXYZ ON JAN. 3, 1939 AS A 15-MINUTE SERIES IN DETROIT ONLY. LIKE THE LONE RANGER AND THE GREEN HORNET, THE ADVENTURE WAS CREATED BY GEORGE TRENDLE & WRITTEN BY TOM DOUGALL; EDITED BY FRAN STRIKER.

THE SERIES WENT ON THE ABC NETWORK JUNE 12, 1947 (MONDAY-WEDNESDAY-FRIDAY, ALTERNATING WITH THE GREEN HORNET)

THE SHOW WAS HEARD ON MBS FROM 1950 TO 1955

ANNOUNCERS: FRED FOY, JAY MICHAEL

DEWEY COLE BARKED AS "YUKON KING"

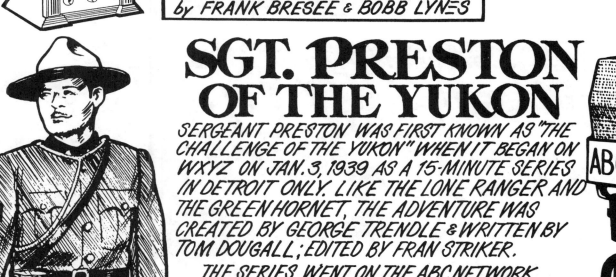

FAMOUS OPENING:
(GUNSHOT-RICHOCHET)
" NOW, AS GUNSHOTS ECHO ACROSS THE WINDSWEPT, SNOW-COVERED REACHES OF THE WILD NORTHWEST, QUAKER PUFFED WHEAT.....
(GUNSHOT-RICHOCHET)
AND QUAKER PUFFED RICE.....
(GUNSHOT-RICHOCHET)
THE BREAKFAST CEREAL SHOT FROM GUNS...
(TWO GUNSHOTS)
PRESENT, THE CHALLENGE OF THE YUKON!
(YUKON KING BARKS)
ITS YUKON KING, THE SWIFTEST AND STRONGEST LEAD DOG IN THE NORTH-WEST, BLAZING THE TRAIL FOR SERGEANT PRESTON OF THE NORTHWEST MOUNTED POLICE, IN HIS RELENTLESS PURSUIT OF LAW BREAKERS!
(PRESTON: ON, KING! ON YOU HUSKIES!)
GOLD! GOLD, DISCOVERED IN THE YUKON! A STAMPEDE TO THE KLONDIKE IN THE WILD RACE FOR RICHES! BACK TO THE DAYS OF THE GOLD RUSH, WITH QUAKER PUFFED WHEAT AND QUAKER PUFFED RICE BRINGING YOU THE ADVENTURES OF SERGEANT PRESTON AND HIS WONDER DOG YUKON KING, AS THEY MEET THE CHALLENGE OF THE YUKON!"

JAY MICHAEL WAS THE FIRST PRESTON; PAUL SUTTON, THE BEST REMEMBERED......

SPONSOR: QUAKER CEREALS

MAJESTIC THEME MUSIC: "DONNA DIANA OVERTURE"

DIRECTOR: FRED FLOWERDAY
PRODUCER: CHARLES D. LIVINGSTON

RADIO'S GOLDEN YEARS ©

by FRANK BRESEE & BOBB LYNES

THE WEED OF CRIME BEARS BITTER FRUIT! THE SHADOW KNOWS.... HA-HA-HA-HA-HA-HA-HA-HA

WHO KNOWS WHAT EVIL LURKS IN THE HEARTS OF MEN?......

The SHADOW

THE SHADOW CAME TO RADIO IN AUGUST 1930 ON CBS' "DETECTIVE STORY" BASED ON STREET & SMITH'S SHADOW NOVELS WRITTEN BY WALTER GIBSON. JAMES LACURTO WAS THE NARRATOR-HOST (THE SHADOW) WHO TOLD THE STORIES. LATER HOSTS WERE FRANK READICK, GEORGE EARLE & ROBERT HARDY ANDREWS. THE SHOW WENT TO NBC IN 1932, THEN BACK TO CBS AS A TWICE-A-WEEK PROGRAM SPONSORED OFF & ON BY BLUE COAL...

BRET MORRISON

IN 1937 THE SHADOW BECAME THE STAR OF THE SHOW..."A MYSTERY MAN WHO COULD "CLOUD MEN'S MINDS SO THEY CANNOT SEE HIM" PLAYING THIS SHADOW WAS 22 YEAR OLD ORSON WELLES WITH AGNES MOOREHEAD AS HIS "FRIEND AND COMPANION" MARGO LANE

WILLIAM JOHNSTONE

FRANK READICK

JOHN ARCHER

MUTUAL LONGACRE THEATRE
SUN. NOV. 19 1944
'blue coal' PRESENTS THE SHADOW

WOR, NEW YORK

LATER CRANSTON/SHADOWS WERE WILLIAM JOHNSTONE, JOHN ARCHER, STEVE COURTLEIGH & BRET MORRISON WHO PLAYED THE PART UNTIL THE SERIES ENDED DEC. 26, 1956

'blue coal' presents

The SHADOW

SPONSORS: GOODRICH, BLUE COAL

ANNOUNCERS KEN ROBERTS, ANDRÉ BARUCH

THEME SONG: OMPHALE'S "SPINNING WHEEL"

OTHER MARGOS WERE MARJORIE ANDERSON, GERTRUDE WARNER, MARGO STEVENSON, LESLEY WOODS & FINALLY GRACE MATTHEWS

Goodrich SAFETY Silvertown

212

RADIO'S GOLDEN YEARS©

by FRANK BRESEE & BOBB LYNES

"....FU MANCHU IS ONE OF THOSE INGENIOUS PEOPLE.... BORN ONCE EVERY THREE OR FOUR GENERATIONS, WHO HAVE THE ABILITY TO CHANGE THE WORLD FOR GOOD...."

THE SHADOW OF FU MANCHU

FU MANCHU WAS A PRINCE OF DARKNESS, MASTER SCIENTIST AND EVIL GENIUS. HE MIGHT HAVE CHANGED THE WORLD FOR GOOD, BUT HE CHOSE THE PATH OF EVIL INSTEAD....

THE RADIO SERIES WAS BASED ON THE POPULAR SAX ROHMER BOOKS AND WENT ON THE AIR IN 1929 AS PART OF THE COLLIER'S HOUR ON CBS. BY 1932 FU MANCHU HAD SETTLED INTO ITS OWN SPOT ON CBS. IN LATER YEARS, THE SHOW WAS SYNDICATED, LASTING UNTIL 1940....

FU MANCHU: JOHN C. DALY, LATER TED OSBORNE, HAROLD HUBER

SUPPORT CAST: BOB WHITE, CHARLES WARBURTON, SUNDA LOVE, ARTHUR HUGHES, GALE GORDON, HANLEY STAFFORD AND CHARLOTTE MANSON

Collier's 5¢

SPONSORS: COLLIER'S MAGAZINE AND CAMPANA BALM

JOHN C. DALY

LOVE

WARBURTON

HUGHES

WHITE

MANSON

ANNOUNCER: GERALD MOHR

RADIO'S GOLDEN YEARS. ©

by FRANK BRESEE & BOBB LYNES

THE ADVENTURES OF Sherlock Holmes

DURING ITS RADIO HISTORY, SHERLOCK HOLMES WAS ON THE AIR FROM OCTOBER 20, 1930 TO SEPTEMBER 4, 1956; RE-RUNS CONTINUED ON NPR INTO 1982.... BASED ON SIR ARTHUR CONAN DOYLE'S CLASSIC DETECTIVE STORIES IT WAS VERY POPULAR ON RADIO...THE MOST FAMOUS BROADCASTS STARRED BASIL RATHBONE AS HOLMES AND NIGEL BRUCE AS WATSON FROM 1939 TO 1945

OTHER ACTORS WHO PLAYED HOLMES & WATSON: WILLIAM GILLETTE, CLIVE BROOK, TOM CONWAY, JOHN STANLEY, ALFRED SHIRLEY, BEN WRIGHT & ERIC SNOWDEN

NBC AIRED A BBC-VERSION IN 1954 WITH JOHN GIELGUD AND RALPH RICHARDSON & ORSON WELLES AS HOLMES' ARCH ENEMY MORIARTY!

KNOX MANNING, HARRY BARTELL

JOSEPH BELL

ANNOUNCERS

RADIO SCRIPTS WERE WRITTEN BY EDITH MEISER, DENIS GREEN & ANTHONY BOUCHER

THEME: "MARCH OF THE ANCESTORS" BY GILBERT AND SULLIVAN

SPONSORS: G. WASHINGTON COFFEE, BROMO QUININE, PETRI WINE & CLIPPER-CRAFT CLOTHING

CLIPPER CRAFT

Petri WINES

G. WASHINGTON'S Makes 35 Cups INSTANT COFFEE

RADIO'S GOLDEN YEARS

by FRANK BRESEE & BOBB LYNES

SHOWBOAT

SHOWBOAT WAS A MINSTREL VARIETY SHOW WHICH TOOK PLACE EACH WEEK ON A MYTHICAL BOAT, THAT MOVED UP THE MISSISSIPPI RIVER, FILLED WITH HAPPY VACATIONERS THE SHOW FEATURED SOME OF RADIO'S GREATEST PERSONALITIES AS GUESTS WITH SONGS AND SKETCHES FROM THEIR CAREERS.

CHARLES WININGER STARRED AS "CAPTAIN HENRY"

SPONSOR: MAXWELL HOUSE COFFEE

REGULAR CAST: HATTIE McDANIEL AND PICK MALONE & PAT PADGETT AS BLACKFACE COMEDY TEAM "PICK N' PAT"

VOCALISTS: MURIEL WILSON, ANNETTE HENSHAW AND LANNY ROSS

ORCHESTRAS: DONALD VOORHEES & AL GOODMAN

ANNOUNCERS: "TINY" RUFFNER, WARREN HULL

RADIO'S GOLDEN YEARS ©
by FRANK BRESEE & BOBB LYNES

SILVER THEATRE

SILVER THEATRE WAS A POPULAR CBS FEATURE FROM OCTOBER, 1937 TO AUGUST 1947, PRESENTING HEAVY DRAMAS AND DELIGHTFUL COMEDIES STARRING TOP FILM STARS OF THE DAY INCLUDING: JAMES STEWART, LORETTA YOUNG, CLARK GABLE, BRIAN DONLEVY, JOAN CRAWFORD AND MORE

HOST: CONRAD NAGEL

"SILVER THE... (FINAL REVISION)   3:00 - 3:30 P.M. PST

"LOVE IS WHERE YOU FIND IT"
SUNDAY, MARCH 5, 1939

ORCHESTRA: (OPENING SIGNATURE)
CONTE: INTERNATIONAL SILVER COMPANY presents the
"Silver Theatre!"
(MUSICAL PROGRESSION)
ORCHESTRA: Starring Lee Tracy and Shirley Ross in "Love Is Wher...
CONTE: You Find It" -- directed by Conrad Nagel.
(MUSICAL PROGRESSION)
ORCHESTRA: Brought to you in behalf of tv...
CONTE: in Silverware...International
...er...and 1847 Rogers

1847 ROGERS BROS.
for 102 years
America's Finest Silverplate

SPONSORS: INTERNATIONAL SILVER COMPANY

THE SERIES WAS BROADCAST EACH SUNDAY AFTERNOON COAST-TO-COAST FROM CBS' HOLLYWOOD COLUMBIA SQUARE STUDIOS ON SUNSET BOULEVARD.....

ANNOUNCER: JOHN CONTE

RADIO'S GOLDEN YEARS ©

by FRANK BRESEE & BOBB LYNES

THE SIX-SHOOTER

"THE MAN IN THE SADDLE IS ANGULAR AND LONG-LEGGED, HIS SKIN IS SUN-DYED BROWN. THE GUN IN HIS HOLSTER IS GREY STEEL AND RAINBOW MOTHER-OF-PEARL..... PEOPLE CALL THEM BOTH..... THE SIX SHOOTER"

CREATED AND WRITTEN BY FRANK BURT, THE SIX-SHOOTER CAME TO NBC ON SEPT. 30, 1953, BUT LASTED ONLY ONE SHORT SEASON......

THE SERIES TOLD OF THE ADVENTURES OF COWPOKE-GUNSLINGER "BRITT PONSET" DURING THE FINAL DAYS OF AMERICA'S WILD WEST.

HOLLYWOOD'S BEST RADIO ACTORS WERE HEARD: PARLEY BAER, HOWARD McNEAR, SAM EDWARDS, JEANETTE NOLAN, LARRY DOBKIN, WILL WRIGHT, JACK KRUSCHEN & MORE

ANNOUNCER: HAL GIBNEY

ACADEMY AWARD WINNING ACTOR JAMES STEWART WAS BRITT PONSET

DIRECTOR: JACK JOHNSTONE

RADIO'S GOLDEN YEARS.©

by FRANK BRESEE & BOBB LYNES

RED SKELTON

RICHARD "RED" SKELTON, AMERICA'S CLOWN, BEGAN HIS LONG CAREER AT AGE 10, JOINING A TRAVELING MEDICINE SHOW; THEN INTO VAUDEVILLE & BURLESQUE BY 1928. RED'S RADIO DEBUT WAS ON THE RUDY VALLEE SHOW AUGUST 12, 1937. LATER HE WAS A REGULAR ON AVALON TIME IN 1939. HIS OWN NBC SERIES BEGAN ON OCTOBER 7, 1941.

RED WAS IN THE ARMY FROM MAR. 1944 TO DEC. 4, 1945

HIS SHOW WAS HEARD ON NBC AND CBS UNTIL 1953

MUSICAL DIRECTORS: DAVID FORRESTER, DAVID ROSE

OZZIE NELSON'S BAND MADE THE MUSIC, HARRIET HILLIARD SANG & ACTED ON THE EARLY SERIES

SPONSORS: RALEIGH CIGARETTES, TIDE SOAP & NORGE

REGULAR CAST: LURENE TUTTLE, PAT McGEEHAN, ROD O'CONNOR & VERNA FELTON
RED'S FAMOUS CHARACTERS: JUNIOR (MEAN WIDDLE KID), CLEM KADIDDLEHOPPER, DEADEYE, WILLIE LUMP-LUMP & BOLIVAR SHAGNASTY

RADIO'S GOLDEN YEARS ©

by FRANK BRESEE & BOBB LYNES

SKY KING!

SKYLAR KING WAS AN EX-FBI AGENT AND NAVY PILOT, WHO BECAME A COWBOY RANCHER AND BATTLED THE FORCES OF EVIL.

WITH HIS AIRPLANE "THE SONGBIRD" SKY KING FLEW INTO ADVENTURES FROM HIS ARIZONA RANCH, OFTEN WITH HIS NIECE PENNY AND NEPHEW CLIPPER... MANY ADVENTURES TOOK THEM TO EXOTIC LOCATIONS AROUND THE WORLD

ROY ENGEL

EARL NIGHTINGALE

JACK LESTER

"AMERICA'S FAVORITE FLYING COWBOY" SKY KING WAS PLAYED BY ROY ENGEL; LATER: JACK LESTER AND EARL NIGHTINGALE

ANNOUNCER: MYRON (MIKE) WALLACE

SPONSOR: PETER PAN PEANUT BUTTER

DERBY Peter Pan PEANUT BUTTER

REGULAR CAST:
PENNY...
BERYL VAUGHAN
CLIPPER...
JACK BIVANS

HEARD ON ABC FROM OCT. 28, 1946 TO JUNE 2, 1950; LAST FOUR YEARS ON MBS, ENDING ON JUNE 3, 1954

RADIO'S GOLDEN YEARS©

by FRANK BRESEE & BOBB LYNES

SMILE TIME

SMILE TIME WAS A DAILY 15 MINUTE SUSTAINING COMEDY SERIES HEARD ON MBS DURING THE MID-FORTIES....

THE PROGRAM OPENED WITH THE CAST SINGING THE HAPPY SMILE TIME THEME...

FOLLOWED BY STEVE & WENDELL CONVERSING, THEN A DAILY FEATURE WHICH OFTEN WOULD PARODY POPULAR RADIO SHOWS OF THE DAY SUCH AS: DR.I.Q.(DR.ICE CUBE), LIFE CAN BE BEAUTIFUL (LIFE CAN BE BLAH) AND YOUNG DR.MALONE (YOUNG DR.MAGOON).....

REGULAR CO-STARS WERE WENDELL NOBLE AND JUNE FORAY

MUSIC BY EDDIE TRUMAN, LATER: SKITCH HENDERSON

THE SHOW WAS CREATED BY AND STARRED COMEDY GENIUS STEVE ALLEN

THE PROGRAM WAS BROADCAST FROM THE MUTUAL-DON LEE STUDIOS ON MELROSE IN HOLLYWOOD

RADIO'S GOLDEN YEARS.©

by FRANK BRESEE & BOBB LYNES

SMILIN' ED'S BUSTER BROWN GANG

Looked... NEW RADIO JUST FOR YOU

SMILIN' ED'S BUSTER BROWN GANG DEBUTED ON NBC IN 1944 AND RAN FOR 8 YEARS, ALWAYS BROADCAST LIVE EVERY SATURDAY MORNING FROM HOLLYWOOD.

BUSTER BROWN, A CBS SERIES BASED ON THE FAMOUS COMIC STRIP, RAN IN 1929. BUSTER WAS A BOY WHO LIVED IN A SHOE; HIS DOG, TIGE, LIVED THERE TOO. THE CHARACTER BECAME THE LOGO FOR BUSTER BROWN SHOE COMPANY WHICH SPONSORED THE SHOWS.

BUSTER BROWN SONG:
"I GOT SHOES, YOU GOT SHOES, WHY, EVERYBODY'S GOT TO HAVE SHOES! THERE'S ONLY ONE KIND OF SHOES FOR ME, GOOD OLE BUSTER BROWN SHOES!"

SMILIN' ED McCONNELL, A VETERAN OF VAUDEVILLE, WAS FIRST HEARD ON RADIO IN 1922 AND BY 1940 WAS ON THE NBC AND CBS NETWORKS MONDAYS THRU SATURDAYS.....

HIS IMAGINARY CAST: SQUEAKY THE MOUSE, MIDNIGHT THE CAT, GRANDIE THE PIANO & FROGGY THE GREMLIN....

FROGGY WAS INVISIBLE UNTIL HE "PLUNKED HIS MAGIC TWANGER" SO HE COULD BE SEEN! (MOST VOICES WERE DONE BY ED McCONNELL)

SMILIN' ED TOLD STORIES (FULLY DRAMATIZED WITH MUSIC, SOUND EFFECTS & ACTORS: JUNE FORAY, LOU MERRILL, TOMMY COOK, KEN CHRISTY, CONRAD BINYON & TOMMY BERNARD

MEMBER BUSTER BROWN — SQUEAKY

MEMBER BUSTER BROWN GANG — MIDNIGHT

MUSIC BY: JOHN DUFFY (ORGAN)
KEN CAMERON (PIANO)

PRODUCER - FRANK FERRIN
DIRECTOR - HOBART DONAVAN

ANNOUNCER ARCH PRESBY

221

RADIO'S GOLDEN YEARS©
by FRANK BRESEE & BOBB LYNES

the Jack Smith show

THE OXYDOL SHOW STARRING JACK SMITH WAS A FIVE NIGHT A WEEK, 15 MINUTE PROGRAM ON CBS...

BROADCAST FROM HOLLYWOOD. THE SHOW FEATURED POPULAR MUSIC & GUEST SINGERS

Smith's Favorite Son Skyrocketing to New Fame

Jack Smith
RADIO'S NEWEST STAR
WITH A SONG IN HIS HEART AND A SMILE IN HIS VOICE FOR YOU

"BIG TIME THRUSHING"
—says Walter Winchell

"SINGS with a JAUNTY BOUNCE"
—says Time Magazine

OXYDOL PRESENTS
The Jack Smith Show

Starring JACK SMITH
WITH DON HANCOCK, EARL SHELDON'S ORCHESTRA AND A NEVER-ENDING PARADE OF
FAMOUS GUEST STARS

CBS STATIONS—EVERY NIGHT
MONDAY THRU FRIDAY
TUNE IN—SEE LOCAL PAPER FOR EXACT TIME OF BROADCAST

IN THE EARLY YEARS, MUSIC WAS PROVIDED BY EARL SHELDON'S ORCHESTRA; LATER FRANK DeVOL WAS THE LEADER.

THE SHOW BEGAN IN 1945 AND RAN UNTIL 1951

EXTRA ACTION
Tide
AMERICA'S FAVORITE
Tide's In... Dirt's Out

SPONSORS: PROCTOR & GAMBLE, OXYDOL AND TIDE

OVER THE YEARS, DINAH SHORE & MARGARET WHITING WERE REGULARS ON THE SHOW...

RADIO'S GOLDEN YEARS ©

by FRANK BRESEE & BOBB LYNES

KATE SMITH

THEME SONG: "WHEN THE MOON COMES OVER THE MOUNTAIN..."

KATE SMITH WAS DISCOVERED BY RECORDING MANAGER TED COLLINS IN 1930 WHEN SHE WAS SINGING ON BROADWAY. COLLINS TOOK CHARGE OF HER CAREER......

KATE WAS FIRST HEARD ON NBC, THEN IN 1931 BEGAN HER LONG ASSOCIATION WITH CBS, BEGINNING THE KATE SMITH HOUR IN 1936....

RECORDING FOR COLUMBIA AND RCA-VICTOR, SHE INTRO'D MANY STANDARDS, SELLING MILLIONS OF DISCS

IN 1939 TIME MAGAZINE NAMED HER "THE FIRST LADY OF RADIO"

SHE INTRODUCED IRVING BERLIN'S "GOD BLESS AMERICA" ON HER SHOW AND MADE IT A HIT!

HER GREETING: "HELLO EVERYBODY, THIS IS KATE SMITH"

FAMOUS TAGLINE: "THANKS FOR LISTENIN'"

KATE SMITH INTRODUCED MANY FUTURE STARS ON HER SHOW: ABBOTT & COSTELLO AND "THE ALDRICH FAMILY"

ANDRÉ BARUCH   TED COLLINS
ANNOUNCERS

SPONSORS: A&P, LA PALINA CIGARS, HUDSON MOTORS, GENERAL FOODS

SHE DID OTHER SHOWS OVER THE YEARS: "KATE SMITH SPEAKS," "KATE SMITH SINGS" & "KATE SMITH CALLS"

DURING THE FORTIES SHE WAS ON ABC AND MUTUAL, THEN BACK TO CBS, ENDING HER RADIO DAYS IN 1951

223

RADIO'S GOLDEN YEARS ©

by FRANK BRESEE & BOBB LYNES

TOM CORBETT SPACE CADET

TOM CORBETT, SPACE CADET BEGAN ON CBS-TV OCT. 2, 1950 AND CONTINUED TELECASTS ON NBC-TV, ABC-TV & DUMONT-TV BEFORE MOVING TO ABC-RADIO JAN. 1, 1952. LIKE SPACE PATROL, THE JUVENILE INTERPLANETARY ADVENTURE WENT FROM TV TO RADIO!

BASED ON BOOK "SPACE CADET" BY ROBERT HEINLEIN

THE TV CAST ALSO DID THE RADIO SERIES: FRANKIE THOMAS WAS TOM CORBETT, JAN MERLIN WAS ROGER MANNING, AL MARKIM PLAYED CADET ASTRO & ED BRYCE WAS CAPT. STRONG

JACKSON BECK ANNOUNCED <u>AND</u> PLAYED PARTS ON THE SHOW

THE SERIES WAS ORIGINALLY AIRED AS A 30-MINUTE MON. THRU FRI. OFFERING, ENDING AS A TUES. & THURS. SHOW 'TIL THE FINAL ENTRY DEC., 1952

NOW... AS ROARING ROCKETS BLAST OFF TO DISTANT PLANETS AND FAR-FLUNG STARS, WE TAKE YOU TO THE AGE OF THE CONQUEST OF SPACE, WITH.... TOM CORBETT, SPACE CADET!!

SPONSOR: KELLOGG'S PEP CEREAL

Kellogg's PEP

TV TO RADIO

224

Space Patrol

CREATED BY MIKE MOSER, SPACE PATROL WAS FIRST SEEN ON TV (15 MINUTES, MON.-FRI. ON KECA-ABC, LOS ANGELES) IN SEPT. 1950 AND LATER MOVED TO THE FULL ABC-TV NETWORK...

OPENING: ROCKET BLAST-OFF..... "HIGH ADVENTURE IN THE WILD, VAST REACHES OF SPACE! MISSIONS OF DARING IN THE NAME OF INTERPLANETARY JUSTICE! TRAVEL INTO THE FUTURE WITH BUZZ CORRY COMMANDER-IN-CHIEF OF THE SPACE PATROL!

THE 30 MINUTE ABC RADIO SHOW BEGAN LATER IN 1950 WITH THE SAME CAST FROM TV. WAS HEARD TWICE WEEKLY THEN MOVED TO SATURDAYS FROM 1951, ENDING IN 1955

REGULAR RADIO CAST: ED KEMMER WAS "BUZZ CORRY," LYN OSBORN WAS "CADET HAPPY"

VILLAINS, ETC. WERE PLAYED BY BELA KOVACS, KEN MAYER, LARRY ROBERTSON, NORMAN JOLLY, VIRGINIA HEWITT AND NINA BARA

DIRECTOR: LARRY ROBERTSON

ANNOUNCERS: DICK TUFELD DICK WESSON

SPONSORS: RALSTON CHEX CEREALS, NESTLÉ CHOCOLATE DRINK

EVER READY NESTLÉ'S SWEET HOT COCOA

NEW RICE CHEX

WHEAT CHEX

MAIN VILLAIN WAS "PRINCE BACCARRATTI" (BELA KOVACS)

WRITERS: LOU HUSTON AND NORMAN JOLLY

TV to RADIO

RADIO'S GOLDEN YEARS.©

by FRANK BRESEE & BOBB LYNES

STARS OVER HOLLYWOOD

THE PLAYS WERE LIGHT COMEDIES AND ROMANCE AND SOMETIMES MYSTERY OR SUSPENSE STORIES

STARS OVER HOLLYWOOD WAS PART OF THE SATURDAY MORNING CBS SCHEDULE, DEBUTING IN 1941 AND RUNNING UNTIL 1954

THE ANTHOLOGY SERIES FEATURED TOP MOVIE STARS INCLUDING: JOAN CRAWFORD, BASIL RATHBONE, ALAN LADD, BONITA GRANVILLE, ALAN HALE, MARY ASTOR, MERLE OBERON, ETC...

MANY OF HOLLYWOOD'S BEST RADIO ACTORS SUPPORTED: LURENE TUTTLE, CONRAD BINYON, JANET WALDO, TOM COLLINS, MARY JANE CROFT, HANS CONRIED, PAT McGEEHAN, ECT...

MUSIC: IVAN DITMARS ORCH.

DIRECTORS: PAUL PIERCE, LES MITCHELL

Armour and Company

SPONSORS: DAIRY-RICH, ARMOUR & COMPANY & CARNATION MILK

JIM BANNON

ART GILMORE

FRANK GOSS

ANNOUNCERS:

RADIO'S GOLDEN YEARS ©
by FRANK BRESEE & BOBB LYNES

STOOPNAGLE & BUDD

STOOPNAGLE & BUDD WAS ONE OF RADIO'S EARLIEST COMEDY SHOWS, RUNNING ON THE AIR FROM 1931 TO 1938 ON CBS; LATER ON NBC THE SERIES WAS BEST KNOWN FOR SPOOFING OTHER SHOWS, AND RADIO ITSELF!

DURING THEIR YEARS ON THE AIR, THEY OFFERED MANY CRAZY PREMIUMS SUCH AS WATERING CANS WITH NO HOLES FOR PEOPLE WHO DON'T LIKE TO WATER AND ROUND DICE FOR LISTENERS WHO WOULD RATHER PLAY MARBLES!

MUSIC BY: DONALD VOORHEES, PETER VAN STEEDEN AND MARK WARNOW ORCHESTRAS

VOCALIST: GOGO DE LYS

FREDERICK CHASE TAYLOR WAS "COL. LEMUEL Q. STOOPNAGLE"

WILBUR HULICK WAS "BUDD"

ANNOUNCERS: HARRY VON ZELL, ANDRÉ BARUCH

SPONSORS: IVORY SOAP, PONTIAC, GULF OIL, IPANA AND SAL HEPATICA, MINUTE TAPIOCA, FORD AND CAMEL CIGARETTES

STOOGES: JOAN BANKS, ALICE FROST & SNAG WERRIS

RADIO'S GOLDEN YEARS.©
by FRANK BRESEE & BOBB LYNES

STOP THE MUSIC!

STOP THE MUSIC WAS A MUSICAL QUIZ SHOW THAT OFFERED POPULAR TUNES AND FABULOUS PRIZES WORTH THOUSANDS OF DOLLARS EACH WEEK, BEGINNING IN 1948 ON ABC, HOST BERT PARKS WOULD MAKE RANDOM PHONE CALLS TO VARIOUS PARTS OF THE COUNTRY...
A MUSICAL NUMBER WAS PLAYED & WHEN A PHONE CONNECTION WAS MADE, PARKS WOULD SHOUT: "STOP THE MUSIC!"

FROM THE START THE SUNDAY HOUR-LONG QUIZ WAS IN THE TOP TEN ON THE RATINGS CHARTS PHONE CONTESTANTS WHO GUESSED THE CORRECT TITLE OF THE SONG GOT A CHANCE AT THE "MYSTERY MELODY," WORTH $20,000 IN CASH & PRIZES

ANNOUNCER: DON HANCOCK

CREATED BY LOUIS G. COWAN, DIRECTED BY MARK GOODSON, THE SHOW MOVED LATER TO CBS (HOSTED BY BILL CULLEN) LASTING A TOTAL OF 8 YEARS

SINGERS ON THE SHOW WERE: KAY ARMAN, DICK BROWN, LATER JACK HASKELL & JILL COREY

SPONSOR: OLD GOLD CIGARETTES

Old Gold CIGARETTES

Made by Lorillard, a famous name in tobacco for nearly 200 years

MUSIC BY HARRY SALTER'S ORCHESTRA

BILL CULLEN

RADIO'S GOLDEN YEARS.©

by FRANK BRESEE & BOBB LYNES

STRAIGHT ARROW

MBS

KA-NEE-WAH, FURY!!

STRAIGHT ARROW CAME TO MUTUAL IN EARLY 1949, ORIGINALLY TO PROMOTE AND SELL NABISCO SHREDDED WHEAT CEREAL, AND BECAME VERY POPULAR, LASTING UNTIL 1951.

OPENING:
"KEEN EYES FIXED ON A FLYING TARGET..(MUSIC STING) A GLEAMING ARROW SET AGAINST A RAWHIDE STRING... A STRONG BOW BENT ALMOST TO THE BREAKING POINT, AND THEN.....(SOUND: ARROW HITS TARGET)..... STRAAAIIIGGGHHTT ARROW!"

NABISCO shredded wheat presents - STRAIGHT ARROW - a thrilling new adventure story from the exciting days of the old West!....To friends and neighbors alike, Steve Adams appeared to be nothing more than the young owner of the Broken Bow cattlespread. But when danger threatened innocent people and when evildoers plotted against justice - then Steve Adams, rancher, disappeared - and in his place came a mysterious stalwart Indian, (MUSIC: PICK UP INDIAN MOTIF HERE) a Comanche - wearing the dress and war paint of galloping out of the darkness to take up the cause of law and order throughout the west - comes the legendary figure of STRAIGHT ARROW!
FINISH INTRO AND UNDER:

HOWARD CULVER

PRODUCER-DIRECTOR: TED ROBERTSON

ANNOUNCER: FRANK BINGMAN

NABISCO

HOWARD CULVER PLAYED STEVE/ARROW HIS SIDEKICK, PACKY WAS FRED HOWARD

OVER A TOM-TOM BEAT: "N-A-B-I-S-C-O NABISCO IS THE NAME TO KNOW; FOR A BREAKFAST YOU CAN'T BEAT, TRY NABISCO SHREDDED WHEAT!"

RADIO'S GOLDEN YEARS ©
by FRANK BRESEE & BOBB LYNES

STUDIO ONE

STUDIO ONE FEATURED DRAMATIZATIONS OF LITERATURE'S BEST KNOWN WORKS. THE WEEKLY HOUR LONG PROGRAM, ORIGINATING IN THE NEW YORK STUDIOS OF CBS, ALSO PRESENTED POPULAR BROADWAY PLAYS......

THE SERIES PRESENTED SUCH MEMORABLE WORKS AS: "A TREE GROWS IN BROOKLYN", "RED BADGE OF COURAGE" AND "A FAREWELL TO ARMS"

STUDIO ONE FEATURED BROADWAY'S FINEST RADIO ACTORS SUPPORTING SUCH STARS AS: ROBERT YOUNG, EDWARD G. ROBINSON, CHARLES LAUGHTON AND MADELEINE CARROLL

HOST-DIRECTOR: FLETCHER MARKLE

PAUL STEWART, PAUL McGRATH, ROBERT DRYDEN, JOE DeSANTIS, EVERETT SLOANE, MERCEDES McCAMBRIDGE

ANNOUNCER: LEE VINES

DEBUTED ON APRIL 29, 1947 & RAN ONE YEAR

RADIO'S GOLDEN YEARS ©

by FRANK BRESEE & BOBB LYNES

LOOK.... UP IN THE SKY!!
IT'S A BIRD! IT'S A PLANE!
IT'S SUPERMAN!

BASED ON THE COMIC BOOK, SUPERMAN BEGAN ON SYNDICATED RADIO IN 1940, LATER WAS HEARD AS A DAILY 15 MIN. SERIAL ON MUTUAL UNTIL 1949; ENDING AS A 30 MINUTE WEEKLY SHOW ON ABC IN 1951.....

SPONSORS:

SUPERMAN/CLARK KENT WAS BUD COLLYER....

REGULAR CAST INCLUDED JOAN ALEXANDER (LOIS LANE), JACKIE KELK (JIMMY OLSEN) & JULIEN NOA (PERRY WHITE)

ABC

Brach's

Kellogg's PEP WHOLE WHEAT FLAKES

MATT CROWLEY GUESTED AS "BATMAN" RONNY LISS WAS "ROBIN"

ANNOUNCER-ACTOR JACKSON BECK

30 MIN. SERIES STARRED MICHAEL FITZMAURICE

BUD COLLYER

RADIO'S GOLDEN YEARS.©

by FRANK BRESEE & BOBB LYNES

"THIS IS THE MAN IN BLACK... WELCOMING YOU TO RADIO'S OUTSTANDING THEATRE OF THRILLS!"

SUSPENSE!!

FOR 20 YEARS (COAST-TO-COAST ON CBS) SUSPENSE WAS THE ULTIMATE HORROR/MYSTERY PROGRAM ON RADIO (1942-1962). EACH WEEK A TOP MOVIE OR RADIO ACTOR WOULD STAR IN CLASSIC AND ORIGINAL LITERARY WORKS:.....

EARLY HOST: BERRY KROEGER

JOSEPH KEARNS

STARS INCLUDED: CARY GRANT, ORSON WELLES, VINCENT PRICE, EDWARD G. ROBINSON, JOAN CRAWFORD & AGNES MOOREHEAD

LONGTIME SPONSORS: ROMA WINES, AUTOLITE SPARKPLUGS

ROMA WINES

DIRECTORS WERE WILLIAM ROBSON, WILLIAM SPIER, ELLIOTT LEWIS...

TRUMAN BRADLEY

HARLOW WILCOX

ANNOUNCERS:

GEORGE WALSH

MOST POPULAR SUSPENSE STORY WAS LUCILLE FLETCHER'S "SORRY, WRONG NUMBER" WITH AGNES MOOREHEAD, BROADCAST 8 TIMES.....

RADIO'S GOLDEN YEARS ©

by FRANK BRESEE & BOBB LYNES

BOB SWEENEY & HAL MARCH

THE SWEENEY AND MARCH SHOW, STARRING BOB SWEENEY AND HAL MARCH, BEGAN AS A VARIETY SHOW IN 1946 AND WITHIN A SHORT TIME BECAME A HILARIOUS SITUATION COMEDY......

THE SHOW REVOLVED AROUND THE ADVENTURES OF TWO YOUNG RADIO COMEDIAN/ROOM-MATES WHO WERE GIVEN A COMEDY SERIES ON CBS

CAST INCLUDED: HANS CONRIED, JANE MORGAN, FLORENCE HALOP

BOB SWEENEY – A VERY BUSY CHARACTER ACTOR ON RADIO AND TV, HE LATER WAS A VERY SUCCESSFUL TV SITUATION-COMEDY DIRECTOR

HAL MARCH – IN THE MID-1950s HE BECAME HOST OF THE WELL-KNOWN $64,000 QUESTION TV QUIZ SHOW

ANNOUNCER: BOB LEMOND

MUSIC: WILBUR HATCH; LATER, LUD GLUSKIN

RADIO'S GOLDEN YEARS©

by FRANK BRESEE & BOBB LYNES

TAKE IT OR LEAVE IT

IN 1940 ONE QUIZ SHOW WOULD DOMINATE THE RADIO AIRWAVES.... BROADCAST FROM NEW YORK WITH OCCASIONAL REMOTES FROM LOS ANGELES, TAKE IT OR LEAVE IT WAS ALSO KNOWN AS THE $64 QUESTION PROGRAM

BETWEEN 1940 AND 1950 THE SHOW WAS HEARD AT TIMES ON CBS & NBC CONTESTANTS WERE CHOSEN FROM THE STUDIO AUDIENCE, BROUGHT TO THE STAGE & HAD A CHANCE TO WIN UP TO $64 BY ANSWERING QUESTIONS CORRECTLY...

COLUMBIA BROADCASTING SYSTEM
COLUMBIA SQUARE PLAYHOUSE
6121 SUNSET BLVD · HOLLYWOOD

No. 926

STUDIO A CBS

EVERSHARP PRESENTS
"TAKE IT OR LEAVE IT"
starring
PHIL BAKER
with
EDGAR FAIRCHILD AND HIS ORCHESTRA

Sunday OCT. 18
1942
7 to 7:30 p.m.
Doors Close at 6:30 p.m.

No. 926
"TAKE IT OR LEAVE IT"

CHILDREN UNDER 18 YEARS WILL NOT BE ADMITTED

EVERSHARP

SPONSOR: EVERSHARP

OVER THE YEARS MANY EMCEES HOSTED THE SHOW: PHIL BAKER, BOB HAWK, GARRY MOORE, EDDIE CANTOR & JACK PAAR

ANNOUNCERS: DAVID ROSS, KEN NILES & & JAY STEWART

CATCH PHRASES: "YOU'LL BE SORR-EE!" (WHEN CONTESTANT WAS TRYING FOR THE $64)

RADIO'S GOLDEN YEARS©

by FRANK BRESEE & BOBB LYNES

TARZAN OF THE AIR

TARZAN WENT ON THE AIR IN SEPTEMBER, 1932. BASED ON EDGAR RICE BURROUGH'S' TARZAN OF THE APES, IT WAS ONE OF THE EARLIEST NATIONALLY SYNDICATED RADIO SERIES. A WEST COAST SPONSOR WAS SIGNAL GASOLINE

IN THE EARLY DAYS IT WAS A DAILY 15 MINUTE ADVENTURE STARRING JIM PIERCE AND WIFE JOAN (BURROUGH'S DAUGHTER) & FEATURING SUCH RADIO STARS AS GALE GORDON, JOHN McINTIRE AND JEANETTE NOLAN...

FROM THE HEART OF THE JUNGLE COMES A SAVAGE CRY OF VICTORY... THIS IS TARZAN..... LORD OF THE JUNGLE!!

SIGNAL TARZAN RADIO PREMIER
SEPT. 10 SAT. MIDNITE 11:30
FOX PANTAGES
6233 HOLLYWOOD BLVD.
MIDNITE 1932 ADMIT ONE

SIGNAL TARZAN RADIO PREMIER
FOX PANTAGES
MID SAT. EVE.
NITE SEPT. 10

A PROGRAM WITH A **READYMADE AUDIENCE**

PRODUCED AND DISTRIBUTED BY

EDGAR RICE BURROUGHS, INC. TARZANA, CALIFORNIA

JIM PIERCE AND JOAN BURROUGHS PIERCE

THE DEBUT PROGRAM OF THE SERIES WAS RECORDED AT THE HOLLYWOOD PANTAGES THEATRE ON SEPT. 10, 1932

IN 1952 & 1953, A 30-MINUTE VERSION OF TARZAN STARRING LAMONT JOHNSON WAS HEARD SATURDAYS ON CBS, SPONSORED BY GENERAL FOODS

RADIO'S GOLDEN YEARS ©

by FRANK BRESEE & BOBB LYNES

TERRY AND THE PIRATES

TERRY AND THE PIRATES WAS BASED ON THE VERY POPULAR COMIC STRIP OF THE SAME NAME CREATED BY MILTON CANIFF...CAME TO RADIO IN 1939 AND FOR OVER TEN YEARS TOLD THE ADVENTURES OF TERRY LEE & HIS FRIENDS PAT RYAN, FLIP CORKIN, CONNIE-THE-COOLIE & HOTSHOT CHARLIE

IN 1943, TERRY TEAMED UP WITH HIS OLD ENEMY, THE DRAGON LADY (ON THE SIDE OF THE CHINESE) TO DESTROY A JAPANESE SUPPLY DEPOT NEAR THE YELLOW RIVER....

TERRY WAS PLAYED BY JACKIE KELK (OF THE ALDRICH FAMILY) LATER BY CLIFF CARPENTER & OWEN JORDAN HIS SIDEKICK PAT RYAN WAS CLAYTON (SUPERMAN) COLLYER, LARRY ALEXANDER, WARNER ANDERSON & BOB GRIFFIN THE DRAGON LADY WAS AGNES MOOREHEAD & ADELAIDE KLEIN; FLIP CORKIN WAS TED DE CORSIA

EACH DAILY 15-MINUTE SHOW OPENED WITH THE SOUND OF A GONG...THEN CYMBALS & A GROUP OF CHINESE JABBERING. IT FEATURED ALL THE INTRIGUE OF THOSE ROMANTIC YEARS IN THE MYSTERIOUS FAR EAST.....

THE SERIES WAS HEARD ON NBC-BLUE, LATER ON ABC

ANNOUNCER: DOUG BROWNING

TUNE IN *TERRY AND THE PIRATES* MONDAY THRU FRIDAY 5:00 P.M. WEBR

RADIO'S GOLDEN YEARS ©

by FRANK BRESEE & BOBB LYNES

TALES OF THE TEXAS RANGERS

TALES OF THE TEXAS RANGERS FEATURED STORIES BASED ON ACTUAL CASE HISTORIES FROM THE FILES OF THE TEXAS RANGERS....

WHILE THE AUTHENTIC RE-ENACTMENTS TOOK PLACE IN MODERN-DAY TEXAS, RANGER JACE PEARSON MANY TIMES RELIED ON HIS HORSE TO BRING THE BAD GUYS TO JUSTICE

THE SERIES BEGAN ON NBC ON JULY 8, 1950 AND RAN FOR 2 YEARS

NARRATOR WAS TONY BARRETT

ANNOUNCER: HAL GIBNEY

PRODUCER-DIRECTOR: STACY KEACH

WRITER: JOEL MURCOTT

SUPPORT CAST: PEGGY WEBBER, ED BEGLEY, PARLEY BAER, KEN CHRISTY, HERB VIGRAN, BARNEY PHILLIPS, SAM EDWARDS, HARRY BARTELL AND NESTOR PAIVA

MOVIE STAR JOEL McCREA WAS THE STAR EACH WEEK AS JACE PEARSON

SPONSORS: WHEATIES AND NBC

NBC

WHEATIES

"Breakfast of Champions"

RADIO'S GOLDEN YEARS.©
by FRANK BRESEE & BOBB LYNES

THE THIN MAN

THE ADVENTURES OF THE THIN MAN WAS BASED ON THE POPULAR MGM FILM SERIES OF THE SAME NAME. IT FEATURED NICK CHARLES AND HIS WIFE, NORA, AS THEY FOUGHT CRIME & CRIMINALS AND BROUGHT BAD GUYS TO JUSTICE

LES DAMON

DAVID GOTHARD

JOE CURTIN

RETIRED PRIVATE EYE NICK CHARLES WAS PLAYED OVER THE YEARS BY LES DAMON, LES TREMAYNE, DAVID GOTHARD & JOSEPH CURTIN. NORA WAS ALWAYS CLAUDIA MORGAN

THE SERIES BEGAN ON NBC IN 1941, MOVED TO CBS IN 1942, BACK TO NBC IN 1948, ENDING ON ABC IN 1950....

PRODUCER-DIRECTOR HIMAN BROWN

ANNOUNCERS: RON RAWSON, ED HERLIHY

SPONSORS: POST CEREALS, SANKA COFFEE, WOODBURY SOAP, PABST BEER & HEINZ

Pabst Blue Ribbon

WOODBURY FACIAL SOAP

SANKA COFFEE

HEINZ 57 VARIETIES

Post

RADIO'S GOLDEN YEARS ©
by FRANK BRESEE & BOBB LYNES

TOM MIX STRAIGHT SHOOTERS

THE TOM MIX RALSTON STRAIGHT SHOOTERS WAS ONE OF THE EARLY DAILY MONDAY-FRIDAY 15 MINUTE WESTERN-MYSTERY SHOWS DEBUTED ON SEPTEMBER 25, 1933

CALLED "RADIO'S BIGGEST WESTERN-DETECTIVE PROGRAM", IT WAS BASED ON THE TRUE ADVENTURES OF REAL-LIFE COWBOY STAR TOM MIX...

THE ORIGINAL STARS IN THE 1930'S WERE ARTELLS DICKSON, JACK HOLDEN AND RUSSELL THORSON; FROM JUNE, 1944 JOE "CURLEY" BRADLEY <u>WAS</u> TOM MIX UNTIL THE END ON JUNE 23, 1950..

SPONSOR: RALSTON CEREALS

CURLEY BRADLEY

JACK HOLDEN

RUSSELL THORSON

ANNOUNCER: DON GORDON

TOM MIX'S HORSE WAS "TONY"

TOM MIX SHOW THEME:
"SHREDDED RALSTON FOR YOUR BREAKFAST,
STARTS THE DAY OFF SHINING BRIGHT.
GIVES YOU LOTS OF COWBOY ENERGY,
WITH A FLAVOR THAT'S JUST RIGHT.
IT'S DELICIOUS AND NUTRITIOUS,
BITE-SIZE AND READY-TO-EAT.
TAKE A TIP FROM TOM,
GO AND TELL YOUR MOM:
SHREDDED RALSTON CAN'T BE BEAT!"

REGULARS ON THE SERIES:
"SHERIFF MIKE SHAW" (HAL PEARY, WILLARD WATERMAN, LEO CURLEY) HANDYMAN-COOK "WASH" (FORREST LEWIS) & TOM'S YOUNG WARD "JANE" (JANE WEBB)

ONE OF THE FIRST SHOWS TO OFFER PREMIUMS FOR A BOX-TOP AND A DIME: WHISTLING BADGE & RING, COMIC BOOKS, SET OF 5 BUTTONS WITH CAST PICTURES, GLOW-IN-THE-DARK COMPASS, SPURS, FINGERPRINT SET, WOODEN GUN AND MORE!!
THE ADDRESS: TOM MIX, BOX 808, ST. LOUIS, MO.

HEARD OVER THE YEARS ON NBC-BLUE AND MUTUAL

RADIO'S GOLDEN YEARS ©

by FRANK BRESEE & BOBB LYNES

ARTHUR TRACY
"THE STREET SINGER"

ARTHUR TRACY, "THE STREET SINGER" BEGAN HIS RADIO CAREER ON NEW YORK'S WMCA IN 1929 AND BY 1931 BECAME A NATIONAL SENSATION HEARD BY MILLIONS COAST-TO-COAST ON THE CBS NETWORK

DURING HIS HEYDAY HE RECEIVED THOUSANDS OF LETTERS WEEKLY, MADE VERY POPULAR RECORDS AND WAS IN "THE BIG BROADCAST" WITH BING CROSBY, BURNS & ALLEN, KATE SMITH AND OTHERS

HIT RECORDS: "PENNIES FROM HEAVEN" AND "MARTA" (HIS LONG-TIME THEME SONG)

Pillsbury
BEST XXXX

SPONSORS: PILLSBURY, GROVES LAB-ORATORIES

WHEN HE CELEBRATED HIS 97TH BIRTHDAY IN 1996 HE BECAME THE OLDEST LIVING SHOW BUSINESS PERSONALITY AND CONTINUES TO SING AT VARIOUS FUNCTIONS & CONVENTIONS IN THE U.S. AND ENGLAND.

RADIO'S GOLDEN YEARS ©
by FRANK BRESEE & BOBB LYNES

OPENING: HELLO THERE, WE'VE BEEN WAITING FOR YOU! IT'S TIME TO PLAY....

"AREN'T WE DEVILS?"

TRUTH or CONSEQUENCES

RALPH EDWARDS CREATED AND HOSTED TRUTH OR CONSEQUENCES FOR ITS LONG RADIO RUN FROM APRIL 3, 1940 TO SEPT. 15, 1956 FIRST ON CBS, LATER ON NBC.

TRUTH or CONSEQUENCES WAS MOSTLY SLAPSTICK, WITH CONTESTANTS BEING BELTED IN THE FACE WITH PIES OR DROPPED IN A TUB OF WATER

"BEULAH THE BUZZER" INDICATED THAT THE CONTESTANT HAD FAILED TO TELL THE TRUTH (ANSWER A QUESTION) AND MUST PAY THE CONSEQUENCES

IN 1948 T or C HAD A CONTEST IN WHICH JACK BENNY WAS FEATURED AS "THE WALKING MAN"... THE CONTESTANT WHO IDENTIFIED HIM RECEIVED $22,500.....

RADIO'S MOST FAMOUS ANNOUNCERS WERE FEATURED OVER THE YEARS: CLAYTON "BUD" COLLYER, MEL ALLEN, JAY STEWART, MILTON CROSS, ED HERLIHY, HARLOW WILCOX, KEN CARPENTER & CHARLIE LYON

DUZ

PROCTOR & GAMBLE'S DUZ SOAP SPONSORED THE SHOW FOR 10 YEARS (A RECORD!)

MUSIC THEME: "MERRILY WE ROLL ALONG"

OVER THE YEARS THE SHOW HELPED RAISE MILLIONS OF DOLLARS FOR CHARITIES; HEART FUND, ETC.....

RADIO'S GOLDEN YEARS.©

by FRANK BRESEE & BOBB LYNES

the RUDY VALLÉE Show

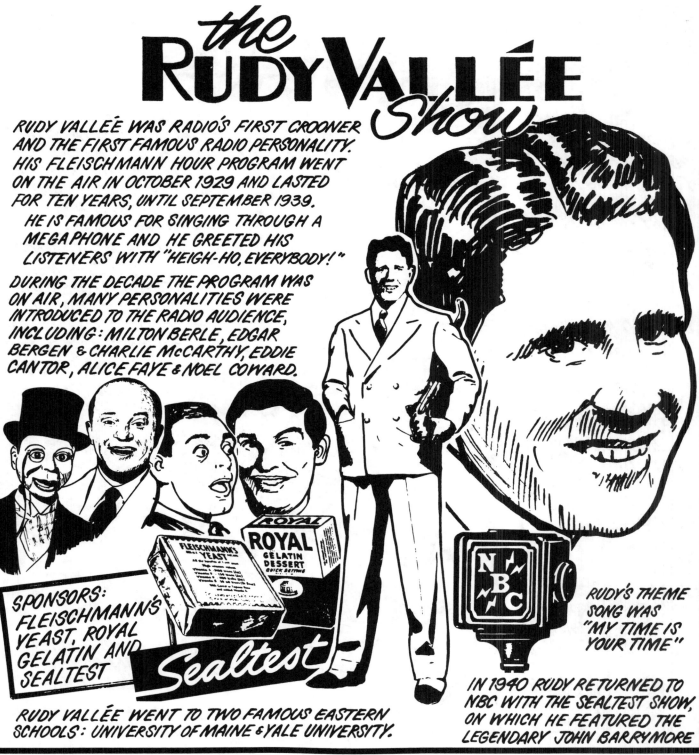

RUDY VALLÉE WAS RADIO'S FIRST CROONER AND THE FIRST FAMOUS RADIO PERSONALITY. HIS FLEISCHMANN HOUR PROGRAM WENT ON THE AIR IN OCTOBER 1929 AND LASTED FOR TEN YEARS, UNTIL SEPTEMBER 1939.

HE IS FAMOUS FOR SINGING THROUGH A MEGAPHONE AND HE GREETED HIS LISTENERS WITH "HEIGH-HO, EVERYBODY!"

DURING THE DECADE THE PROGRAM WAS ON AIR, MANY PERSONALITIES WERE INTRODUCED TO THE RADIO AUDIENCE, INCLUDING: MILTON BERLE, EDGAR BERGEN & CHARLIE McCARTHY, EDDIE CANTOR, ALICE FAYE & NOEL COWARD.

SPONSORS: FLEISCHMANN'S YEAST, ROYAL GELATIN AND SEALTEST

RUDY VALLÉE WENT TO TWO FAMOUS EASTERN SCHOOLS: UNIVERSITY OF MAINE & YALE UNIVERSITY.

RUDY'S THEME SONG WAS "MY TIME IS YOUR TIME"

IN 1940 RUDY RETURNED TO NBC WITH THE SEALTEST SHOW, ON WHICH HE FEATURED THE LEGENDARY JOHN BARRYMORE

RADIO'S GOLDEN YEARS ©

by FRANK BRESEE & BOBB LYNES

VIC & SADE

VIC & SADE WAS ONE OF THE EARLIEST OF ALL RADIO SERIAL COMEDIES DEBUTING IN JUNE 1932 AND RUNNING OVER THE YEARS ON BOTH CBS AND NBC UNTIL LATE 1946. THE SHOW RELATED THE DAY TO DAY STORY OF THE ECCENTRIC GOOK FAMILY (VIC & SADE AND THEIR SON, RUSH) IN THE LITTLE TOWN OF CROOPER, ILLINOIS

ART VAN HARVEY "VIC"

BERNARDINE FLYNN "SADE"

ANNOUNCERS RALPH EDWARDS, ED ROBERTS, ED HERLIHY AND BOB BROWN

BILLY IDELSON "RUSH"

CLARENCE HARTZELL "UNCLE FLETCHER"

THE RADIO GENIUS WHO CREATED AND WROTE "VIC & SADE" WAS PAUL RHYMER

THE GOOKS LIVED IN "THE LITTLE HOUSE HALFWAY UP IN THE NEXT BLOCK".....

Crisco FINEST VEGETABLE SHORTENING

SPONSOR: PROCTOR & GAMBLE

THERE ARE GROUPS OF FANS (FRIENDS OF VIC & SADE, VIC & SADISTS, ETC.) THROUGHOUT THE COUNTRY WHICH CONTINUE TO PAY TRIBUTE TO VIC & SADE AND TAPES OF THEIR SHOWS ARE IN GREAT DEMAND BY COLLECTORS....

THEME SONG: "CHANSON BOHEMIENNE"

RADIO'S GOLDEN YEARS©

by FRANK BRESEE & BOBB LYNES

VOYAGE OF THE SCARLET QUEEN

THE VOYAGE OF THE SCARLET QUEEN STARRED VERSATILE RADIO ACTOR ELLIOTT LEWIS IN A SERIES OF HIGH ADVENTURES WHICH SAW HIM AS MASTER OF THE KETCH "SCARLET QUEEN, THE PROUDEST SHIP TO PLOW THE SEAS". THE "QUEEN" ROAMED THE SOUTH PACIFIC IN SEARCH OF EXCITEMENT.....

OPENING:
"LOG ENTRY....THE KETCH SCARLET QUEEN, PHILIP CARNEY, MASTER. POSITION: 3 DEGREES, 7 MINUTES NORTH, 104 DEGREES, 2 MINUTES EAST. WIND: FRESH TO MODERATE. SKY: FAIR"

THE PROGRAM WAS CREATED BY ELLIOTT LEWIS AND SOME OF HIS BUDDIES FROM HIS DAYS IN ARMED FORCES RADIO

ELLIOTT LEWIS: "PHILIP CARNEY"

ED MAX: "FIRST MATE, MR. GALLAGHER"

CAST: MARVIN MILLER, BILL CONRAD, GLORIA BLONDELL, BARTON YARBOROUGH, CATHY LEWIS, HERB BUTTERFIELD, JOHN DEHNER, MORE

MUSIC: DICK AURANDT

ANNOUNCER: CHARLES ARLINGTON

WRITERS: GIL DOUD, ROBT. TALLMAN

THE SERIES WAS HEARD ON MUTUAL BEGINNING JULY 3, 1947

RADIO'S GOLDEN YEARS ©
by FRANK BRESEE & BOBB LYNES

Walter Winchell

"GOOD EVENING MR. & MRS. NORTH & SOUTH AMERICA... AND ALL THE SHIPS AT SEA, LET'S GO TO PRESS! FLASH!"

FAMED NEWSPAPER COLUMNIST WALTER WINCHELL, WENT ON RADIO ON AUGUST 30, 1931 AND HIS SHOW WAS A POPULAR FEATURE FOR 26 YEARS.... ON HIS NEWSCAST HE SPOKE 215 WORDS A MINUTE, THE FASTEST IN RADIO! AT ONE TIME HIS SUNDAY NIGHT PROGRAM WAS HEARD BY MORE THAN 33 MILLION LISTENERS

OVER THE YEARS HIS PROGRAM WAS HEARD ON CBS, NBC, ABC & MUTUAL

HIS LONGTIME SPONSOR WAS JERGENS LOTION (JERGENS JOURNAL) LATER, GRUEN WATCHES & KAISER-FRAZER AUTOMOBILES

HE BEGAN HIS CAREER AT THE AGE OF 13 WHEN HE JOINED HIS BOYHOOD FRIENDS EDDIE CANTOR AND GEORGE JESSEL IN A MUSICAL ACT.

HIS LONGTIME ANNOUNCER: BEN GRAUER

JERGENS LOTION

GRUEN

DURING THE 1930s WINCHELL HAD A PHONEY RADIO "FEUD" WITH BANDLEADER BEN BERNIE

IN THE 1950s WINCHELL'S SHOW WAS ALSO SEEN ON ABC-TV; HE LATER NARRATED THE VERY POPULAR "UNTOUCHABLES" SERIES

RADIO'S GOLDEN YEARS©

by FRANK BRESEE & BOBB LYNES

WEBER & FIELDS

JOE WEBER AND LEW FIELDS WERE ONE OF THE MOST POPULAR TEAMS IN VAUDEVILLE; THEY WERE ALSO ONE OF THE EARLIEST COMEDY DUOS TO APPEAR ON RADIO.... THEY WERE HEARD ON WEAF, NEW YORK ON THE EVEREADY HOUR, THE FIRST MAJOR VARIETY SHOW ON RADIO. THE PROGRAM BEGAN IN 1923 AND WITH THE FORMATION OF NBC (11-15-26) IT BECAME THE FIRST BIG NETWORK VARIETY SHOW

OVER THE YEARS, IN ADDITION TO RADIO AND VAUDEVILLE APPEARANCES, WEBER AND FIELDS MADE MOVIE SHORT SUBJECTS AND~BETWEEN 1912 & 1916 PRESENTED MANY OF THEIR ROUTINES ON PHONOGRAPH RECORDS

THEY PASSED AWAY WITHIN A YEAR OF EACH OTHER: LEW FIELDS IN 1941 AND JOE WEBER IN 1942.....

RADIO'S GOLDEN YEARS ©

by FRANK BRESEE & BOBB LYNES

WILD BILL HICKOK

WILD BILL HICKOK WAS ONE OF A HANDFUL OF TV SERIES THAT ALSO MOVED TO RADIO, DEBUTING ON MBS DECEMBER 31, 1951 RUNNING THROUGH 1956....

WILD BILL HICKOK WAS PLAYED BY GUY MADISON

JINGLES JONES, HIS CHUBBY SIDEKICK, WAS ANDY DEVINE

MBS

Kellogg's SUGAR CORN POPS

Kellogg's SUGAR CORN

Kellogg's SUGAR CORN POPS

"YIP-EE!
A rip snortin' cereal—
a rootin' tootin' snack!"

SPONSOR: KELLOGG'S CEREALS

TV TO RADIO

BASED ON THE LEGENDARY ADVENTURES OF REAL-LIFE WESTERN LAW-MAN, JAMES BUTLER HICKOK, THE SHOW FEATURED HOLLYWOOD'S BEST CHARACTER ACTORS: RALPH MOODY, TYLER McVEY, CURLEY BRADLEY, PAUL DUBOV, HOWARD McNEAR, KEN CHRISTY & EARLE ROSS...

RADIO'S GOLDEN YEARS.

by FRANK BRESEE & BOBB LYNES

THE WITCH'S TALE

MIRIAM WOLFE (AGE 13)

OPENING: "WELCOME TO THE WITCH'S TALE! THE FASCINATION OF THE EERIE! WEIRD, BLOOD-CHILLING TALES....TOLD BY NANCY, THE WITCH OF SALEM... AND SATAN, HER WISE BLACK CAT. THEY ARE WAITING.... WAITING FOR YOU NOW!..".

THE WITCH'S TALE WAS ONE OF THE EARLIEST HORROR SHOWS TO BE BROADCAST. IT BEGAN IN 1931 ON WOR-NEW YORK, AND WITHIN THREE YEARS IT WAS HEARD COAST-TO-COAST ON THE MUTUAL BROADCASTING SYSTEM..

THE SERIES FEATURED STORIES OF TERROR AND SUPERNATURAL AS INTRODUCED BY "OLD NANCY," KEEPER OF THE KEY TO THE MASTER BOOK OF HER GHOST STORIES

OLD NANCY WAS PLAYED BY ADELAIDE FITZ ALLEN, LATER BY MIRIAM WOLFE (AT 13 YEARS OLD!) AND MARTHA WENTWORTH

CAST MEMBERS: DON McLAUGHLIN, MARIE FLYNN, MARK SMITH

MARTHA WENTWORTH

RADIO'S GOLDEN YEARS ©
by FRANK BRESEE & BOBB LYNES

WLS NATIONAL BARN DANCE

THE FIRST RADIO BARN DANCE DEBUTED ON CHICAGO'S WLS IN APRIL, 1924, DURING THE STATION'S FIRST WEEK ON THE AIR. THE WEEKLY SHOW FEATURED SQUARE DANCES, HILLBILLY SONGS, BARBERSHOP QUARTETS, COWBOY, FOLK & FIDDLE MUSIC, COMEDY SKITS AND DRAMA.

FOUNDER GEORGE D. HAY, "THE SOLEMN OL' JUDGE"

LONG-TIME HOST WAS JOE KELLY

ANNOUNCER: JACK HOLDEN

SPONSORS: ALKA-SELTZER, PHILLIPS MILK OF MAGNESIA

GENUINE PHILLIPS MILK OF MAGNESIA

Alka-Seltzer

THE FINAL LOCAL WLS NATIONAL BARN DANCE BROADCAST WAS ON APRIL 30, 1960

EARLY STARS: HENRY BURR, GRACE WILSON, BRADLEY KINCAID, GENE AUTRY, LULUBELLE & SCOTTY, THE HOOSIER HOT-SHOTS, RED FOLEY, PAT BUTTRAM, SMILEY BURNETT, PAT (UNCLE EZRA) BARRETT, GEORGIE GOBEL, PATSY MONTANA, LOUISE MASSEY & WESTERNERS; LATER DINNING SISTERS, BOB ATCHER & REX ALLEN...

THE SHOW BECAME THE NATIONAL BARN DANCE WHEN A 60-MINUTE PORTION OF THE 4-HOUR SATURDAY NIGHT SHOW BEGAN ON NBC-BLUE (FROM SEPT. 30, 1933 TO 1946). MOVING TO ABC IN 1948, IT ENDED IN 1950

WLS
THE PRAIRIE FARMER STATION - - CHICAGO

ORIGINALLY OWNED BY SEARS, ROEBUCK AND COMPANY... WORLD'S LARGEST STORE

ABC

RADIO'S GOLDEN YEARS©

by FRANK BRESEE & BOBB LYNES

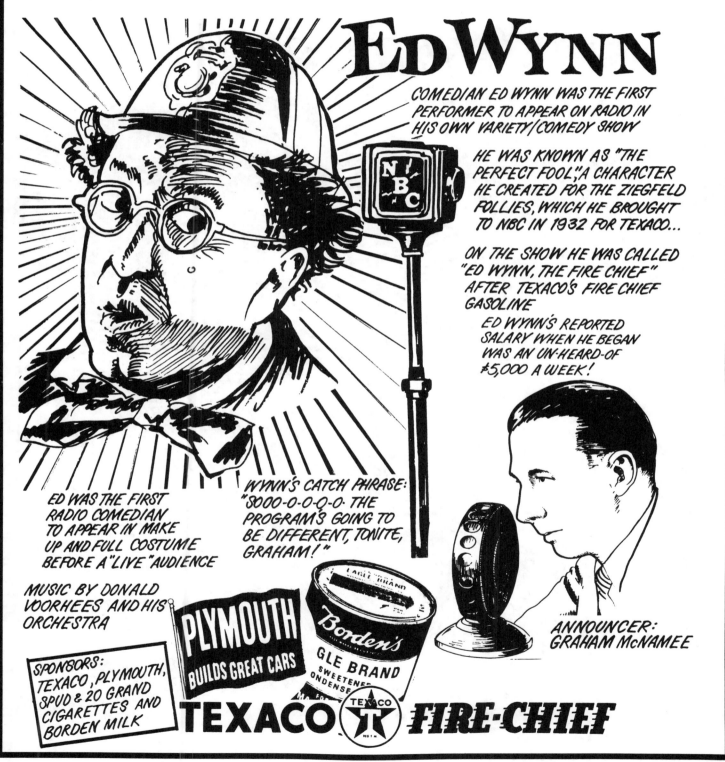

ED WYNN

COMEDIAN ED WYNN WAS THE FIRST PERFORMER TO APPEAR ON RADIO IN HIS OWN VARIETY/COMEDY SHOW

HE WAS KNOWN AS "THE PERFECT FOOL", A CHARACTER HE CREATED FOR THE ZIEGFELD FOLLIES, WHICH HE BROUGHT TO NBC IN 1932 FOR TEXACO...

ON THE SHOW HE WAS CALLED "ED WYNN, THE FIRE CHIEF" AFTER TEXACO'S FIRE CHIEF GASOLINE

ED WYNN'S REPORTED SALARY WHEN HE BEGAN WAS AN UN-HEARD-OF $5,000 A WEEK!

ED WAS THE FIRST RADIO COMEDIAN TO APPEAR IN MAKE UP AND FULL COSTUME BEFORE A "LIVE" AUDIENCE

WYNN'S CATCH PHRASE: "SOOO-O-O-O-O- THE PROGRAM'S GOING TO BE DIFFERENT, TONITE, GRAHAM!"

MUSIC BY DONALD VOORHEES AND HIS ORCHESTRA

ANNOUNCER: GRAHAM McNAMEE

SPONSORS: TEXACO, PLYMOUTH, SPUD & 20 GRAND CIGARETTES AND BORDEN MILK

PLYMOUTH BUILDS GREAT CARS

Borden's EAGLE BRAND SWEETENED CONDENSED

TEXACO FIRE-CHIEF

RADIO'S GOLDEN YEARS

by FRANK BRESEE & BOBB LYNES

X-MINUS ONE

OPENING:
"COUNTDOWN FOR BLAST-OFF...
X-MINUS 5,4,3,2, X-MINUS 1... FIRE!
(ROCKET BLAST) FROM THE FAR
HORIZONS OF THE UNKNOWN
COME TRANSCRIBED TALES
OF NEW DIMENSIONS IN TIME
AND SPACE. THESE ARE STORIES
OF THE FUTURE, ADVENTURES IN
WHICH YOU'LL LIVE IN A MILLION
COULD-BE YEARS ON A THOUSAND
MAYBE WORLDS. THE NATIONAL
BROADCASTING COMPANY, IN
COOPERATION WITH GALAXY
SCIENCE FICTION MAGAZINE
PRESENTS...X-X-X-X-MINUS-
MINUS-MINUS-MINUS-ONE
ONE-ONE-ONE....."

SOME STORIES: "MARS IS HEAVEN," "AND
THE MOON BE STILL AS BRIGHT," "ALMOST
HUMAN," "A GUN FOR DINOSAUR," "TUNNEL
UNDER THE WORLD," "HELLO, TOMORROW,"
"THE OUTER LIMIT," "NIGHTFALL," "TIME
AND TIME AGAIN" & "MARTIAN SAM"

X-MINUS ONE WAS ALMOST A CONTINUATION OF
DIMENSION X (NBC'S EARLIER SCIENCE FICTION
SERIES; ENDED SEPT. 1951) WHICH BEGAN ON
APRIL 24, 1955. IT ALSO FEATURED RADIO
ADAPTATIONS OF SOME OF THE ERA'S BEST
STORIES WRITTEN BY THE GREAT SCIENCE
FICTION AUTHORS: ROBERT HEINLEIN, RAY
BRADBURY, ISAAC ASIMOV, POUL ANDERSON,
THEODORE STURGEON & ROBERT BLOCH

ACTORS: SANTOS ORTEGA, JACK GRIMES,
JOE JULIAN, BOB HASTINGS, JOHN GIBSON,
MASON ADAMS, RAYMOND EDWARD JOHN-
SON, LUIS VAN ROOTEN, STAATS COTSWORTH,
WENDELL HOLMES, MANDEL KRAMER,
JOHN LARKIN, JOE DeSANTIS, MORE

X-MINUS ONE ENDED
ON JANUARY 9, 1958

SCRIPTS WERE BY ERNEST
KINOY & GEORGE LEFFERTS
DIRECTOR: DANIEL SUTTER

ANNOUNCER:
FRED COLLINS

RADIO'S GOLDEN YEARS©

by FRANK BRESEE & BOBB LYNES

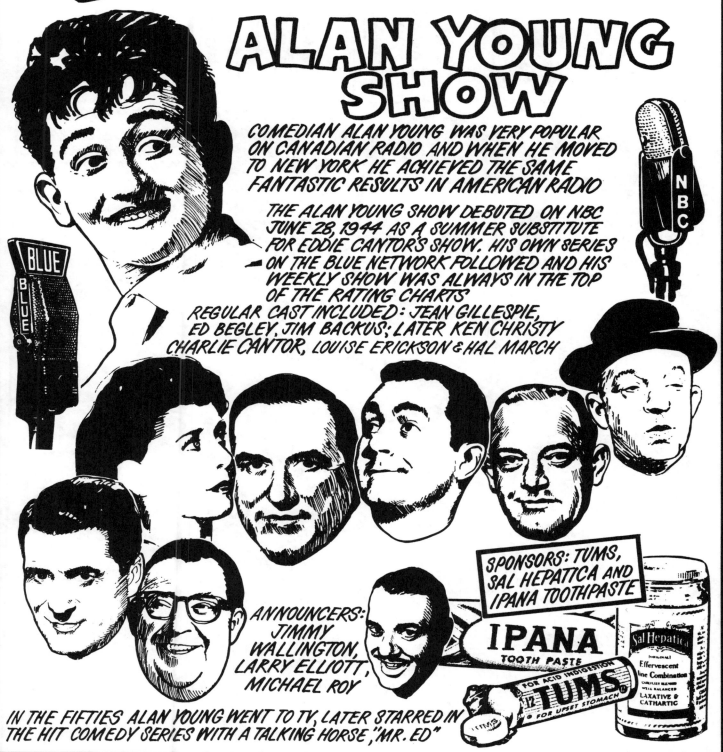

ALAN YOUNG SHOW

COMEDIAN ALAN YOUNG WAS VERY POPULAR ON CANADIAN RADIO AND WHEN HE MOVED TO NEW YORK HE ACHIEVED THE SAME FANTASTIC RESULTS IN AMERICAN RADIO

THE ALAN YOUNG SHOW DEBUTED ON NBC JUNE 28, 1944 AS A SUMMER SUBSTITUTE FOR EDDIE CANTOR'S SHOW. HIS OWN SERIES ON THE BLUE NETWORK FOLLOWED AND HIS WEEKLY SHOW WAS ALWAYS IN THE TOP OF THE RATING CHARTS

REGULAR CAST INCLUDED: JEAN GILLESPIE, ED BEGLEY, JIM BACKUS; LATER KEN CHRISTY CHARLIE CANTOR, LOUISE ERICKSON & HAL MARCH

SPONSORS: TUMS, SAL HEPATICA AND IPANA TOOTHPASTE

ANNOUNCERS: JIMMY WALLINGTON, LARRY ELLIOTT, MICHAEL ROY

IN THE FIFTIES ALAN YOUNG WENT TO TV, LATER STARRED IN THE HIT COMEDY SERIES WITH A TALKING HORSE, "MR. ED"

RADIO'S GOLDEN YEARS ©

by FRANK BRESEE & BOBB LYNES

Your HIT PARADE

LUCKY STRIKE
"IT'S TOASTED"

THE ONLY SPONSOR: LUCKY STRIKE CIGARETTES

"YOUR HIT PARADE" WAS THE MOST POPULAR MUSICAL PROGRAM OF ALL TIME, DEBUTING ON APRIL 20, 1935 AND RUNNING UNTIL JANUARY 16, 1953. EACH WEEK THE SHOW WOULD FEATURE THE TOP 7 SONGS OF THE WEEK, SUNG BY SUCH STARS AS FRANK SINATRA, DORIS DAY, DICK HAYMES, GINNY SIMMS, ANDY RUSSELL, BERYL DAVIS

ANNOUNCER BASIL RUYSDAEL

ANNOUNCER ANDRÉ BARUCH

VOCALISTS IN THE EARLY YEARS WERE GOGO DE LYS, BUDDY CLARK, LANNY ROSS AND BEA WAIN. BRIEFLY, IN THE LATE 30's COMEDIAN W.C. FIELDS WAS A REGULAR ON THE SHOW!

THE FAMOUS TOBACCO AUCTIONEERS HEARD WEEKLY ON THE LUCKY STRIKE COMMERCIALS WERE L.A. (SPEED) RIGGS AND F.E. BOONE....

DURING THE 1950s THE SHOW WAS ALSO SEEN ON TV AND WAS VERY POPULAR

The following pages contain an index of the programs and stars featured in this collection. Broadcast references are listed in italics.

INDEX